D1376550

Three's a
Crew

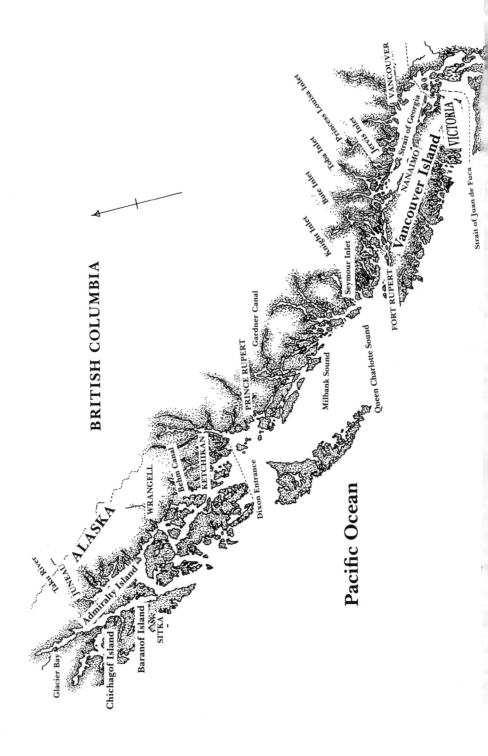

Three's a
Crew

Kathrene Pinkerton

HORSDAL & SCHUBART

Horsdal & Schubart Publishers Ltd.

Box 1, Ganges, BC, V0S 1E0, Canada

The publishers thank Charles Lillard for bringing this lovely and long-out-of-print book to our attention, and for writing the foreword.

Cover painting "Grassy Point", by Carol Evans, Dayspring Studio, Fulford Harbour, BC.

Map drawn by Suzanne Gagnon, Ganges, BC.

Photographs are by the author and Stewart Edward White, from the original edition of this book.

The body of the text is a facsimile reprint of the original edition.

Design and typesetting of the front matter by The Typeworks, Vancouver, BC.

Printed and bound by Hignell Printing Limited, Winnipeg, Manitoba

Canadian Cataloguing in Publication Data
   Pinkerton, Kathrene, 1887-1967.
      Three's a crew

      ISBN 0-920663-11-7

      1. Northwest Coast of North America—Description and travel.   2. British Columbia—Description and travel—1901-1950.*   3. Alaska—Description and travel—1896-1959.   4. Pinkerton, Kathrene, 1887-1967.   I. Title.
   F852.P55 1991   917.95′0443   C91-091149-5

CONTENTS

FOREWORD

SOME DAYS ON ENTERING A new cove or inlet we'd instinctively cut our engines and drift, the magic was that strong. Later we'd move on, rowing, almost silently moving into the mystery. Sometimes there would be abandoned homesteads, tumbledown mining camps, or overgrown logging sites to explore; frequently what lay ahead was an unnamed creek with ponds so blue, so clear, that diving into them was like diving into the sky itself. That's how it was at places like Traitors Cove and Helm Bay in the Southeast Alaska of the mid-1950s.

Some of us never learned how to live comfortably with this magic. It contained too many dimensions; but more than the wilderness of greens and blues, more than the silence and bedrock-deep serenity, the magic was more enigma than enchantment. We had a history but could not find it. There at the head of some cove, camped beside a creek, we knew our story; but what about the stories of those early settlers, miners, loggers? Of them we knew nothing. Behind our camp, only a few yards upstream, likely as not, there were the remains of ancient weirs. What of the Indians who had fished and camped at this very spot?

Where had all these stories—this history—gone? Only once in a while did we discover real images that we could study. Sometimes it was a photo in an old magazine, now and again it was encounters with men like Wildcat Ander-

son and Ben Marr, men whose time on the coast went back
to the turn of the century or beyond.

This wasn't much to build on. Then one day, for me, the
picture began to change. I discovered Stewart Edward
White's *Wild Geese Calling*. Set near my home, the novel was
a fictionalized account of how C.R. Johnstone and his wife
made their way upcoast from Puget Sound to Alaska. To
give the novel other levels of validity, Johnstone's grandchildren were schoolmates of mine, and I'd sat on the small
float near the outfall of Roosevelt Lagoon listening to
Handlogger Jackson's tales, and Handlogger was
Johnstone's son-in-law. Twenty years later Jackson would
add several posthumous panels to this tapestry when his
Handloggers was published.

Thus our local history began to gain shape. How large it
was became clear when I learned that some 20 years before
Wild Geese Calling appeared, White had cruised the B.C.-
Alaska coast with Robert and Kathrene Pinkerton, both of
whom were also writers. It took time but I finally located a
copy of Kathrene Pinkerton's *Three's a Crew*, her account of
her family's years cruising the Inside Passage. Suddenly
our coast became one end of a much larger fabric, one that
was international and important; how valuable this history
was, and is, continues to go unacknowledged by specialists
and schoolbooks.

On reading *Three's a Crew*, I discovered that the Pinks—
as they called themselves—were as fascinated as was White
by the life and times of C.R. Johnstone (Pinkerton spells
the name Johnston). For them he was a new breed of fron-
tiersman, an image highlighted, in their eyes, by his always
being one jump ahead of them. And by 1924, when *Three's a
Crew* begins, it was not easy to get the jump on Kathrene
and Robert Pinkerton.

Robert was born in Wisconsin in 1882. After a stint at the University of Wisconsin, he worked his way west to Denver, Colorado, as a newspaperman. In 1911 Robert married Kathrene Gedney, a native of Minneapolis five years his junior and a field secretary for the Wisconsin Anti-Tuberculosis Association. Ill health forced Robert to give up newspaper work not long after their marriage; that was when they decided to go north, "to pioneer in the Canadian wilderness," as they told an interviewer in 1941.

And north they went with a $150 nest egg, the result of a 30,000-word novelette that they had written in five days. They lived in the northern Ontario bush, trapping, fishing—and teaching themselves how to write. Their first publication had proven to be a fluke: two years passed before they sold anything else.

Five years later, when they returned to the United States, both were professional writers, selling regularly to a wide range of pulp magazines. By this time both were fiddlefooted so it was not long before they took off on a leisurely transcontinental drive in 1917. After various long stops—Denver, the Redwood country, Los Angeles, the art colony at Carmel—the Pinkertons reached San Francisco, which became their base until 1924.

Bobs Pinkerton, who plays such a major role in her mother's book, and who is still fondly remembered in Victoria by friends she made as a student at the Strathcona School for Girls, was born while her parents lived in the Canadian wilds. She went on to become a magazine editor and writer, but Bobs never achieved the brief fame her parents knew.

About 1927, after selling an uncounted (and today uncountable) number of articles and stories (some 4,500,000 words, according to their figures) in collaboration with her husband, Kathrene began working alone. It would seem from the public record that while her career accelerated, his slid toward oblivion. For years he wrote a book-length serial for the pulp market every 28 days, but none of this material has been collected. He did publish a number of novels in the 1920s (several in collaboration with Kathrene) but if he's remembered at all today it is due to his *The Gentleman Adventurers*, a history of the Hudson's Bay Company published in 1931.

On the other hand, Kathrene Pinkerton made a solid mark with *Wilderness Wife* (1939), *Three's a Crew* (1940), *Two Ends to Our Shoestring* (1941), a number of juvenile novels set in Ontario, and several still-fascinating juvenile novels (written as late as the 1950s) set on the B.C.-Alaska coast. These books are still available in many large libraries, and their prices, when they can be found, in secondhand book stores suggest they are still in demand. Realizing this, in 1976 a New York publisher reprinted *Wilderness Wife* as *A Home in the Wilds*.

Her Northwest Coast memoirs and novels make Pinkerton one of the most prolific of coastal writers; unknown to most, she's also the first woman to write about coastal cruising. And as far as 20th-century coastal cruising is concerned, the only work to predate *Three's a Crew* is Stewart Edward White's curious (and radiantly defective) *Skookum Chuck*. Prior to this, book-length cruising literature (some of it dating back to the 1880s) was written from the perspective of a coastal steamer or freighter.

In 1968 the first Canadian edition of M. Wylie Blanchet's *The Curve of Time* appeared and quickly reached small-c classic status in British Columbia. The book was a virtual follow-up to *Three's a Crew* and much about the books was similar: the authors were educated women cruising with families, both enjoyed writing well, and each loved the same coast, albeit at slightly different times. Then, in 1985, the next-to-impossible happened: Beth Hill brought out *Upcoast Summers,* a book that is, in effect, a sequel to Pinkerton's and Blanchet's books. This trilogy forms an increasingly important account of west-coast life between 1924 and the outbreak of World War II.

Historians suggest this was a period when time stood still. The Roaring Twenties had little effect on the coast, and the Dirty Thirties changed things but slightly. It was a period bordered at one end by a generation who did not return from the trenches, and at the other by men boarding eastbound troop trains in 1939.

But on reading Pinkerton, Blanchet and Hill, we find that life did not stand still during those two decades; very subtly things were changing. The handloggers were going, fishing was increasingly unpredictable, the logging camps were mechanizing, floatcamp life was becoming little short of a floating hell for many wives and mothers. (And elsewhere, although it is never stated in *Three's a Crew,* conditions in the publishing industry made it impossible for writers like White and the Pinkertons to continue their lives afloat.)

In their seven years cruising the Pinks saw a good deal of coastal life, and being frontiersmen of a kind, they saw it in a way undiluted by social theory or romantic vision. Better yet, what Kathrene Pinkerton saw, she could write about; consequently there are pages in this book that are unrivalled as history (the descriptions of handloggers), sociology (floatcamp life and mores), and literature (the poetry of her descriptions). In this book Kathrene Pinkerton was so enamoured of her subject she writes like a lover, a woman who needs to be understood, and must win over her readers.

Like so many books published as North America got its world-war footing, *Three's a Crew* was lost in the shuffle, as were the Pinkertons, so to speak. What Robert and Kathrene wrote during the mid-1930s is not a matter of record. Bobs was on her own during most of this time, and married one John Clarke McIntyre about 1939 or 1940. What happened to her husband and any children is unknown; in 1990 one of Bobs' long-time friends said that in all the years he'd known her, she had not once mentioned this part of her past.

During most of the mid-to-late depression years, Kathrene worked in office jobs; then, in a short burst, she wrote the three books about her family's travels and activities. There was another decade of silence before her last spate of juvenile novels began appearing in the 1950s; she then fell silent again. Kathrene Pinkerton died in 1967, Robert in 1979, and when Bobs died in 1988 she took with her the only complete account of the Pinkerton saga.

Today, *Three's a Crew* remains our first cruiser's-eye view of the Northwest Coast. By the thousands, men and women in their boats have unknowingly followed the courses laid out by the *Triton's* captain, but the Skipper and his crew ploughed along in no one's wake. The magic they discovered in the 1920s was alive and well in Alaska 30 years later. Today it continues to thrive in a thousand coves and inlets between Seattle and Haines—ask anyone who has spent days exploring Desolation Sound, Behm Canal, or Boca de Quadra's quirky waterways.

Charles Lillard

The Yakima *Points North*

Bobs Inspects a
Sixty Pound Salmon

We
Watched the
Yucluetaws
Run at
Henry's An-
nual Picnic

I

"GOING FOREIGN"

WE HAD BEEN TO SEA IN SHIPS, never in small craft, but that did not affect our planning. Other lubbers had bought cruisers and sailed away and we saw no reason why we should not. What we never dreamed was that most of the following seven years would be spent afloat.

In those first three days aboard our whole attention was devoted to getting the little *Yakima* ready for sea. We lay at a mooring in Lake Union, in the center of Seattle, and amid city streets and sounds we could have no vision of scores of quiet harbors in which we would anchor throughout the thousand miles that stretch into Southeastern Alaska. The ship canal that led from lake to salt water held no hint of long arms of the Pacific twisting into the very heart of the majestic coast range. City skyscrapers could not help us to imagine mountains standing with their feet in the sea.

We had strangeness aplenty in merely being afloat, and we were very much engaged in cramming a summer's supplies for a family of three into a thirty-six-foot cruiser. We did not need a glimpse of the years to come, of glaciers and icebergs, whales and sea lions, big brown bears and rivers choked with salmon. That lay in the future. We were occupied in preparation.

When Robert and I decided to take Bobs, our daughter

13

of nine, and spend a summer cruising the intricate coast line of British Columbia, the procedure appeared to be comparatively simple. We'd buy a boat, stow supplies aboard and depart. Bobs had never been on shipboard, and Robert and I had never navigated or lived in a cruiser, but freshness would add zest to the adventure.

Having made our decision, we put it into execution in our usual forthright fashion, for we get on faster by trying out a scheme than thinking about it. Summer vacation was almost upon us. We were living in San Francisco, but Seattle was the doorway to cruising waters and a good place to shop for boats. Since the best way to learn about cruisers was to visit the market, Robert went to Seattle. After two days of waterfront prowling he sent a jubilant telegram announcing that we were the owners of a seagoing craft. Bobs and I took the first train for Seattle.

A taxi conveyed bags and family directly from station to mooring pier. Robert was very anxious that we like his purchase. Our praise was gratifying but of no other value. Bobs and I, never having seen a cruiser, considered any small boat equipped with living quarters a minor miracle. Robert's knowledge was much wider, for he had seen the boats he didn't buy while he searched for one within our modest budget. Now he tried to share this knowledge by describing the impossible crafts he had avoided.

I noticed the white paint of the *Yakima's* cabin was very fresh. The boat smelt of cleaning powders and Robert appeared quite tired. But the effect of the *Yakima* on Bobs and me was all that he could wish.

The boat was thirty-six feet long, with a cockpit and a hunting type cabin. The cockpit was covered by a canopy and could be enclosed with curtains. A wheelhouse amidships was open aft. From this a companionway led below.

The cabin contained a large locker forward, transom berths, a combined engine room and galley, and a tiny bathroom.

The heavy duty twelve-horsepower Frisco Standard engine sat squarely in the center of the galley. Dresser and sink were on one side and stove and food lockers on the other. I mistrusted the arrangement and feared the motor would interfere with my culinary routine. Later I discovered that my viewpoint was quite wrong. A cook ranked lower than an engine and I had to adjust my activities to its needs. As I worked at the dresser the huge revolving flywheel threatened my calves and the rocker arms shot up and down beneath my chin. They offered a fine opportunity for mechanized attachments, but Robert remained cold to my suggestion that they operate a master mixer.

Our first inspection was unmarred by too much knowledge. The microscopic bathroom, reached aft through the galley and containing a toilet and a bowl, delighted us with its ship plumbing. Pumps and a folding basin were novelties to Bobs. And I, who had never heard the word "gangway," didn't realize that the path to the bathroom was also my galley floor space. Later I recognized a traffic problem.

Robert opened the buffet locker forward to show the space for clothes and pulled down the dining table which was hinged against a bulkhead. This cabin was our living and dining room, and a moment later he transformed it into a stateroom by swinging the hinged backs of the transom berths into position. Then we stood in a center aisle between four upholstered shelves. The *Yakima* had been advertised as "sleeping four," but without our extra upper we'd have had to take our clothes to bed.

Thus far our plan to own and operate a cruiser was as

simple as we had imagined. In the next three days the
adventure did not dim, but we discovered that going to sea
for a summer entailed much contriving. As we intended
to cruise a coast which had only a few tiny settlements,
needs of three months had to be anticipated. I awakened
in the night to write items on a lengthening list.

And all that impedimenta had to be crammed into a few
lockers which, unlike cupboards, had a way of petering out
to nothing at the bottom. Boxes and square packages meant
wasted space. The lockers balked at our solution of the
laundry problem—bales of paper towels and napkins.
Everything had to be unpacked and poked into odd corners and crevices.

"Stowing," Robert called it in trying to set a proper ex-
ample in sailoring vernacular for Bobs and me, and then
he'd say, "Bring me that stuff from the hind end."

But no sea term covered our despairing search for places
to put a typewriter, books, medical supplies, food and
clothing. We reduced possessions to the minimum and then
discarded half of them. Everything had to promise service
to pay its passage.

When I had assembled a small mountain of articles
which I proposed to put into the lockers of our eight-foot
cabin, Robert came below and stared in fine male horror.

"Once you and I traveled light," he said.

Although we'd already done it twice, we again searched
for discards. Oilskins, rubber boots, sweaters and Mackinaw coats passed inspection. So did shirts, underwear,
woolen hose, footwear for the boat and ashore, playsuits
for Bobs and slacks for me. Robert reluctantly conceded
"shore clothes," one outfit each for him and me and spares
for Bobs because garments of an active youngster are subject to stress.

Books must be carried, and ours were chosen for triple duty. We could all share Conrad, McFee, Fabre, Masefield, sea and clipper ship stories. Bobs' paints, drawing pads, paper and pencils got by with a question as to whether one girl could actually cover that amount of blank paper in a summer.

"She'll have to do something in her hours aboard," I said. "You're lucky she doesn't go in for games."

His eyes lighted on a model yacht he had given her to sail in San Francisco parks to encourage water-mindedness. Now he scowled at it.

"You won't need that when you've a dinghy to row," he said.

Bobs looked at him with that unreasonable logic which develops in females even at an early age.

"But, dad!" she protested. "I can sail it better from a rowboat than from the shore of a lake."

Robert's abrupt departure was a complete male rout, but he returned a half hour later with a ship's carpenter. Then our stowing was complicated by boards, sawdust and quick drying stains and varnish, while main cabin, bathroom and even cockpit were equipped with lockers.

The morning when the miracle of stowing was finally accomplished, Bobs and I lounged in deck chairs while Robert and a mechanic worked on the motor. Three days aboard a boat had taught us that women are not welcome when there is engine trouble, especially when the motor sits squarely in the center of the galley.

The portentous tones of the mechanic led us to expect the worst, but at last we heard the steady sound of the exhaust. Robert was cheerful when he came on deck. The mechanic with his kit of tools looked like the doctor who has just saved the patient.

"She's jake now," he said. "I suppose you folks are anxious to pull out."

Robert nodded. "Everything's aboard."

I listened with a sense of shock. A green skipper and a greener mate who had never taken even a rowboat to sea were about to pilot a cruiser through the locks into Puget Sound and head north into the unknown. The *Yakima,* which had seemed very modest until that moment, suddenly grew up to be an ocean liner.

For the first time I wondered if we had been sane on that day when we had so abruptly decided to cruise along the British Columbia and Alaska coasts. Twenty-two months of steady writing had entitled Robert to a vacation, and those months had completed five years in one locality. Almost unconsciously we had been relinquishing our foot-loose instincts and accepting the creed that a family should "stay put." We deserved no credit for this attitude. By the time we had followed the usual parental routine of proper schools, dancing classes, the inevitable orthodentia for a growing child and a decent neighborhood in which to bring up a daughter, had added a few outlets for ourselves in golf, theaters, concerts and dinner parties, there were no funds with which to do anything but "stay put." And after we had bought these routine requirements with our writing, there was no energy to expend in wandering.

When confronted with a vacation, I had suggested a motor trip, though without brilliant ideas as to where. Five years of routine had crippled my imagination.

Robert was not enthused. "We need a new outdoor game," he said.

I proposed a voyage on a freight ship.

He shook his head. "I mean a game we can play. How about running our own boat?"

I was startled. Sea ventures were common in West Coast newspapers. Pictures of treasure seekers or the odd pair sailing to the South Seas would be prominently displayed, and a few weeks later these individuals would reappear in a brief notice that they had been rescued off the coast of Lower California.

The waterfront of San Francisco, where ships from every port are docked, had fascinated us. We had looked wistfully at a freight ship or two but continued to regard the sea more as a spectacle than the realm of our own adventures. Our wanderings had been done on land. When the unconscious western urge had brought us to the Pacific we had halted. Distant and exotic lands had not beckoned. Our instinct was for pines and mountains. Our compass had always pointed north.

"Finest cruising country in the world off the B. C. coast," Robert said. "And beyond that is Alaska."

"Boats cost money," I said.

Robert looked around our living room as a crustacean must regard his last season's shell. "If we didn't have this town stuff on our necks, we could take a flyer with a small cruiser."

The *Yakima* was the outcome of that speech. Robert's telegram found Bobs and me with our possessions in storage and ourselves in readiness to make whatever craft he bought our only home for the next three months.

We slept aboard the boat while fitting out. We were encircled by Seattle. We could see street cars and hear the honking of automobiles, but land and its activities seemed remote. All day our home rocked gently to passing water traffic. Ships from the Pacific, impressive white yachts, small cruisers equally gleaming in bright varnish, tugboats with tows, Cape Flattery salmon trollers, tankers and oil-blackened work boats, all proceeded endlessly up and down the fairway. The shores were lined with services for these boats, wharfs to sell them fuel, marine railways for their haul-out, sprawling shed-like structures for repairing and building, and long floats jutting out into the lake for mooring.

We lay in a community of small craft. Behind a long pier and shutting off the street was a marine outfitting store in which we and other boat owners bought paint and tackle, hardware and gadgets, and exchanged reports on that annual frenzy known as "spring overhaul."

Chats at the store welded us into a fellowship with other cruisers and helped induct us into our new world. Bobs' and my education in small craft broadened swiftly. We knew the arrangement below decks of every boat at the floats, and their owners knew ours. If our home rocked in the wash of passing craft, other homes were rocking too, and this communal rocking made the situation normal. A pier for a doorstep seemed more natural when other home-owners fared likewise. And my foot-square galley dresser and even smaller sink were palatial in comparison with other galleys.

Bobs spent hours visiting. Like an investigative puppy, she scampered about the floats and went aboard wherever a hatch was open. Her favorite chum was Tommy Drake, one of those lone sea rovers who had crossed the Pacific and the Atlantic in a tiny schooner he'd built himself. He was outfitting his third for a voyage to Europe. His first two had been wrecked in the Far East and on the Cuban coast, and his present craft was destined to be lost on the sandbanks off Holland. Bobs came home crammed with first-hand yarns of sea adventure.

She also reported that we were the only motor craft

"going foreign," waterfront parlance for cruising in other than U. S. waters, and I understood why many of our callers had been wistful and respectful.

All this exchange of boatcraft had given me an illusion of having become a sailor. I overlooked completely the fact that safe days alongside a float provide no grounding in seamanship, until I heard Robert say, "Everything's aboard."

But my sudden sense of inadequacy for the role of mate could not hold back the swift movement of departure. Our good-bys were said. Robert rocked the huge flywheel and, although I hoped it wouldn't, the motor answered in dutiful staccato. The *Yakima* nosed out into the channel and the crowded mooring fell astern.

We were pledged to Neptune.

II

A SKIPPER'S DUTY NEVER ENDS

THE MOMENTOUS OCCASION
of casting off our mooring lines for the first time called for
a gay and jaunty speech, but I could only ask the skipper
if he was scared.

"I'll be less so when we're through the locks," he said.
He was wrong, but he didn't know it then.

We had never seen the locks, the second largest in the
world. A regulation calling for sixty-foot bow and stern
lines was a bit dismaying, but the large group of sightseers on the pier was more so. They made our maiden voyage a public demonstration. No one had told us that tourist
spectators were a permanent feature of lock passage, and
I suggested that we wait for a quiet rehearsal hour. The
War Department had given us stage fright, too, with its
printed warning that defective mechanism might cause
damage to the gates, wreck a ship and be responsible for
loss of life. We knew nothing of the *Yakima's* lock manners.

The lock attendant who took our lines appeared incredibly calm and cheerful. He regarded lock passage as a
minor incident. "Move down to the lower gate, Captain,"
he said to Robert.

This first public use of Robert's official title registered
with Bobs. It did with me, although I had no reason to believe that a twenty-minute run down a canal had endowed

our skipper with sea wisdom. Robert beamed in pleased surprise.

We made fast in the lock's smaller chamber alongside a salmon troller. The narrow intervening space lost its slight reassurance when I thought of the sixty feet of lines on which we were to dangle. Then two more boats entered. The bluff bow of a seventy-foot halibuter towered above our stern, and the *Yakima* looked like a Pomeranian taking chances with a mastiff.

The rear gates swung shut. The man who rode them verified the closing and raised his arm in signal. We waited for further orders, but no one spoke or looked in our direction. Then we felt the boat move as the *Yakima* started its descent in a watery elevator.

After that we didn't need orders. Robert at the bow, I at the stern, struggled to achieve a compromise between paying out lines and keeping them taut. The *Yakima* went lower. A wet cement wall rose above us to three-story height. Disappearing over its top, apparently into nothingness, were our lines. No one was in sight. Tautness seemed imperative to me and I clung to my line so tightly we scraped marine growth from the dripping cavern's sides. The skipper pled with me to spare the rails.

We came to rest at last in the bottom of a well. The lock attendant who had stood companionably beside the *Yakima* peered down at us from a great height. I had an odd feeling of having jumped through a looking glass and was relieved that someone apparently cared what had happened to us. But he didn't. He only wanted to know where to fling our lines, and they landed smartly on deck and after canopy. The din of four motors filled that narrow chamber. The gates, which divided the fresh water world from the salt, swung open. The Pacific lay before us.

A new tang came to our nostrils. I was conscious of coolness and a breeze brought the distinctive odor of a beach at ebb tide. I turned to congratulate the skipper on the lock behavior of his ship and his crew, and found him engrossed in a traffic problem.

The sea was not vast and empty as we had expected. It was as crowded and busy as a downtown street. A ferry scuttled from its berth. A large ship approached on our starboard. Rowboats trolling for salmon dotted the water ahead. A tanker rounded a point. Our faster lock companions demanded passage.

A boat astern signaled its intention as to course and the shrill toots precipitated a panic aboard the *Yakima*. I thought the skipper knew the rules of the road. He had thought he did, but in sudden doubt he demanded a reading. Quite literally I began at the beginning.

"Not all that!" he barked. "What's the rule on an overtaking vessel?"

I began a futile search that was ended by the skipper snatching the pamphlet. Somehow he tooted back the proper answer, although the other boat must have begun to wonder.

"We'd better get those rules down cold," the skipper said.

That was obvious. We couldn't go into conference every time a ship whistled at us.

We intended only a short run, and when we were past the Ballard Blinker I looked longingly across the sound at the friendly shores of Bainbridge Island. This wandering on the Pacific with all our goods and chattels gave me a sense of being homeless. I wanted to get our hook down, be stationary again and catch my breath. But such a suggestion was not seemly from a first mate, especially as Bobs was ecstatically studying charts under Robert's equally delighted coaching. I went below. When I returned a few moments later I found that not only had Bainbridge Island disappeared but also the shore astern. A light fog had cut off even visual contact with land.

"We'll anchor in Port Madison," the skipper said.

The words "port" and "anchor" appealed to me. Navigation was a tiring business and now we had to steer by compass. I watched the skipper move parallel rulers over the chart. It looked quite nautical and I almost said, "Aye, aye, sir," when he announced the course.

Robert's preparation for the new game of cruising was far better than was mine. Also his responsibility was greater. He had taken on the double job of captain and engineer, while I, as mate, had only to relieve him at the wheel and carry out orders. Of his two jobs, he was better prepared as an engineer. Mechanics spoke of him as being "handy around a motor." In his first encounter with one, a temperamental two-cycle engine in a launch we had owned in the Canadian woods, he had solved the mystery of its bad manners. He had added to his understanding of internal combustion principles during a transcontinental motor trip in the early days of roads, not highways, when machine shops might lie a hundred miles apart.

His knowledge of salt water methods and hazards came almost entirely from books. We had both read many sea stories and to these he had added motor boat magazines and a handbook on small craft. Our fresh water experience was valuable. We had paddled several thousand miles in a canoe and, while we knew little of tides and tidal currents, we did know a great deal about water and air in motion. Boatmen call it "water savvy," that instinctive handling of a craft and an ability to estimate rough water.

But our best defense against mishap was psychological. We had not attacked the salt water game in a cocksure spirit. A very wholesome respect for the sea was our chief asset as mariners. We knew imprudence and overconfidence asked for trouble, and would undoubtedly bring it.

"We'll stay safe by being scared all the time," Robert had said.

Looking for danger, we found it, and before we'd been a half hour at sea. I chanced to glance astern and saw a score of huge black fins cutting the water. The fins curved backward. Some were six feet high, others half that. All were coming swiftly toward us.

I let out a shrill yelp of terror.

"Holy Mackinaw!" Robert said, and he swung the bow sharply.

His decision to get out of the way was instantaneous, but the fins spread on both sides of our course and were rapidly overhauling us. Huge black bodies rolled up under the curving fins. The largest was the size of the *Yakima*, and all were ten times as active.

"What are they?" Bobs demanded.

No one knew.

Robert guessed they might be blackfish, sometimes called pilot whales, although really a large species of porpoise. But educating a child in natural history was not so important at that moment as giving those huge creatures an unobstructed passage.

To dodge a school of sportive whales cruising in loose formation and in the same general direction requires agility. The *Yakima* weaved and looped and weaved again. Whenever we thought we'd shaken them off, Bobs or I, acting as lookouts, would call, "Here's another," as a large black fin came toward us, and the skipper would throw the wheel hard over.

Bobs was less terrified than we, but she had been fed on the robust deeds of sea adventures. Probably she thought this invasion was to be expected, though her question showed that the situation had not been covered in sea fiction.

"Do boats always have to run away from whales?" she asked.

Her inquiry went unanswered while whales popped up all around us. Their method of travel only added to their threat. They rolled over like enormous revolving disks, disappearing and coming up a short distance beyond. Thus every empty bit of water held a menace. We never knew but that one of those thirty-foot, ten-ton masses of surging energy would come up beneath the boat. Even a flip from a tail would have crushed our planking. The *Yakima* rushed about like a terrified herring. It may have been undignified but we didn't care.

When the last had passed we turned limply to each other.

"Of all the dangers I've conjured up in the middle of the night," I said, "I never thought of that one."

"Those Lake Union sailors!" Robert said. "Warning us of everything but—"

"Here comes a lot more!" Bobs called.

We looked astern to see a second section, another thirty whales, bearing down upon us.

The *Yakima* resumed its weaving tactics and I began to wonder if we were to be in flight from whales all summer. Robert must have contemplated the same possibility. As a big bull rushed toward us, the *Yakima's* bow remained steady.

"I'm through dodging," the skipper said.

The bull came up for air close off the starboard counter and we heard plainly the loud "shu-s-s-sh" of his exhalation. He rolled under, and the next need for breath would bring him up beneath us.

We did nothing, although my immobility was due to plain panic. I scarcely breathed as we sailed across an empty stretch of sea. Finally, off to port, we saw the whale break water. I couldn't believe the miracle of our escape.

"I was betting that the sound of our propeller would send him down," Robert said. "Otherwise boats couldn't leave port with whales as thick as this."

We tried this theory of whale behavior on the laggards. When they proved the soundness of the skipper's reasoning, we boldly held our course. Robert instructed Bobs in natural history, but I kept an apprehensive eye astern.

It took weeks and the assurance of many seamen to convince me that our first hour on the sound was unusual. Whales are a frequent sight in the North Pacific and we saw many, blackfish, humpback and finback. The sight of these enormous animals always thrilled us for it is impossible to become blasé about a whale. But never again did we encounter two large schools in quick succession.

Apparently an important whale regatta was being held in Puget Sound and the whales knew where they were going, fog or no fog. They were better navigators than we, for when the excitement was past we discovered we were lost. By course and speed we should be near Port Madison but there was no sign of shore. Robert checked and re-checked and tried not to look as worried as he was.

My report of the dim outlines of a bold headland off the port bow made matters worse, for according to "The Coast Pilot" I should have seen a low point. Then the skipper broke down and admitted, "I don't know where in hell we are." That this had happened a mere stone's throw from Seattle was mortifying and did not add to our safety. We could wreck a ship as successfully within ferrying distance of the city as a thousand miles north.

The skipper threw out the clutch and, while we drifted helplessly in a gray world, wondering just what navigators did in such a situation, a salmon fisherman rowed into the circle of our fog horizon. He looked a bit startled when we asked if we were near Port Madison.

"You've got the wrong President," he said. "This is Port Jefferson."

We'd mistaken more than the name. We'd made a navigating error of two miles on a four-mile course, a free, wide and handsome stab at coastwise piloting. At that rate we might pile up on the Rocky Mountains.

The skipper took a compass bearing on the headland and, I suspect, a couple of quick guesses, and we departed. Evidently the needle was not so tricky on southerly courses for we found Port Madison, and found it, too, a snug harbor. We baptized our sounding lead in salt water and I began my first lesson in use of clutch, throttle and wheel as the anchor was let go and I moved the *Yakima* ahead to bite the hook solidly. I thought we rode to a lot of cable.

"You'll have to pull up all that rope in the morning," I warned when Robert came aft.

"A scope of three to one is a good rule," he said. "If you anchor right you don't worry."

He was psychic, but how psychic we didn't know until the next morning.

For the first time since we had owned her, the *Yakima* rode at the end of an anchor cable. As if in celebration of the occasion, a breeze swept away the fog and we watched the last gray wisps driven from the timbered ridges. The small cove in which we lay was sun-drenched, warm and very much our own domain.

We went below to inspect our pocket home. At the moorings it had seemed impossible that three people could sleep, eat, dress, store belongings and lounge and read in the evenings in that tiny cabin. Now, at anchor, the expanse of water around us made it seem larger and the *Yakima* suddenly became a compact, self-sufficient home. My housekeeping instincts were stirred and I planned a real dinner. While fitting out we'd had time only for snacks or had eaten at a restaurant. Now a regular life was beginning.

Bobs announced the occasion warranted a swim, dropped her few garments in the cockpit and went overside. We decided that our liquid ceremony should be celebrated otherwise.

"Happy Voyage!" we said as we clicked glasses.

An hour earlier such a toast would have been only a gallant gesture on my part, but in the peace and quiet of harbor all the panics of our first day seemed remote.

In that moment the compass was our only problem, but we had known of that. In Seattle a compass expert had refused to risk an inaccurate adjustment on so small an instrument and boat. The compass was directly above the motor and a vertical water tank. He had not approved of the arrangement but had said that much trial-and-error running would enable us to make our own compass card. Immediate need of knowing the vagaries of our compass had been proved that afternoon.

"We'll go south, up sound," the skipper said. "By running courses in every direction, we'll learn how badly off it is."

Two days in the vicinity of settlements seemed a good scheme. Our blithe departure for the north had allowed no time for working out the inevitable bugs of initial operation. A green crew could better adjust itself to sea behavior in small and quiet waters. At the risk of appearing to be a sissy, I confessed my delight at this short postponement of our northern cruise.

It was dark when we went on deck for a last inspection. Bobs was asleep in an upper berth and our own were made up. The cabin looked like a compartment in a Pullman. I was so exhausted I could have fallen into my bed as I made it, but a last turn around the ship seemed a mate's duty.

"It's breezing up a bit," Robert said as we stood in the cockpit accustoming our eyes to the darkness.

Small waves rippled along the hull and halyards beat a quick tattoo against the mast. The dinghy no longer cuddled sociably at our stern but rode to a tight line. Its bow slapped the surface of the water and the sound carried a vague warning.

I thought it might be just my first night's fear until Robert read the barometer. It had fallen in an hour.

"Isn't this hell?" he said. "I've read of anchor watches and prowling around wet decks in pajamas. And now we draw that the first night out."

He looked as tired as I felt. I made the proper gesture of a first mate and offered to take my turn on watch. To my great relief, he refused.

"Don't worry if you hear me up," he added gallantly. "But Ye Gods! It's going to be cold and wet out there in pajamas!"

"Call me if the wind gets bad," I said as I snuggled down in my warm berth.

I planned to sleep with one eye open and dozed off feeling sorry for him. A skipper's responsibility never ends. And that was the last I remembered.

I wakened to a cabin bathed in sunlight. Robert's berth was empty, but it had been slept in. I heard him slushing down the deck and cockpit. When I joined him, although he looked rested, I inquired guiltily if he'd had a hard night.

"Never woke up," he said. "That wind must have died down."

There was no evidence of wind or turmoil in the glassy calm of the bay or in the blue sky where lazy little puffs of white clouds floated. I'd never seen a fresher morning.

"That'll teach us to stop reading the barometer," I said. "After this let's use our judgment."

We were laughing at the dread into which a small needle had sent us when we heard oars. A man, rowing fisherman fashion, standing and facing the bow, came alongside.

"You seem to have come through it all right," he said.

I wondered if our first voyage across the sound had become a matter of public interest. I smiled and nodded and tried not to appear baffled. Robert looked thoughtful.

"I saw you folks come in," our caller said. "Wondered if I'd find you here this morning. A couple of fishing boats dragged, but you folks don't seem to have moved."

This had no meaning for me. Robert's answer was the height of diplomacy as he lined up a point and agreed that we had not moved. And then he added, "I had out plenty of cable."

"Good rule to follow," the man said. "But who'd expect a breeze like that in summer? About midnight I thought it was going to blow the top of the world off."

He pushed on his oars and went away. I didn't know whether to snicker or not. Perhaps I did, for the skipper was testy.

III

DECEPTION PASS

WHEN THE "YAKIMA" FI-
nally turned north we had more than a corrected compass
card to our credit. Our sea legs were stiffening, our sea
manners were improving and the crew had been shaken
down. We might become sailors, and already we had titles.

Bobs had chosen hers after deep thought and resort to
sea fiction. "Deckhand" had not appealed. She distrusted
so wide a gap between her rating and our own, and a nine-
year-old's wariness of the odd job role warned her it might
be only a polite term for the official polisher of brass. Her
final choice of bo'sun made her also an executive. True,
she had no underlings to carry out orders, but neither had
we. Boat work was relieved of embarrassment as all three
scrubbed decks, washed paint work and polished brass together.

We had made the surprising discovery that ship life was
very busy with tricks at the wheel, odd jobs about the boat
and galley duties, while above decks was a constantly
changing scene, a world of movement and fresh interests.
The sea was never empty—a new variety of birds, a sudden screaming flight of gulls which had sighted booty, a
tiny settlement ashore that existed for no apparent reason,
and always passing boats. Land traffic may become monot-
onous for encounters on the highway are momentary and
automobiles much alike. But every boat is different and

33

remains in sight for a long time. When one appears across
the bows it has time to impress its personality before it
finally drops astern. One never forgets a boat.

This changing life had made the wheelhouse a gathering
place. When under way, it was our social center. We
hadn't seen so much of Bobs since she had gone to school.
She and I joined the skipper as soon as below deck tasks
were finished in the morning. We ate lunch as we cruised,
on what we called "our bridge," a long seat built aft of the
wheel, with the top of the cabin serving as a table. The
nearness of the bridge to the galley allowed the cook to
keep track of events above deck. It was the first outdoor
game we had found in which travel and routine of living
could go on simultaneously. I was always popping up,
armed with a basting spoon or a fork, to salute a whale or
a passing tug.

The few days afloat had been a period of discovery.
"Ship's discipline" had always suggested the behavior of a
group of worthy individuals and I had wondered if our
family could meet this test. But we found that the impressive words were only a term for logical behavior. Meri-
torious conduct grew out of the situation rather than out
of the individual.

When no one in the family could dress, move around or
eat breakfast until blankets had been stowed and the berths
transformed into seats, public opinion compelled prompt
rising. And when the chop from an afternoon breeze
would roll loose objects to the floor, no one left his pet
possessions lying around. The skipper and I were relieved
from exhortations on orderliness. The sea spoke for us, and
its first rebuke was effective. We were all on the bridge
enjoying the gentle motion of the boat when a crash sent
Bobs dashing to the companionway. We looked down to

see her unscrambling drawing pad, cakes of paint and small tins which had contained water.

The same inexorability applied to ship's duties. I had to be free to take the wheel when we anchored or lifted the hook in order to maneuver while the skipper was on the foredeck. Bobs had to lead the trailing dinghy forward so that the painter would not become entangled when we reversed. Grave consequences hung on failure to discharge these tasks. Bobs and I weren't under skipper's orders. We were under orders of the sea, and at the first sound of a slowing motor we rushed to stations. Going to sea being a communal project, our pride was involved and we would have been mortified had we proved undependable.

A small boat with only one dinghy, and an existence new to all three, acted as a great leveler. The usual gap between the adult and child world was closed because we did everything together. Had this situation been contrived in town, where school, playmates and adult activities compel separate paths, it would have been a false and tiresome arrangement. But in a home cut off by the sea, communal participation developed naturally.

And everything was as interesting and different for us as it was for Bobs. Basically our physical world was altered. We had exchanged land for water, a stable home for one of constant movement; we no longer walked out of our front door but stepped into a dinghy and rowed. In the sharing of these new experiences we got as chummy as a group of sightseers in a bus.

Danger, too, held us together as a crew-family. We were learning to take precautions automatically. We discussed perils and faced their possibility in the future. Now, as we cruised north, we thought of what lay just ahead, our first encounter with a tidal rapids, Deception Pass.

In Seattle all advice had begun and ended with a warning about Deception Pass. Even its name, given to it by Vancouver the explorer, suggested treacherous water.

"The Coast Pilot" was equally pessimistic. Usually I tried to rise above that volume's lugubrious cautions lest my desire to go cruising be completely shattered. One would gather from its pages that the Inside Passage was one long succession of rock-cluttered channels, swift currents and narrow passages and that a skipper who did not possess local knowledge had much better take to the open Pacific.

The government's guide for mariners was very definite about Deception Pass. After describing the narrow channel between an arm of Puget Sound and Juan de Fuca Strait, it added that the pass was "only eligible for such small vessels and steamers as are well acquainted with the locality. The tide sets through it with great velocity." Since we had never seen this or any other tidal rapids, we read the statement with deep misgiving.

The physical facts were terrifying enough without warnings. The pass was a cut between sheer rocky walls and the current, at strength, ran at ten knots. We had been cautioned to attempt these rapids only at dead slack, when the current ceased to run in one direction and turned to flow in the other. Slack differed from tidal change by shore because water which raised and lowered a vast indented area had to flow through this bottle neck. Time was required for the process just as a huge flask is filled or emptied more slowly than a wide-mouthed pail.

Government current tables stated the hours of slack, and because our first tidal rapids seemed to demand the fresh energies of early morning, we dropped anchor one afternoon within a short distance of the pass. When we went to bed we had very much of a "just before the battle" feeling and our anchor was up early. We were taking no chances on being late for slack in the Pass, for we intended to go through in dead water if possible. We arrived with time to spare.

A tug with a tow of logs lay in the shelter of a point, holding the sections of logs against the shore much as a nervous brood hen might guard her chickens. We drew alongside for information and advice. While we did not admit that this was our first tidal rapids, the captain could easily have deduced it from our manner. And he upset all our careful timing. According to him, the government's current tables were quite wrong. He used his own and most elaborate method to determine the hour of change.

We listened intently and then fell back to work out this new system. I circled the *Yakima* slowly while Robert worked on such data as mean lower low water, tidal differences and constants and ratio of range. It meant nothing to me, perhaps because arithmetic never had. But I realized for the first time that mathematical problems are not devised solely to make life difficult for students. These figures had a distinct bearing on our safety.

Robert had just determined that we had more than an hour to wait when we saw the tug pull out from behind the point. We did not know then the canny attitude which towing logs develops in tug captains. This one was merely seeking the most advantageous start of his snail's pace during the brief slackening of the current, but we assumed that slack had come.

Robert speeded up the motor. "I'm taking no chances in that narrow channel with a tow of logs," he said.

We were well out in the current when we realized our mistake. The towboat captain must have wondered at the source of our sudden courage. Safe near shore, he stared out of his wheelhouse as the navigators who had been over-cautious ten minutes before now gaily started through while the tide was running.

We bore down on a maelstrom.

"You girls are in for a ride!" Robert warned. "Hang on."

The twisting force of the current gripped our hull. A whirlpool spun us to one side and an eddy flung us toward a rocky wall. The deck careened alarmingly. And then another eddy flung us back into the center of the channel. Robert gripped the wheel and watched the surface of the water. He did not know tidal rapids but he had water-savvy. The *Yakima* skirted a line of small whirlpools which marked the edge of the back eddy. The propeller labored in heavy water and then raced as we went with the current. In another moment we were out in a wide channel.

I looked back a bit dazed. It had happened so quickly I could not believe Deception Pass lay behind us.

"That was easy," Robert said. "After this I wouldn't be afraid to try it an hour, either way, of slack."

"But your mate was scared," Bobs said.

I had been, and still was. I thought the skipper had experienced a few bad moments, but I didn't say so. Even a family-style skipper has a right to his private doubts and fears.

We turned now into Rosario Straits. They lay sparkling, blue and inviting across our bow. Mount Baker towered astern. Abeam were the white peaks of the Olympics. Off to the westward the Straits of Juan de Fuca led to the open Pacific. Deception Pass was the doorway to the real cruising waters.

I offered to begin my education in steering by compass

even though it seemed unnecessarily nautical when we could so easily aim at a point. But point-to-point piloting would not be possible in fog or at night, or even in the larger waterways. I thought the skipper looked a bit smirky when he turned the wheel over to me. I was sure of it five minutes later when I struggled with a whirling compass. The *Yakima* weaved until our wake looked as though I were trying water writing. Like all beginners, I tried to swing the compass to the lubber point instead of the lubber point to the compass, and it was weeks before I became convinced the needle didn't move.

It was a field day for the bo'sun and the skipper. When I finally found myself headed east while the course I wanted lurked stubbornly at the bottom of the compass, their laughter threatened to destroy my mate's rating. I suggested that the bo'sun take a trick at the wheel.

She fell into the trap, and she was so small and so sure I was sorry for her. Her head barely topped the spokes. Her stance was very quartermasterly. So was her manner until that first look of horror as the compass started off on a mad swing.

Equality in lubberishness having been restored, I carried on my training in peace and quiet, or at least as much peace as the strong currents would permit. There were no snickers when I got lost in the tide rips.

"Where did you learn to steer by compass?" I asked Robert, when I finally got the lubber line under fair control.

"Dodging blackfish in Puget Sound that first afternoon," he said.

By sneaking sights over the bow, I made our landfall, a point on one of the San Juan Islands. The whole group was enchanting, a northwood's fairyland thrust up from the sea. Pines grew from tide mark. In narrow channels we caught inviting glimpses of small bays and winding arms. To explore them would take days or even weeks. It seemed silly to rush past such beauty and start across the big Gulf of Georgia.

"And we might pile up before we found anything better," the skipper added, a speech we were to remember a few days later.

But our exploration of the San Juan group began and ended at the town of Friday Harbor that afternoon. Bobs and I returned to the municipal float with rare shopping booty, native spring lamb, green peas and fresh strawberries, to find a visitor aboard. He was in fisherman's uniform, his shirttail tied in a little knot behind and his hip boots cuffed down at the knee like a medieval swordsman.

"Mr. Willis has been telling me about the coast," Robert said. "He's been all along British Columbia and in Alaska."

"And I'd like to be going again," Mr. Willis said. "It's a great trip you've planned."

As we stowed our packages in the galley I heard our guest suggest an anchorage. A mobile home is a great convenience for we dropped the hook just off Mr. Willis's small white house and went ashore for an afternoon call. He met us on what he called his "foredeck," and the railed veranda thrust out over the water did give the feel of shipboard. He explained the nautical atmosphere of his home very simply. "Knew how to keep ship, but keeping house would have bothered me."

Mr. Willis may have lived on land, but he had never really left the sea. He was born on the islands and as a lad he and his brother had rowed entirely around Vancouver Island. They made the voyage in winter. Hundreds of miles of open ocean along one of the worst coasts in the world! His only comment was that it had been "a very pretty trip." Later he was the first fisherman to troll for salmon in the tide rips off Cape Flattery.

"I built my own boat," he added. "A man's got to know what's under him out there."

I looked at the pioneer of the famous Flattery fishermen and then at his small troller. It was the last of a line of home-built craft and he was proud of it. I asked why he lived on land.

"It's on account of my sisters," he said, a trifle shamefaced. "They got to feeling that living in a boat isn't quite respectable. So I promised to build me a house. Want to look around?"

We followed him through his sop to respectability. He was quite confident that his sacrifice had been appreciated, but I wondered if his home ashore had really relieved his sisters' minds. The "main cabin" was as fine a piece of ship's carpentry as I ever saw on land. It was quite narrow, had built-in lockers and two transom berths facing each other across three feet of floor space. The table was hinged neatly against the wall. That room could have set out to sea and not a thing would have gone adrift.

The galley must have baffled the sisters completely. Dishes were held in racks and the small ship's stove wore side rails. The stateroom was as nautical. When I saw a kerosene lamp in gimbals I expected it to sway. The only sea gear which he felt demanded an explanation was his ship's berth.

"Been at sea so many years it seemed I couldn't have slept ashore," he said.

In the early evening Mr. Willis rowed out to the *Yakima* and joined us for after-dinner coffee. We got out the charts. If we'd not had any charts aboard, I think he could have drawn them for us. His memory was almost photographic. He described long, winding, sea-floored canyons which penetrate the high mountains, waterfalls which drop so sheerly that a boat's tank can be filled with hose and funnel. He gave details of small hidden harbors. He told of the violence of skookum chucks in which the tides run twelve and even twenty knots. His words had warmth and color. He had not only seen but had felt the beauty of that vast stretch of sea country to the north.

When we described our first encounter with the two schools of blackfish, he confirmed our deductions as to the sound of the propeller.

"Sometimes a big boy, a hump- or fin-back, gets a fellow worried," he admitted. "I've always wondered what would happen if you met up with a deaf whale."

It was long past dark when Mr. Willis pulled his dinghy alongside and said good night.

He left us stirred and eager for farther waters, for white-capped mountains adorned by waterfalls and the jeweled blue of glaciers, for voyages up winding fiords flanked by bold cliffs and forested slopes. He had given us bits of weather wisdom and axioms on winds and currents. He had told us how to make the only possible anchorage at the heads of bottomless inlets. That kindly fisherman never knew it, but he had trimmed our sails for the north.

"Who said anything about cruising the San Juans?" the skipper demanded after his last trip on deck to see that our riding light was burning.

IV

"BREAK OUT THE GROG"

Ceremony marked our crossing of the international boundary. The bo'sun had become a stickler on yacht etiquette and assumed the duty of seeing that our ensign flew at the taffrail each morning and was taken in at sunset. Her offer had sounded handsome, but a glint in her eye made us suspect she enjoyed reminding superior officers they had slipped up several times in this ship routine.

"Dad left the ensign out till bedtime last night," she reported.

She was waiting to see if we would forget the formalities of becoming guests of the British Empire. But the skipper fooled her. He broke out the red ensign and attached it to the halyards. As we crossed the line the bo'sun ran it to the yard arm.

Then we were indeed "going foreign."

Mr. Willis had warned us not to miss the Gulf Islands, which lay just beyond the border. They were as trim and manicured as he had promised. The Vancouver Island side of the archipelago was the stronghold of English county families and they had brought the orderliness of the homeland with them. Small homes dotted the shores. All had a regulation equipment—house, gravel paths, flower garden, float with a white dinghy moored alongside, a sailboat at a buoy, and somewhere in the clearing a smooth green square for tennis. No wonder tennis teas figure so largely in English fiction! Neatly trimmed hedges rebuked pine forests and even the rocky shoreline looked tide washed and scoured.

We dropped anchor in a lovely bay. A secluded cove we had glimpsed around a point promised bathing, and Bobs and I decided to make a bath a major event. Our sixty-gallon tank of fresh water was jealously guarded by the skipper. He didn't actually ration water with a medicine dropper, but the cubic contents of one were considered adequate for tooth-brushing and a pint was rated as a plunge.

Bobs and I, equipped with towels and soap, set off in the dinghy. The cove was as secluded as we had hoped and we took possession. A shelving rocky ledge at the head had warmed the incoming tide. Rock out-croppings gave it a rugged aspect and we were searching for a pool when we came upon a magnificent natural bathtub.

Neptune himself might have scooped out that huge depression for his favorite mermaid and thrown up the rocky wall which screened it. Smooth, clean granite sides led gradually to waist depth. Not even a barnacle threatened the skin and the tide had filled it with clear tepid water. We sudsed and scoured and chatted. When we were clean we experimented with salt water laundry. A cake of Captain's soap, which lathered in sea water, didn't accomplish a cleansing miracle on my shirt, but it had done a great deal for Bobs and me.

We believed we were alone until we heard voices from the rock above us. We looked up into the startled and indignant faces of an Englishman and his three sub-teen daughters. They stood in a line like steps. Baggy black bathing suits apparently bought for them to grow in, and white towels clasped to their bosoms, made them look like a row of enraged penguins.

The man's ruddy coloring was turning purple in his rage, and even his sandy mustaches quivered. I feared an apoplectic stroke and the girls stared fearfully from him to us. Apparently they could not quite believe that any person could have done this to him and be allowed to go on living.

Bobs made hospitable gestures toward the girls while I attempted a polite speech. Both overtures were received in icy silence.

This desecration of the family tub could not be passed over lightly. The affair promised the importance of an international incident, and we adapted the only diplomatic course left open by ignominiously collecting towels, wet shirt and Captain's soap from under their frozen glances. I tried to make my retreat to the dinghy appear both leisurely and dignified, but I am sure I slunk. When we rounded the point they were still standing staring after us, a frieze of British wrath and outrage.

"Do you suppose they'll ever bathe in that tub again?" Bobs asked in a tone of awe.

I doubted it. The tide would carry out all traces of our Captain's soap but nothing short of a tidal wave could cleanse the cove of the pollution of our presence. Even the harbor might be spoiled for them so long as we lay at anchor. I became increasingly convinced of this.

"We've got to get out of here," I said as we scrambled from the dinghy into the *Yakima*. "I washed my shirt in an Englishman's bathtub."

The skipper stared. He knew a single-track mind sometimes caused me to do odd things, but this demanded an explanation.

When he could stop laughing he began to scoff at my determination to leave the harbor. Neighbor trouble, he pointed out, didn't enter cruising life.

"Because it's so simple to change the neighborhood," I said.

In the end we did just that. We pulled up the hook and sailed away until we found a cove without a house on shore. It was dusk then, we were tired and dinner was late, and the skipper didn't think the incident so funny.

"Hope this gives you a good night's sleep," he said.

His speech was a cue to the news he broke soon after midnight when he shook me awake.

"We're aground," he said.

His recognition of disaster proved at least that he had become skipper-conscious. Even in his sleep he had caught that first stiffening of a craft whose keel rests on a solid substance. His startled leap from the berth had tipped the boat a few inches and it had not swung back. The balance of a waterborne craft was gone.

In two seconds flat I joined him on deck, where he was trying to shove off with a pick pole. I added my efforts with an oar but we were far beyond the shoving stage. The *Yakima* didn't budge.

"Would the motor help?" I asked.

"Might," he said. "But I've got to make sure there are no rocks astern."

Exploring in the dinghy, he found we were on a reef but caught forward.

"Better waken Bobs," he said as he went below to start the motor.

Bobs sat up in her berth and surveyed us with wide-eyed astonishment. The motor did nothing. We were fast aground and getting more so every minute as the tide ebbed. Robert stopped the motor.

"We'd better get dressed," he said. "We'll get off in the dinghy."

Bobs and I began to pull on clothes. Taking to a small boat in the middle of the night conformed so perfectly with the pattern of sea disasters that haste automatically entered the picture. I grabbed the first clothes I could find. Bobs too was donning a strange assortment.

"Dress warmly," the skipper cautioned. "You girls may have to wade in three feet of water."

He intended only a light reminder of unpredictable events, but its effect on Bobs was sobering. She speeded dressing in silence. When she was finally accoutered for the sea, boots, overalls and heavy Mackinaw, she remarked suddenly, "You two can wade in three feet of water. But what do I do in it?"

The practicability of her question helped to restore morale. We were laughing when we stepped overside into the dinghy, and then suddenly it didn't seem so funny any more. I wondered if we had lost the boat and asked Robert what we were taking with us.

"Cash, traveler's checks and a flashlight," he said.

That sounded serious. I thought of several things we might have brought. Food was one, but Robert objected to my proposal that we go back.

"No telling what our weight would do," he said.

We circled our grounded craft. We could see little in the darkness, but we knew the *Yakima* was caught forward and amidships. As the water was deeper on the port side, apparently the reef shelved off. With heavy timbers we might still shore up the hull. The beach where we went to search didn't promise much, but partly by feel and partly by sight, we found some pieces of driftwood. They were of varying lengths and Robert thought them almost too frail to bother with. To me, even finding them brought comfort. We were doing something to save our boat.

We carried them to the dinghy and I was beseeching Robert to hurry when we heard a fearful racket.

The *Yakima* had heeled over. Cans, dishes, kettles, objects big and small, slammed and crashed and clattered inside that craft. Every starboard locker must have dumped itself to port. After a moment of silence we heard a final heavy thud.

"What was that last thing that fell?" the bo'sun asked.

It sounded as though it might have been the stove or even the motor. We abandoned the driftwood and rowed out. By flashlight we looked at the *Yakima* as she lay far over on the shelving reef, now bared by the falling tide. All hope of any help from us was past. She would have to take her chances.

The behavior of any boat when beached is problematical until it has been proved. Boats have been known to lie supinely on their sides and fill. Others lift with the rising water. The *Yakima* drew three feet. One of her best features was her deadrise. That was now a handicap. So also was her long cockpit. It looked very vulnerable as she lay far to port.

I asked the skipper if he thought she had a chance. His answer was an equivocal comment on her deadrise and her cockpit.

"And if she fills?" I asked.

"She'll slip off into deep water," he said.

The tide was still ebbing. It would be several hours before flood would determine the outcome. We went ashore and built a fire, a blaze as despondent as was our spirits. I broke a long silence to ask the skipper if we had marine insurance.

"This is a swell time to think of that," he said.

So I knew we had none.

With first officer's tact, I had refrained from discussing causes. I suspected an incorrect computation of the tidal range. To me, a mathematical error would be as inevitable as any other act of God and should automatically absolve the skipper.

But Robert was apparently seeking some other explanation when he went for a dinghy prowl in the first gray trace of daylight. When he returned I asked why we had gone aground.

"Because you washed your shirt in an Englishman's bathtub," he said.

"No," I said. "I mean really how did it happen?"

"I told you," he insisted. "When we finally found this harbor, I got careless and let out a lot of cable and misjudged the distance to the reef. When the breeze let up, we swung onto it. All on account of a shirt."

"And I didn't even get it clean," I mourned.

A few days earlier, when I'd been puzzling over current tables, I had asked him how he intended to cope with tidal problems. He had answered that he expected to mix mathematics, common sense and trial and error, and that he'd pull some boners. He had added that he'd try not to pull them twice.

I referred to this now in an attempt to be cheerful. "Just some boners we won't pull twice."

"We may not have a chance to."

His tone was sober. I knew it meant more than the monetary loss. That was serious enough, but emotional values were involved. Already we were planning, some time and somehow, to get a larger boat and really cruise the North. Now I wondered what would happen to the bigger venture if this exploratory cruise ended so soon in disaster and in the mortification of a skipper who had lost his ship.

With the first pink flush of sunrise the incoming tide began to lap the reef on which the *Yakima* lay. Robert suggested that we could see better from the dinghy. We rowed out. Our disjointed efforts to make conversation didn't conceal our tension. Each knew the other was talking only because silence made the anxious moments longer. Bobs sat in the bow. Until we saw her sober face we hadn't realized how much the summer had meant to her. None of us had realized how much we had been counting on the cruise until the end was threatened. A very disconsolate trio sat with their eyes focused on the cockpit as the sea crept higher.

When the water was within two inches of the top of the combing I looked away. I didn't want to see the tide cross it. I was wondering if I could bear to be there as the *Yakima* made that sideways slip into deep water, when I heard Robert's exultant yell.

"She's started up!"

The port side was lifting, slowly but perceptibly. We sat in the dinghy and encouraged that craft much as one might talk to a rallying patient. There was a new affection in our tones. Robert forgave her the cockpit. He reminded her that she had been built by a good builder. And once or twice he called her a good girl. It didn't help the *Yakima* a whit, but it was an easement of our tension as we watched her struggle to an even keel, and then float free.

Aboard at last, we found below decks the shambles we had feared. Neither the stove nor the motor had moved but every other piece of equipment had done so or was draped with some object which had projected itself across the cabin. We decided that the last heavy thud had been a stove lid. It had landed neatly on a pile of china. The galley showed what can happen when an improperly stowed boat moves quickly. The lesson was cheap at that, for it lasted through many years and probably saved much equipment when we hit heavy going. The dresser looked as though a giant with no food inhibitions had started to shake himself up a meal. A can of motor oil had merged with molasses to form a batter thickened with dried fruits, pickles, soap powders and condiments. A bottle of capers had been added as an afterthought. A jar of preserved eggs which had gone adrift had not helped the floor much, but they were now slowly dripping into the bilge.

We three crowded into the companionway to look.

"What happens," the skipper asked our authority on ship etiquette, "after a disaster at sea?"

And Bobs, who had her own private stock of ginger beer, said promptly, "Break out the grog."

V

AS OUR SHIP HAD TO BE EN-
tered at the first foreign port, we moored at the municipal float in Nanaimo. The entire crew walked to the government building. This was very improper. A crew should
not leave an unentered vessel. I had time to regret our
informality while the customs official read and reread the
ship's papers which the skipper had laid diffidently on the
desk. It didn't seem possible that a six-ton vessel warranted
such deep thought on the part of a maritime power. Finally
Great Britain demanded the reason for our cruise.

The skipper hesitated, suspecting a trick question, but I
am always willing to go exhaustively into our past. I was
about to do so when the official supplied the missing answer.

"For health and pleasure," he prompted briskly, and he
stamped the document and pushed it toward us.

Legitimately ashore now, we went shopping for dishes
to repair the galley wreckage and a summer's liquor supply.
The skipper decided that a gallon of overproof rum would
help to cement coast friendships and I celebrated our return to Canada with Scotch.

Equipped now for callers, we had one immediately. A
canine head was thrust through a cabin window and a
medium-sized white dog looked us over. A black spot

above one eye gave him a jovial leer as he asked, "How about it?"

Our laughter brought him pell-mell into the cabin where he went immediately to the galley dresser in a barefaced demand for a handout. He didn't definitely say that for months he had vainly tried to find work, but his pitiful look implied such a story.

"Perhaps he's lost," the bo'sun suggested hopefully.

Although he accepted the last of the San Juan lamb with considerable tail wagging, he didn't eat like a famished dog. I was suspecting that he was not a worthy object of charity when we heard the exhaust of an approaching boat. Our caller pricked up his ears, finished his lamb with a sudden air of haste, stopped for a brief wag of thanks on the companionway steps, and departed. Most evidently he had an appointment.

When we reached the float he was already absorbed in the latest arrival. Before the lines were made fast he had disappeared in the wheelhouse.

"Of course he was in a hurry," Robert said. "He heard his master's boat."

This credit for canine devotion was immediately ruined by our white dog appearing with a large bone. He cut us dead as he sauntered off to shore. A man looked out of the wheelhouse and laughed.

"That's the float bum," he said. "Been working boats for years."

Bobs renewed her suggestion of adoption though she gave up the idea when we learned that boats had attempted to give him a home and had pulled out with him aboard. He had always got back to the float to continue the art of panhandling and now everybody accepted him for what he was—the most engaging canine rascal who ever worked

his personality to earn a living. Cooks saved bones and
tidbits for him and his attentions were considered a tribute
to the craft.

"You can't tell me that dog don't know boats which
feed the best," the captain of the new arrival said. "If he
didn't come aboard us, the crew would begin to growl
about the chow."

In the early afternoon we nosed out into the Gulf of
Georgia. A strong northwest wind was blowing. The
skipper didn't like to start a five-hour crossing as there was
no knowing what the wind might become before we could
get to shelter. My insistence that it was only the usual
afternoon westerly was not an attempt to be a weather
prophet. I have a fundamental dislike of turning back.

"If Vancouver could wait over in Departure Bay, we
can," Robert said as he turned the bow of the *Yakima*
back toward harbor.

I didn't feel quite so bold when we found two tugs at
anchor, shepherding their booms of logs. Steam in the
boilers was the only sign of life except for white-aproned
Chinese cooks who came on deck occasionally with cans
of garbage. I wanted to discuss weather, but it wasn't until
evening that any member of the crew appeared.

We rowed over in the dinghy. A man leaned on the rail
and answered questions. The westerly, he told us, might
blow out that night, or it might last three days. He was as
disinterested in its duration as he was in us. His manner
suggested that weather was out of our control and might
as well be accepted.

The skipper wrested an admission that the gulf was no
place for us that day, and on our row home he looked a

bit smirky. I remarked that towing logs apparently made men lethargic.

"Even you'd become philosophical aboard a tug," he said. "A two-mile speed hour after hour with the same point in sight all day—you'd calm down or go crazy."

The westerly did not blow out that night nor the next day. The tug's crews provided a lesson in patience. They didn't even come on deck to look at the weather. Those somnolent tugs became more and more annoying when cited as a model for my own deportment.

For the first time we three were cooped up aboard the *Yakima* with none of the excitement of travel to speed the dragging hours. I spent the first day of our imprisonment in an orgy of activity.

The long lockers underneath the berths had seemed an inspired receptacle for food stores until I discovered that we had almost to take the cabin apart to find a suddenly required item. Now I restowed. Canned butter, grapefruit, oils and everything which would keep better in a cool place were laid below hatches against the hull. The large lockers in the cockpit were converted into a day-by-day grocery storage which could be replenished from the main supplies below the transom berths.

I listed the location of every bit of food aboard the boat and was rather proud of my ready use of the nautical terms, port, starboard, forward, aft and amidships. It was a whole day's job, but never again would I have to unset the dining table, fasten it to the bulkhead, chain up the upper berths, lift the lowers and grope through a heterogeneous collection of packages because we had inopportunely run out of sugar.

I devoted the second day of our imprisonment mainly to gazing at the gulf while the bo'sun and skipper jeered.

"Mother thinks she can make the wind stop by looking at it," Bobs confided to her father.

Their conduct was as annoying as that of the tugs. They put a rope fender around the gunwale of the dinghy. Bobs practiced rowing with Robert coaching from the stern seat. They brought the model yacht into the cabin and made extensive changes on its rigging. They lay stretched out on berths at either side and read. And they talked for hours. Their demeanor suggested that the westerly should be allowed to settle its own affairs, whether it blew for one day or seven.

I was beginning to wonder if I cared about my family when the wind died suddenly the third morning of our stay. I was elated. The skipper glanced at the tugs, neither of which showed signs of departing.

"Wish I knew why they're not pulling out," he said, as though their reasons should guide us.

"Are we sailors, or are we logs?" I demanded.

"You'll find out how much of a sailor you are before we're across the gulf," he said.

He started the motor and raised the anchor in that decisive wait-and-see manner men adopt to indicate their opinion of feminine logic, and we departed. At the end of three hours I almost felt sorry for him. Except for a rather delightful ground swell, the sea was calm. Distant islands were not low, as farther south. Each had its own mountain, while on the mainland ahead and on Vancouver Island off our port quarter great white peaks lifted into a blue sky.

Suddenly the wind came up from the southeast and blew harder after its short rest. No wonder the tugs had remained at anchor. I began to wish I were a log and not a sailor.

"I told you the gulf could get dirty," the skipper said. "It'll take an hour to get to shelter."

The westerly had blown hard and steadily and honestly. This wind came in gusts and kicked up a quick sea. A straight line was not the safest distance between two points. Quartering away from that sea became too dangerous and we headed into it.

I looked at the shores with some yearning. There is nothing to do with a boat but sail it.

"Boats should have wheels or wings," I said.

"You'll think so before we reach the mainland," Robert said.

When we lifted to a crest I could see waves breaking on the sheer point of an island. Spray drenched the stunted firs growing in rocky crevices above. The continuous onslaught of the sea on those rocks told me something of what we were in for.

Heading into the sea cut our speed and the steersman had to fight every instant. Our course lay to port but we could edge off only between the larger waves. They grew so big it was necessary to meet them full and with a half closed throttle. The skipper could not relax for a moment, and I saw him use the same technique I had known when bucking a head sea in a canoe.

Bobs and I sat in the cockpit and became victims of the strange hypnosis that comes from watching the creamy crests of waves hiss along the sides and fall astern. I was beginning to enjoy it when Robert called me forward.

"Take the wheel," he said.

I didn't even pretend to look eager.

"Better get the knack of easing into them while I'm here to help," he said.

Until then I had not considered the complications of a

two-man boat. Motor trouble would leave me at the wheel alone. And what would Bobs do while I stood the trick? A big wave could pop that small body overside like a pea out of a pod. I said so to Robert.

"Bobs!" he called. "Come up on the bridge."

I steered under the coaching of my tutor.

"Easy," he would caution. "Get ready for that big one. Less throttle! Hit it square!"

The last was usually delivered with considerable more vehemence than the first. Fortunately I was beginning to get the hang of it when the motor stuttered.

The skipper dived below. His head reappeared a moment later as he reported a clogged feed line.

"If I have to stop the motor we're in for a rolling," he said. "But don't worry."

I didn't have time or energy to worry. There is no better antidote for fear than a definite problem and I discovered one reason why a storm is so much more terrifying to passengers than crew.

Measured by combers, each of which had to be appraised and dealt with, Robert was gone a long time. Actually he was gone only a few minutes.

"Trouble worked itself out," he said. "Had enough?"

"Plenty!" I said.

But it was relief to know that I could handle the boat in rough weather and after the skipper had complimented me I did a bit of boasting.

"I'll take another trick a little later," I said quite casually. "Call me when you're tired."

I didn't take a trick. I sat with Bobs on the stern seat of the cockpit and hoped I would not be impressed into service when we came about and started to run before a sou'easter which was getting bigger and better every minute. The *Yakima* was never designed for running and, when she turned the full lines of her stern to the combers, seas crept up behind, lifted her high and tried to throw her into the trough.

The trailing dinghy followed doggedly. When we lifted to a crest, it lay far beneath us, climbing the hill of green water like a tired horse. And when we wallowed in the trough it rode far above our heads. Bobs and I were laughing at its antics when the skipper turned and saw us. He took one look at the small boat towering directly above us.

"Come away from there!" he yelled. "Do you want that dinghy landing in your laps!"

Mate and bo'sun were in disgrace for seeing humor in real danger. After that we settled down beside him and watched the gray-green seas rush past. The wind increased until it tore white spume from the crests and bore it away laughing. There was malevolency in that laughter.

And suddenly all the noise, confusion and motion ceased as the *Yakima* rounded a point toward which we had been wallowing. I looked astern to see if the wind could actually still be blowing. Beyond the point the whitecaps were still steadily marching north.

"After this I do what tow boats do," I admitted.

Robert was tired, but he looked happy.

"That breeze was nothing," he insisted. "No boat's been to sea until it's had a dusting."

I'd always wondered what rated as a dusting. But at least our crew of three had proved that we were sailors and not logs.

VI

WE LEARN FROM CROWS

Norwegian fishermen have told us that the inlets of British Columbia are more beautiful than the fiords of their native land, and few can dispute them because both fiords and inlets have been seen by few except our fishermen friends. The fiords of Norway are remote, and close to the northwest corner of the United States is one of the most spectacular coast lines in the world. Yet we have been in inlets never visited by tourists.

For a thousand miles north of Puget Sound this coast once extended farther into the Pacific. Its mountains were much higher than at present. An outer range rose from the sea. Behind it was a deep valley and behind that a stupendous range with deep narrow canyons cut by ancient rivers. Before the last glacial period the whole coast sank, tilting seaward, and the sea flowed in. The outer range became a vast archipelago extending from Puget Sound through Southeastern Alaska and the first valley is now the Inside Passage. Former foothills and mountains have become islands, and spaces between the peaks form a fascinating network of straits, channels, sounds, bays and arms.

Even the great mainland range sank, but the mountains permitted the sea to take only the steep walled canyons of the ancient rivers. Today these canyons are long inlets. The sea has invaded but the mountains remain. Neither makes concession to the other. The mountains rise straight from salt water and one could moor a ship against rocks as to a wharf. One could step from the deck and begin at once to climb.

As we cruised up the narrow winding ribbon of Jervis Inlet, the sea seemed to part the mountains for us. They lifted directly from the sea, forested, with sheer cliffs mossed in bronze. Across their glittering snow peaks traveled dark shapes of cloud shadows. Nearer peaks merged with higher neighbors beyond, but the face they presented to us was complete. Sharp spires reached into the clouds and from the heights our eyes could follow one long sweeping line to the Pacific.

Never until then had I seen a mountain whole.

In such a place even "The Coast Pilot" should break down and become rhapsodic. Hoping for once to catch it off its pessimistic base, I opened the book and found it admitted Jervis Inlet to be remarkable. This seemed a minor triumph until Robert explained that the word was used in the sense of being noticeable.

As we went farther, lofty mountains took more complete possession. We stared back at a reach behind us and the way by which we had come was hidden. The peaks had closed in. That bit of sea was surrounded by inner mountains. It was a detached fragment, cut off from the wide ocean but still a part of it. The tang of salt water was in our nostrils. Great tides left their marks on the shores and gave a sense of movement. The blue sea lay there, victorious in its invasion, but a prisoner.

"This—this—" I tried to find words and then became as inarticulate as was "The Coast Pilot."

"After a summer of it," Robert said, "you'll get peeved when I call you from the galley to have a look. We're only beginning."

We were on our way to Princess Louise, which is an inlet beyond an inlet. It is connected with Jervis near the head by a rocky gorge obstructed at the outer end by rocks and islands. "The Coast Pilot" gave the velocity of the tidal current in the entrance as nine knots and didn't mention a sharp bend.

We had been told much of the beauty of Princess Louise, but I didn't think it could compare with what we were leaving.

The tidal rapids at the entrance was an inspired piece of showmanship. We were so occupied in making the turn with a rushing current that when we looked up it was as though a curtain had been lifted from one of nature's most spectacular performances. Yosemite, with a sea floor, lay before us.

We sailed down a narrow slit in the mountains. Peaks became higher and steep shores more bold and sheer until snowcaps rose from five to eight thousand feet on either side. Yet height was forgotten in the impression of nearness. Intimacy is an odd word to use in speaking of a mountain, but these lofty masses had lost some of their austerity and challenge. They had drawn near and become benign. Granite ledges seemed almost within hand touch. Colors of bronze and old gold mosses on steep shores were repeated by reflection on the water. The young green of fresh growth which had found foothold in high crevices was intensified in the mirroring. One could not determine where the sea left off and the mountains began.

High above us lay snow fields. Everywhere streams tumbled down sheer cliffs. Some were long white shafts against dark rock, others foaming cascades of broken leaps from crag to crag, a robust and not-to-be-denied seeking of the sea. And here and there a crystal pencil left a mountain height as water and was caught and dispelled by sunshine into rainbow mist, a gossamer thing midway between substance and a dream.

Bobs and I climbed atop the wheelhouse in our excitement. It was a new, quiet world up there. The exhaust came to us as a low mutter. We could hear only a sharp tinkle from the bow wave. We counted waterfalls, not because we are by nature statisticians but because we could not believe this abundance. In the last two miles we saw fifty-two.

We anchored at the head of the inlet off a river which followed the general custom and made its entrance as a falls in a last triumphant leap of fifty feet. We wanted to lie within sight and sound of that gorgeous white curtain. The inlet is too deep for even a large ship to anchor, and the bank of silt deposited by the river offers the only bottom a cable can reach.

This bank drops off at an angle of forty-five degrees, and no anchor could cling to it. Mr. Willis had told us how to lie securely, however, and we followed his directions. Robert dropped an anchor in eight fathoms and I ran on toward the shore until it had bitten. He then made the cable fast astern and took the other anchor to shore in the dinghy, its cable fast to our bow.

Now we lay moored bow and stern. We could not be driven ashore, for the heavy anchor would have to be dragged up the steep bank. And that anchor could not drop off into the depths because the bow anchor kept us from drifting off the bank.

Thus we lay securely and enjoyed our waterfall. After dinner we sat on deck and watched our world change from light to darkness. The sun had long since set in our deep water valley. Its light was only a rosy crown on white-capped peaks above a broad band of indigo shadows.

"Mountains, a private showing of a waterfall, and a boat at anchor," I said. "What more could we want?"

"If we had a boat large enough to live in, this sort of thing could be continuous," Robert said. "We'd move our home from one spectacle to another."

He was silent for a moment before he added, "We'd need a fifty-footer. Take some doing—money, navigating and work."

It was then that the bug was hatched.

We had already discovered that days at anchor had to be declared regularly aboard a thirty-six-foot boat. We declared one the next day. The motor required attention. Laundry must be done ashore. And we wanted to explore the river. Another sporting event was called to our attention by the crows.

They began gathering soon after breakfast. A large delegation sat in nearby trees and noisily discussed some matter of public interest. Other crows joined them, flying straight to the meeting place. Newcomers asked questions and received a raucous chorus of information. Every branch held one or more black shining bodies and I became impatient with all this chattering procrastination.

"Now they're here, why don't they do something?" I demanded.

Curiosity kept us on deck. We were almost ready to believe that they had met merely for conversation when a crow suddenly let out an exultant shriek and dived at the shore. In two seconds every bird had followed. The beach at the river-mouth was filled with crows.

"A clam tide!" Robert yelled. "And we've been sitting here wondering what they were waiting for."

Armed with pail and pronged spade, we joined the

crows. The beach was erupting with tiny spurts of water and when I learned each spurt meant a clam I became as excited and voluble as the birds. Robert turned over a spadeful. Not one clam but half a dozen lay in the loosened silt.

I had gone to the beach properly dressed for clamming. I wore gloves and carried a piece of canvas on which to kneel. But with my first sight of this harvest of the sea I went completely atavistic. The canvas lay forgotten. The gloves were dropped. I dug and I scratched. Maybe I cawed.

The crows clammed with us. Robert rested his back and watched them.

"Look at what those smart birds are doing!" he exclaimed.

Bobs and I maintained the first demonstration was an accident until we'd seen a second, and then a third, crow fly over a rock and drop a clamshell. Before it struck, he had swooped to his shucked dinner. Like every good system, the method had a flaw. Gangster crows sat on rocks and waited. One trusting crow lost three broken clams to raiders before he decided there was no percentage in being an aerial waiter.

Neither the crows nor we left the beach until the incoming tide was covering the clams' small jets. The crows flew low to wherever they slept off their orgy. We left our clams in the pail to spit out the sand in water and I read recipes for chowder.

While the skipper worked on the motor that afternoon, Bobs and I explored the shore. At the foot of the falls I found a pool so lovely I became inspired, although by nature I am not a fervent laundress. It lay in a setting of thick foliage. Sunlight filtered through the delicate green of broad-leaved maple and formed a lacery overhead. The pool's clean granite sides were mossy-edged and adorned with flowers. Jeweled dragonflies flitted lazily or alighted to make an extra garnish on a vivid petal. In such surroundings, even the scouring of clothes is fun. The shore looked like a Chinese laundry with sheets, towels and shirts spread on driftwood to dry.

Bobs and I went swimming and showered in icy mist below the falls. Huckleberry bushes growing shoulder-high and loaded with red berries decided us on pie for dinner, but I was soon the sole harvester.

Bobs deserted me for a grotto. It was the first of a large collection of mossy retreats she discovered in many harbors. Tall five-finger ferns concealed the entrance to a fairy room hidden beneath a huge spreading cedar. The ground was carpeted in brown needles and the retreat was dim and cool. At the rear a broad cedar root, upholstered in thick moss, formed a low couch from which one expected to see a wood nymph spring. A single shaft of sunlight picked out and made translucent the tender green of a thick clump of maiden hair.

"See," Bobs said. "They've even put in flowers."

Then I knew that I was trespassing in the world of the little people. Red huckleberries and laundry pools belonged to my age. I returned to them, and as I looked back I saw Bobs pull the fern door shut behind me.

In the late afternoon the skipper ahoyed for transportation ashore. He wanted to know what the river did before its last leap to the sea and all three of us started off with the laudable ambition of scaling the cliff beside the river. It was our first experience with the dense growth of British Columbia mountain sides. We abandoned the project after a half-hour's struggle with an impenetrable barrier of spruce, cedar, dead and down timber, huge boulders, salal brush and a thicket of huckleberries.

The attempt at mountain climbing gave us a fine appetite for clam chowder. The clams were succulent, fat and tender. I admired the crows for their discernment in sea food, but Robert refused to believe they were epicures.

"You mean those crows didn't come from all over the country to this special beach?" I demanded.

"One way to find out. We can wait for tomorrow morning's low tide."

That meant missing low water slack in the entrance and as we sat on deck the next morning watching an empty sky I began to feel a bit foolish. By some verbal chicanery I had been maneuvered into the position of defending a theory that crows carried timepieces and tide tables.

"Not a crow," the skipper said.

As he spoke a dozen winged their way across the inlet and alighted in the trees. Others began arriving. The same question-and-answer cawing went on as the previous morning, and, as before, the swoop of one crow was the signal for the local clam diggers' union to go to work.

"I'll be damned!" Robert said.

The crows' understanding of tides bothered Robert. He decided finally that they watched the shoreline. I would have been quite willing to believe they were mathematicians and added and subtracted with great ease.

Bobs saw nothing strange in their timely arrival. Apparently she expected tide intelligence and I wondered what the *Yakima's* grounding had done to our rating. We probably ranked lower than the crows, but neither Robert nor I took a chance and asked her.

VII

SALMON

GRIEF POINT HAD BEEN IN
sight for hours, ahead, abeam and, at long, long last, astern.
Only then did we know we were slowly eating up the
miles. All day we had been slogging up the Gulf of
Georgia. It was glassy. The glare of sunlight on the water
made me sleepy. Bobs had gone below to read, her solution
of an uneventful afternoon. I yawned and studied the
chart.

Sarah Point lay just ahead. Beyond it was Desolation
Sound. Neither name promised much. I wondered if the
two were associated in Captain Vancouver's mind. Map
naming laid explorers open to psychological probings. The
skipper didn't answer my comment. Sun, a burnished sea,
the steady throb of the motor and the monotony of a low
shoreline had acted as a soporific. He didn't even care
whether he had relief at the wheel.

I had gone below and was intent on an elaborate pudding when I heard him call.

"On deck, crew!"

We rushed up to find Sarah Point astern and the whole
glory and magnificence of Desolation Sound heaped up
before us. Across a stretch of mirror sea, ranks and ranks
of snow-clad peaks extended. They rose straight from the
water and higher peaks behind them crowded closely.
It was a mighty gathering of the mountains. After the low

shores we had been following, this barrage of grandeur came with startling impact.

"And Vancouver named this Desolation Sound," I said.

"May be something to your Sarah theory after all," Robert said. "You girls better stick around."

Bobs forgot her book and I deserted the pudding, but we had heard the finale before the opera. The high peaks of Toba Inlet and the charm of the Rendezvous Islands couldn't touch us. We were still a little numb.

We were making our longest day's run, half the length of the Gulf of Georgia, and we intended to tie up that evening at the float of Henry Maurin, who lived just inside the entrance of the Yucluetaw Rapids.

Even this slight penetration of one of the two large northern passes to the gulf waters made us feel like daring mariners. The passages, Seymour Narrows and Yucluetaw Rapids, are bottleneck openings through which flows the northern tidal water serving the Gulf of Georgia. Twice each lunar day tides raise the level of the gulf and all its channels, straits, inlets, arms, bays and coves from eight to twenty feet. Twice daily all that immense amount of water must flow back to the open ocean. This surge and ebb, this filling and emptying of a large and complicated region, must take place through these narrow channels. The magnitude and the inexorability of this tidal movement stirred my imagination, but nothing I had ever encountered could help me picture the force and violence with which the sea thunders through these two restricted corridors.

Seymour impresses with its might and power, for the channel is fairly straight and the sea pours through in a headlong rush. The Yucluetaws are four miles long, obstructed by islands and reefs, and the channel makes two abrupt turns. Giant whirlpools and boils form, and over-falls mount high above hidden ledges. Four times daily a fury grows until the mountains echo the sullen roar, and then sound and maelstrom fade to what is comparative quiet as the tide turns and prepares again to demand its way.

We had chosen the easterly passage, the Yucluetaws, because it was on the mainland, or inlet, side and also because Stewart Edward White had suggested that we might get in touch with him at Henry Maurin's. Robert had met Stewart and I had wanted to since my north woods days when I read "The Forest." Betty and Stewart White had cruised the two previous summers and had left Seattle before we bought the *Yakima*.

We reached the Yucluetaws just as the last of the flood was pouring out and bucked through the entrance. Taking advantage of an eddy, we made our way along the shore to a small niche in the cliffs where Henry Maurin had stretched boomsticks and built a landing float.

It was fast water. Several boats lay along Henry's boom-stick, among them a fifty-foot cruiser. Robert had only time to remark that he hoped it might be Stewart's boat before I had to go forward and get ready to throw a line.

A man stepped from the cruiser's cabin to help us moor. Robert was maneuvering in tide surges while I stood on the foredeck poised to hurl a line. In my excitement lest we fail to make contact with the boom, I almost knocked our benefactor into the current with a heavy coil of manila.

He was still steadying himself from the impact when Robert stuck his head out of the wheelhouse and called, "Hello, Stewart!"

The man on whom I wanted to make a good impression

glanced quickly in my direction. I thought he might be merely identifying his assailant.

But he laughed. "For Pete's sake, where'd you get that line?" he demanded. "Steal it off a battleship?"

Stewart White was not at all surprised by our arrival for he had suspected that Robert was badly bitten by the cruising bug. In answer to Stewart's call, Betty White appeared on the afterdeck of the *Dawn* and learned the identity of her new neighbors. With her background of African safaris, she too had become a legendary figure and I had expected to meet a woman of almost heroic proportions. Instead, her slight five-foot knicker-clad figure was startlingly girlish. But the moment she came aboard and we heard her voice and felt the vigorous warmth of her glance we caught her amazing "through hell and high water" spirit.

While we were talking a thick-bodied man came from shore on a long boom stick. His deep tan skin and coal black hair made his white undershirt look even whiter. He wore hipped-boots and walked on the almost submerged log as easily as though he trod a pavement.

Stewart introduced "The Pinks" to our host, Henry Maurin.

We had heard something of Henry's history. He had been a Colorado cowpuncher before he drifted out to the coast and saw Indians catching salmon and cod in the Yucluetaws. Needing a job, he offered to deliver live fish to a logging company. Regularity was important for the company had never found a fisherman who could be depended upon to make a weekly delivery.

Henry caught a boatload of silver salmon for the first order and left them in the sea, strung on a cord through the gills. When he returned with a second load he found

only a row of fish heads. A seal had visited the market
first. After that raid Henry kept his live fish in a washtub
in his rowboat.

Now a gas boat, equipped with a live box, had sup-
planted the tub arrangement. Winter and summer, Henry
made weekly deliveries to the logging camp. Only once in
seventeen years had he failed to do so, an impressive record
in face of the obstacles. Each trip to the camp meant running the Yucluetaws twice and in winter he fought gales
and blinding snowstorms.

Henry's first little tent home had also changed. Now,
overlooking the rapids, was a six-room house, surrounded
by fruit trees, vegetable garden and flower beds. Fruit
and vegetables were canned by Henry's wife and in fall
the root house overflowed with jellies and jams, cans of
meat and vegetables, boxes of pears and apples and kegs
of sauerkraut and pickled herring. The Maurins could have
withstood a siege and never missed a meal. It was pioneering housekeeping which made my mouth water.

Henry came aboard the *Yakima* while we were eating
dinner. When he asked if we were fixed for going out
that night, I hadn't the remotest idea what he meant. Nor
had the skipper.

"Which one is the fisherman of the family?" Henry
asked.

The skipper nodded at me.

"Better get your tackle ready," Henry said.

Then I understood the air of purposefulness which had
suddenly descended on the float in late afternoon. Bobs
and I had gone aboard the *Dawn*, and Betty White had
come to visit the *Yakima*. She had found things to admire
in our small boat.

"I can't bear it!" she declared. "You've got a bowl in

your bathroom, which is more than we have. And when you have bathroom traffic the cook can squeeze into a corner. I have to back out of my galley and carry a hot skillet with me."

As Bobs and I beamed to learn other cooks were more put upon than we, Betty had glanced at her watch and made a hurried exit. Evening salmon fishing was so much a part of her Yucluetaw regime it never occurred to her that another woman didn't know all about it.

Twenty minutes later she had called Stewart to dinner. Henry had walked up the hill for his, and the chatting groups on the float had dispersed.

We were eating an early meal only because everyone else appeared to be doing so. Now we left the dishes unwashed and went to the float with Henry. A fisherman who lived in a small boat inside the boom was gathering bait and tackle. We joined him for a conference and Henry introduced Mr. Blair. He was always "Mr. Blair." Only a few knew his French Canadian name and the title was an affectionate tribute to his simple dignity and innate sweetness.

Henry and Mr. Blair equipped me for salmon fishing. Within ten minutes I had cutty-hunk, a spoon which wobbled to resemble a crippled herring, a heavy gaff and a line fathomed with colored string. Mr. Blair showed us how to thread a herring. I began to ask a lot of questions. I'd never caught anything larger than a bass.

"Just watch the others when the run starts," Henry said.

"But how will I know when it's started?" I persisted.

Henry stared in amazement before he laughed. "You'll know," he said.

We set off in our dinghy and followed the others

around the point, where we joined twenty rowboats moving slowly back and forth across the quiet water just inside the current. The scene was very peaceful and an air of sociability prevailed. Each rower nodded to the others as they made the first circle. Friends chatted as they passed. There was no fisherman's anxiety or even impatience. Whatever the event they awaited, they seemed certain it would occur. Except for trailing lines, it appeared that a desire for a quiet evening on the salt chuck had seized a strangely assorted group of people.

Everyone who could get a craft and a line to trail was there. Indians from Church House in patched boats and dugouts, yachtsmen in trim dinghies rowed by paid hands, commercial fishermen with wives starched and bungalow-aproned in the stern, and fishermen rowing singly.

Nothing happened for half an hour. The last rosy tints were fading from the snow fields on Mount Estero's symmetrical peak. The straight high mountain across the channel was clothed in black shadow. The sea was as warmly opalescent as the inside of an abalone shell. I had forgotten the purpose of our coming and was soaking up the beauty and the quiet of the evening when I heard a sharp clatter of oars. A lone fisherman grabbed at the line tied to his thigh, yanked it quickly back and up. Then, standing, he began to pull in while the boat, drawn by an invisible steed, traveled swiftly against the current.

"Did you see how he struck the fish?" Robert asked me anxiously.

I had seen and was filled with a desire to have the chance to strike one, too. We heard rather than saw the end of the battle. From far across the eddy came a sharp tattoo as a great fish thrashed the loose floor boards of a boat. There followed a whanging and a banging when a club came down as often against the hollow sides of the boat as on the fish.

"Do you think you could do it?" Robert asked.

"Which?" I said. "Pull in the fish or beat him to death?"

Landing of the first salmon caused a change. Suddenly purpose galvanized the rowers. They didn't row any faster but they worked harder at it. Soon from all directions came the same sounds of thrashing salmon and blows from heavy clubs. Others turned to watch the struggles, their own excitement growing.

As I was beginning to fear a skunking, a wave of laughter swept the fleet. Fishermen barked shrilly. All were looking at a boat into which a man was lifting a long, white, snake-like body.

"He caught a dogfish," Mr. Blair said as he passed. "How are you doing, Missus? Better come up to twenty feet. It's getting darker."

I wasn't doing at all. And now to my horror of being skunked was added the further fear of having to pull in a dogfish while everyone jeered. There would be no way to hide my shame.

My crew was concerned only with being skunked. The silvery bodies of large salmon had been lifted over gunwales all around us. Bobs and Robert were beginning to question my methods when I felt a mighty yank. I had been tensed for a nibble and the forward thrust of my fist was an instinctive reaction to the ferocity of that attack rather than a cool-headed effort to strike the fish.

"Got him snagged?" Robert demanded.

Either he was, or we were. That salmon was going places and taking a seven-foot dinghy and three people with him. Robert yelled at me to give the fish line and let him tire himself out. The salmon went a long way off. It seemed a bit incredible that we had any connection with an object so far away. Out in the current, past a half dozen boats, a fish broke water. I looked at the distant splash in astonishment.

"Is that my fish?" I demanded.

"Not yet," Robert said.

It wasn't my fish for some time afterwards. When he made a wild dash toward us and the line slackened in spite of my frenzied hand-over-hand hauling, I moaned that I had lost him. When he sounded I seemed to be tugging at the bottom of the ocean. Twice he lay alongside where I could see the gleaming body and even get the half-pound lead aboard. But after lying apparently gentle and quiescent, the fish was off with a tail slap that drenched us.

"He's a whale!" Robert cried. "Don't lose him!"

A third time the fish lay beside the boat, the lead came in and stayed. Robert thought that the fish was tired. He should have been. I was exhausted. And our audience gave me stage fright. The only sure method of landing that fish appeared to be a leap overside and a hand-to-hand encounter. I would have been quite willing. The honor of the family was at stake. Robert reached for the gaff with a "Better let me—"

I grabbed the gaff. "I'm going to land or lose this fish myself," I said.

Robert chuckled and settled back. "Go to it!"

My first salmon had become a public matter. The audience took a hand with shouts. "Lift him! High! High!" They were warning me to keep him off the gunwale.

I didn't lift the salmon very high nor did I manage to achieve that fine free swing of the other fishermen. But I got him aboard.

When he was thrashing on the floor boards, Robert looked at me. "How about the rest of it?" he asked.

I shook my head. "From here on I'm just a poor weak woman."

Safe from the ignominy of a skunking, I felt a full-fledged fisherman. When I saw a huge fish, almost as long as the dinghy, come to the surface, I begged Robert, "Pull over there! Quick!" A tyee, king of salmon, would be a first-night triumph.

Robert rowed briskly in the opposite direction. He, too, had seen that thick body roll over as does a porpoise.

"Snag him and I cut the line," he said, and he added that he didn't intend to drown a whole family to hang up any fishing records.

We had caught three more salmon, none as large or as scrappy as the first, and now the bang and clatter of fighting fish broke the silence only occasionally. Boats were dark shadows on silvered water and Lewis Channel was a gleaming shaft between black shores. Bobs reported the gleam of phosphorus on our trailing fish line. An ominous note had crept into the roar of the rapids.

"Time to quit," Robert said. "Even now we'll get a real ride around the point."

We did, and then rowed through the opening in the boom chains and drew up beside Henry's float. The yellow light of a lantern glistened on oilskin-clad figures around the scales.

"How many?" a voice asked in the darkness.

"Four," I said, trying to make my tone casual.

We laid our fish in the row of gleaming salmon on the float. Measured against the others, mine seemed to have shrunk. And I was disappointed when Robert called the weight, a total of ninety-four pounds with the largest fish a scant thirty.

"What do you expect as a beginner?" Robert asked.

"Beginner!" Mr. Blair shouted. "That's a good one! The whole salt chuck was laughing when she told you she'd gaff that fish herself."

Before Mr. Blair cleaned the salmon catch he rapped sharply on the float with a hatchet and a school of rock cod stuck their noses to the surface. Their spiny fins framed faces which seemed to wear a perpetual look of mild amazement.

"See!" Mr. Blair said proudly. "They know when I call them to supper."

His pets might know the supper gong, but they didn't know the difference between supper and a baited hook. Bobs caught enough for codfish balls for the whole crowd before Betty White called out that a pot of hot chocolate was ready in the *Dawn*.

Fishing, like parties, should be talked over. It was nearing midnight when the gang broke up. I'd had a gorgeous evening and Stewart heaped up the measure when he offered to lend me a salmon rod. I protested that I might break it and he agreed that I probably would. It was his guest rod, equipped with a spare tip.

"Anyone who can get so excited over handline fishing ought to have a chance to play a salmon on a rod," he said.

VIII

THE YUCLUETAWS

Henry's tiny cove was beside the last stretch of the Yucluetaw Rapids and every six hours their roar reached its sullen crescendo and died away. The current boiled and foamed and eddies tugged at our mooring lines and gurgled along the hull and set the boom chains to clanking.

Though violence was rushing past us, life at Henry's had the peace and quiet of a rural Sunday. No one had a task so important it could not be dropped for an hour of yarning. I'd look out the window and see a half dozen men sprawled in the sun on the float, and I didn't need to listen to know they were talking fish, or Henry was telling a story of his adventurous past, or Mr. Blair was explaining the ways of a salmon with a herring. It was common belief in the Yucluetaws that Mr. Blair knew everything transpiring in the mind of a fish.

Betty and I could join our menfolks or carry on those small activities which absorb women in their own homes. It was Betty's third year of cruising and from her I learned much of living afloat while my own sea legs were still wobbly. There is a great deal about boats and equipment that their skippers never suspect. Bobs joined the men at all times and spent hours listening to Henry's animal stories, which he told well because he loved animals.

In the rushing rapids beside us there was always move-

ment. Eagles and gulls and terns fished for herring thrown
to the surface by the violence of the current. Little terns,
tailored in black and white, dived fearlessly to the bottom
of a whirlpool for a meal. Always an eagle could be seen
soaring a half mile above, poised for a power dive of amazing speed should a hake be thrown to the surface by a
boil.

Clouds of gulls fished and screamed their delight in the
violence and turmoil of the rapids. And almost every big
log which raced past us in the current carried a row of
white gulls as passengers. They'd ride until they reached
quiet water and then fly back to thumb another ride.

A world of movement and life lay beneath us, too, and
we didn't need water telescopes to study it. Through the
crystal-clear water we could see the current tearing at the
sand thirty feet below. Long brown streamers of kelp
rippled in the tide. Herring passed in schools. Rock cod
moved lazily through the underwater kelp forest. Clams
left grooved tracks in the sand bottom. Occasionally an
octopus crawled into view, rose and gray and bright
orange, his black eyes staring up at us.

Henry and Mr. Blair would be called to catch him.
Henry used the chopped arms of devilfish for cod bait
and there was usually one in his live box, sulking beneath
a half dozen eighty-pound ling cod awaiting their turn on
the logging camp tables.

Bobs brought us all running when she discovered a six-
foot wolf fish. This rare specimen aroused the interest of
even the old fishermen and we lay on the float with our
faces almost in the water while the beast moved from clam
to clam and an endless stream of crunched shells poured
from the sides of his powerful jaws.

It was peaceful and quiet and very pleasant at Henry's,

but the rapids never let us forget their presence. They governed our lives, our comings and goings. For four hours or more on each tide rowboats remained fast to shore. If it were "boat day" and we expected mail, or needed something at the store outside the rapids, we had to wait for slack. And we hurried to get out and back while the rapids were only murmuring.

When the tide was running the channel was deserted, but as the full force of the current died the Yucluetaws became a busy thoroughfare. Men rowed from one cove to another or went out to the store. Gas boats darted out of holes or shot past on the waning tide. Mrs. Maurin rowed away at eleven-thirty one morning to make an "afternoon call" on a neighbor. She was back in an hour. All life bowed to the rapids.

Huge booms of logs moved southward at slack and with quiet water in sight at last, they seemed to quicken their pace in relief that the hazards of the Yucluetaws were behind them.

In midafternoon everyone grew suddenly restless. There was less talk. Men took lines from drying reels, oiled gear, examined leaders for kinks, polished spoons. Brass on a boat might tarnish but those men could have shaved with the brilliant lures as mirrors. Galley fires were lighted and dinners prepared. There was no real reason for haste, but the dinners were gobbled. Then bait cans were filled with herring from the live box and dinghies were loaded with tackle.

We rowed away swiftly to get down to the point. Still there was no need for haste. Everyone knew the salmon run would not begin for an hour, but no one ever waited. That first leisurely circling of the quiet eddies was a strangely important part of the fishing hour, just as was

the weighing in and hot chocolate and cookies in one of
the boats afterward. But we were alive again, excited. The
day had been only preparation for this.

My second night of fishing was done with Stewart's
guest rod and carried on under his instruction. He volun-
teered to be my tutor and my oarsman. The evening's catch
was not impressive in weight, but I laid two twenty pounders down with a thrill of triumph. I'd earned those fish,
each after a half hour's struggle. Never in that time had the
outcome been certain, and the odds were always on the fish.

I'd reel in line until my arms were loose and I thought
that if the fish took it out again I'd give him the rod too,
and jump in after it to hide my shame. But Stewart would
drive me to resumption of the battle.

I missed the feeling of direct connection with a tugging
fish I'd had with a hand line. That had been a hand-to-
hand struggle. Also I had the feminine idea that one goes
fishing to catch food, and the more fish the better. I could
probably have caught four salmon while I played those
two, but by the time the second was in the boat I knew
I'd had ten times more fun than I'd ever had before. I
hadn't broken the guest rod's tip either, and I determined
right there I'd have a rod of my own.

Henry Maurin was king of the Yucluetaws. He was the
only man who ran them in a gas boat at any stage of any
tide, night or day. Big ships waited for slack, but Henry
played with whirlpools.

"They're not bad," he said, "if you don't buck 'em.
Go with 'em and you can always work out. It's the boils
that are dirty. They'll pick you up and set you on the
beach, and there's nothing you can do about it."

Henry celebrated his kingship each year with a picnic
on Little Dent Island at the north end of the rapids. The

date was selected by the full moon of June, when the biggest flood of the summer poured through the narrows. Everyone went in Henry's boat, leaving on the last of the ebb and mooring behind the island. After we'd carried the baskets across and built a fire and boiled tea we ate lunch on a high rock and watched the Yucluetaws put on their show.

Little Dent Island lies in midchannel and forces the tide into its narrowest and swiftest place. The flood began with a low mutter, and the current swept along, fast and smooth and straight. Eddies formed along the shore with a line of small whirlpools to mark the preliminary skirmish with the torrent. Then, as the tide massed its forces and the great push began, the mutter grew to a dull roar. Current snarled along the shore and there was no longer a smooth straight sweep. Masses of water were deflected by ledges in the depths and broke the surface as upsurging boils an acre in extent. Huge whirlpools formed, spinning dizzily. The resistless power of that steady rush of tide threw the whole rapids into mad confusion.

A great tree trunk came lunging down, and a whirlpool seized it, stood it on end, waltzed it around and sucked it from sight. A quarter of a mile beyond, the tree was spewed out and tossed into a fresh welter of turbulence and confusion.

Rivers and cataracts have settled and regular movement. Here the tide snarled and surged and doubled its might in savage thrusts as it crowded through the narrow channel. And when the great tidal push increased in power, the roar intensified. The whole surface of the channel would lift suddenly. Then I understood why the Yucluetaws had been known to put a large steamship on its beam ends and hold it there, helpless in the rapid's grasp.

We sat tense and thrilled as the spring flood built to a climactic burst of power. I was conscious of a tremendous inner excitement while I watched. Occasionally someone would call attention to a newly forming whirlpool or a mounting boil. I didn't speak. I was exalted. Only a few great symphonies have moved me more. In the end, I was very weak and very tired.

And I began to wonder how the little *Yakima* would fare when we went through the next morning.

IX

Wʜᴇɴ ᴡᴇ ꜰᴏʟʟᴏᴡᴇᴅ ᴛʜᴇ *Dawn* through the Yucluetaws at slack it didn't seem possible that in this channel had been the maelstrom we had watched from Little Dent. The Yucluetaws' slack is comparative, however, for the beast is never entirely still. The water is always restless. Before it has quite settled down after one turbulent rush it begins to stir and prepare for the next mad surge in the opposite direction. Currents swung the bow, lazy whirlpools formed and innocuous boils grasped our propeller and brought groans from the motor.

"Even you could take the wheel through this," the skipper said, and he didn't intend a compliment.

It was a relief to know how tame the Yucluetaws could be. I'd been more pleased than I had dared to show when Betty and Stewart White had suggested that the *Yakima* follow the *Dawn* and that the two boats stop for a day's picnic in Philips River. Even Bobs had looked relieved at the Whites' suggestion of a convoy through the rapids, although like children of her age, she was usually unaware of danger.

Philips River was as charming a trout stream as ever found a gay, twisting channel to the sea. It laughed across gravel bars and murmured over moss-covered rocks. Growth on its banks was tropically luxuriant. Tall stocks

85

of devil's club lifted above our heads as we rowed the dinghies upstream.

Betty and Stewart were, like ourselves, nose-bag picnickers. Each carried his own lunch. Robert wore his lumberjack fashion, tied to his belt and dangling jauntily behind. The rest believed pockets were made for use. Betty could have existed on a desert island with what she carried parked about her small person. We lunched on an island in a lake which we reached in a toy-sized craft that was an essential part of Stewart's trout-fishing equipment.

Betty had christened the fifty-pound pram "B.V.D." It was properly named, architecturally, and also as a suggestion that it would be well to strip to the essentials before embarking.

After lunch we separated for our individual specialties. Robert scaled a cliff. Stewart caught cutthroat for our dinners. Bobs, Betty and I did some bathing to save the skippers the high labor cost of filling our fresh water tanks.

We went home, tired and happy, to our separate dinners. After each crew-family had washed dishes and appeared on the after deck as a declaration that they were now at leisure, we rowed to the *Dawn*.

The skippers brought out the charts and planned a few days of convoy cruising. The decision to do so came about naturally for our regimes and our interests tallied. Each boat was family-crewed. We all had similar ship tasks and each of the five could, and often did, find his own amusement. We liked the same sort of cruising, short runs and shore expeditions.

So for several days the *Dawn* and the *Yakima* sailed companionably together. Our mornings were spent at anchor with everyone too occupied for visiting. In the afternoon we cruised or explored ashore. In the evenings we met on one boat or the other and laughed at the same jokes.

It was our first convoy cruising. We enjoyed it. So did Betty and Stewart White. But unfortunately the *Dawn* had already visited the waters to the west and north. We had not seen that region and our summer's cruise would be incomplete until we did so. So the two boats parted, the *Yakima* to push on farther, the *Dawn* to cruise leisurely, and the two boats to meet at the Yucluetaws in the latter part of August and go south together.

Our next weeks were like skimming the pages of a tantalizing book. Time permitted us to visit only the high spots of the country, and Bobs and I could now use this land term uncorrected. Even the skipper broke down and admitted "country" was what we saw, although we lived afloat. Ordinarily there is a sharp demarcation between land and sea, but this intricate shoreline, with the mountains standing at the water's edge, was a merging of the two. I called it "sea country." Dwellers of the region might live on land, or in a float house moored to shore, but their goings and comings, every condition of their lives and work, were governed by the sea.

We studied charts to determine how much of that deeply indented shoreline we could visit.

"Knight Inlet, the Indian villages, some prowling in Queen Charlotte Sound—it's all we can do," the skipper said. "That'll give us around fifteen hundred miles for the summer."

The east end of Queen Charlotte tested a pilot's skill. No place in the world are there more islands and rocks per square mile of ocean. The small scale chart looked flyspecked. We nosed our way through narrow channels in

which kelp streamed in the current. Kelp, reaching from
rocks to surface, warns of dangers below. It is the marin-
er's friend in those unbuoyed waterways, but unfortunately an in-and-outer. Nature hasn't done a thorough job.
Some rocks, like some heads, are bare.

We wandered through a maze of waterways where
islands, or even whole groups, suddenly detached themselves from a solid shoreline to confuse us. Then having
thoroughly identified themselves as islands, they performed
a disappearing trick by merging again with the green
wooded shores when we looked for them astern to get a
bearing.

Points opened to disclose channels and closed as quickly.
The skipper feared that if we lost the identity of any one
of those countless islands we would stray for days in a
labyrinth of water corridors.

It was my duty to check islands and rocks against the
chart. I came back from a quick trip to the galley to find
the scenery all jumbled.

"This country leaps about so," I protested.

"You can't take your eyes off it for a minute," Robert
said in his most skipperish manner. "It's a lot more important to know where we are than to have apple pie for
dinner."

There were days when whitecapped stretches made
cruising uncomfortable and even unwise. Then we lay in
secluded coves with only waterfowl and seals for neighbors. Terns flew gracefully past. Gulls made derisive comments on the quality of our garbage. Seals circled the
Yakima to observe us. We spent one evening under the
constant surveillance of a group of six, the largest of which
would swim within a few yards of the boat whenever he

thought we were not looking. We three played a game with him. We pretended to be unaware of his approach and then turned suddenly and spoke. Invariably he'd cough deprecatingly and look away as though conscious of bad manners.

We saw a great deal of harbor life that first summer because we were usually abovedeck. We were having our first long vacation in years and the three of us spent hours rowing in the dinghy. We ate dinner in the cockpit, and often breakfast, thus justifying my insistence on bringing a card table which rolled into a compact bundle. The skipper had sworn there was no place for it aboard and then proved otherwise by looping it securely under the top of the wheelhouse. The table more than paid its passage and was so successful that I had difficulty in retaining sole credit for the idea.

It enabled us to make up the stateroom early and sit down for dinner with housekeeping tasks finished. Invariably Robert would remark, "Aren't you glad I found a place to carry this table?"

And when Bobs and I snickered, he'd pretend he'd only been dusting off some family humor.

The jokes of a trio, like a three-cornered game of dominoes, are a cut-throat affair with the alignment constantly changing. Sometimes sex determined it, either two women against the man, or two women in competition for male approval. At other times age pulled together and the skipper and mate were lined up solidly against the bo'sun. Occasionally we came off second best.

Our greatest rout was in the matter of the education of the young. We might be taking a vacation, but we felt that Bobs' summer should be instructive. We had come armed with a textbook on marine life. When I dipped into it, I found it more instructive than stimulating and I noticed that Bobs thumbed quickly through the drawings and scientific terms and laid the volume down.

An unopened book, as useless as a stowaway, bothered the skipper and one wind-bound day we took a magnifying glass, notebook and the treatise ashore. The fire of our enthusiasm over the field report Bobs might present to the science teacher left Bobs very cold. When Robert and I settled down to prepare for the educational foray, she wandered off down shore.

Sea snails appeared simple enough, until we began to read. We were digging in grimly on species, markings, classifications and Latin terms when Bobs looked over our shoulder.

"A bunch of barnacles are eating dinner," she said. "You ought to see how funny they look with their skylights open."

We went to watch. The petaled shells were shoved back and long black feeding tentacles were waving in the water. In the bottom of the pool a number of sea snail shells were moving faster than I'd known snails could travel. Bobs tore a limpet from a rock and held the exposed soft flesh of the mollusk before a moving snail shell. Instantly a crab's claw shot out and grasped the shell, and a hermit crab came partly from his stolen home, held the shell with one claw and fed himself with the other.

It was exactly as though he were eating from a dish.

Robert let out a whoop and began tearing limpets from the rocks and holding these minute oysters on the half shell before hungry hermit crabs. All three of us squatted on the rocks and fed crabs industriously. We had the entire pool of hermit crabs daintily shredding limpets and bearing the minute particles to their mouths. At least they were dainty unless a fight was imminent. When a larger crab tried to steal a prize from a smaller, the little fellow would use both claws if necessary to cram the limpet into his mouth before the raider could bobble over.

Lest we give the first crab colony indigestion we went in search of other pools. I hadn't realized how gorgeous was their coloring. Greens, blues, yellows and deep rich reds, brilliant under clear water, made Persian patterns on the bottom. Gray mosses and bronzed grasses formed miniature marine forests. Tiny grotesque fish swam through the sea growth. Sea urchins like great red pin-cushions were thickly studded. Long yellowish-green sea cucumbers lurked in ledges. Tiny mussels lay in rows.

Bobs handed one to a hermit crab. He seemed a bit overcome with such an enormous meal, but he was holding the shell in one claw and shredding the flesh with the other when he was discovered by a school of minnows. They waited just out of claw reach while he tore off a bite and then darted in and stole it. Their darts were so much swifter than his grabs that he shredded the entire mussel for his tormentors. The crab grew madder at each raid and the stalks of his black pinhead eyes protruded so far we thought he'd lose them as well as his dinner.

We were still laughing when we returned to our dropped book. It didn't seem so important now. Robert picked it up and was about to heave it into the sea when Bobs and I rescued it.

"Every boat should have a reference library," I said. "It was the educational theory that was sour."

My love for wresting booty from the country was completely satisfied. Small streams held trout. A walk to any inland lake produced berries. Although the skipper protested that fruit had no connection with a nautical report,

I entered in the log the fact that on one trail we found
strawberries, yellow and red salmon berries, blackberries,
red and blue huckleberries, wild grapes and salad berries,
all ripening at once.
Food gathering on the tide flats was delightfully communal. At six o'clock one morning we found two eagles, a
dozen tall blue herons and hundreds of gulls and terns already at work. They must have set their alarm clocks a
full half hour earlier than we. A sea lion poked his pointed
nose out of the water, looked at us and then swam off, disgusted with our invasion of his preserve. The eagles
perched in near-by trees and watched us warily, but the
herons only glanced up and then resumed their reflective
poses. Their postures were deceiving, for lightninglike
strokes at passing minnows revealed the tensity of skilled
fishing.

We rowed up a small stream as the tide flowed out and
met a dozen noble crabs swimming to deep water. We
scooped up all with a dip net, although Robert protested
we couldn't eat that many. Bobs incorporated his comments on my hunting instincts in a parody on "Sea Fever."
The first and last lines were spirited, the only ones considered worthy of preservation in the ship's log.

*"I must go down to the flats again, to the fighting crab and
      the clam . . .
And all I ask is a long spear, and light to see them by."*

The fly-specked chart and the name, Beware Passage,
had warned us of trouble, but nothing had prepared us for
a flying blackfish fifty feet long above the brush on an
island. The silhouette was painted modernistically in a bold
black and white design. Bobs and I gasped, and the skipper
almost hit a rock in his astonishment.

We didn't know then that the blackfish is the symbol of death among Queen Charlotte Sound Indians. As we passed the effigy we saw that it marked a native cemetery, and we knew we were near the three Indian villages we were seeking.

Robert and I had known Ojibwas in the Canadian wilderness and were accustomed to birch bark canoes and wigwams and skilled workmanship in tanned skins. The native culture of the Northwest coast is different. This Indian is a builder and a carver. He is famed for seamanship in huge dugout canoes, for the construction of enormous community houses and the decoration of their attendant totem poles.

The three villages were the most southerly mainland settlements of these people. We knew they would be deserted, for the salmon run had called the women to the canneries and the men to the fishing boats. But we wanted to see the handicraft rather than the people. Mamalilaculla and Old Village were the more primitive. Karlukwees had been somewhat modernized by cannery pay checks.

We were fortunate to choose the most interesting village for our first stop. The *Yakima* dropped anchor before a dazzling white beach. Behind it was a row of enormous buildings. Even from the water they were impressive for each was about the size of a town hall. We thought the beach was sand until we stepped from the dinghy and found that we were standing on crushed shells, the kitchen midden of generations of a clam-eating people.

The village boasted pieces of municipal statuary in addition to its totem poles. A carved wooden figure of a boy stood on a point. The features were negroid, and the lips were brightly carmined and eyes and cheeks encircled by white. A figure of a woman, mounted on a tall pole, was staring out to sea. Her hands were extended in a gesture of welcome and, although her beauty treatments must have required the services of a human fly, her lips, too, were brightly carmined and her eyes outlined in white. Bobs asked if she bore any resemblance to the Statue of Liberty, but we thought the native carver had not been inspired by an abstract idea.

As we pushed through a rank growth of head-high nettles we came suddenly upon a rudely carved, crouching figure. The mask-like face wore the same startling makeup. I leaped back, definitely frightened. I didn't know the significance of the primitive carving or of the setting, and I couldn't guess. But my thoughts instinctively turned to the jungle and beat of drums.

The totem poles were the first we had seen in their natural setting. Here they belonged. The conventionalized birds and beasts which crowded up the tall columns were brightly painted in crude reds and blues and blacks and whites and yellows. The symbols serve as crests of families or of communities, or even of a people. From the similarity of the poles in the three villages we decided that the natives must be fearfully intermarried. Later we learned that a chief's crest included those of his wife's and of his sons' wives' families and that each conventionalized symbol represented only a major division of the tribe and did not necessarily imply blood relationship.

The community houses were huge barn-like structures designed to shelter a dozen families. Those still in use were roofed and sided with hewn planks of astonishing width and length. A door of one piece was forty-four inches wide and we measured a hewn plank two inches thick, four feet wide and forty feet long.

The real beauty of the buildings was in the framework. Two uprights at each end supported a transverse beam. The uprights were four feet in diameter and hewn with such beautiful precision that grooves ran the full length of the timbers, giving them the aspect of fluted Greek columns. On these supporting ends rested the two main lengthwise beams. They, too, were four feet in thickness and fluted, and they stretched a hundred feet in an unsupported span.

Robert had fancied himself as a builder of log cabins and he thought he had seen skilled work with the broad ax, but these enormous fluted beams, longer and bigger than any logs he had ever seen and resting high above our heads, left him gasping. He wanted more than anything else to know how the natives got them up there.

The doors of those community houses still intact and occupied were padlocked. We wandered down a row of eleven of the enormous buildings and got only glimpses of dim interiors through cracks in the siding. At last we found a door which was open.

We entered. Sunlight filtering through a crevice and the smoke hole in the center gave an eerie effect to the big darkened auditorium. Firestones in a circle of blackened earth and ashes marked the community kitchen. Extending around the sides was a wide plank platform on which the families lived and slept. In one corner in the rear was a small building, a house within a house. On the back wall the effigies of a pair of enormous thunder birds stretched the entire width. Their huge beaks projected high above our heads and the spread of those huge painted wings dominated the whole interior.

The birds were the only furnishings except for community eating dishes, carved in the form of seals, and hollowed. These stood on broad bases with carved legs and were a yard or more in length.

A machine-made filet lace curtain at the window of the small house in the corner suggested grandeur, but the only opening, a low door through which we would have to crawl, made me think it might be only the dog house. Robert crawled in first. His report of a big brass bedstead decided Bobs and me to follow.

It was evidently the chief's house. That important personage didn't sleep on the divan platform. Since the bed was the only piece of furniture, we decided that otherwise he shared the communal life. The everydayness of a brass bedstead did something to restore normality, for when we crawled forth again the hugeness of those brooding thunder birds seemed less awesome.

Robert, however, could not recover from his wonder over how the mammoth timbers had been handled. He didn't learn until the next year when we met George Hunt, son of a Scotch Hudson's Bay post manager and an Alaskan Indian princess. George had done much work with Franz Boas for many years in gathering material for the Smithsonian Institution, and the first question Robert asked was, "How'd they get up those hundred-foot beams?"

They were raised, George said, by skids and cribbing, and then he answered my question of why the thunder birds dominated every household by telling the legend of the lone Queen Charlotte Island Indian who had traveled far south and had to build his community house unaided. A thunder bird had taken pity on him and helped lift the enormous beams.

George Hunt's soft voice and vivid phrases embellished the legend marvelously. I was in a warm glow of gratitude that Bobs should have heard a folk tale told so colorfully. I was about to thank George when she spoke.

"But," she said, "if there was only one of him, why did he need a community house?"

X

Letters to post and deplen-
ished stores took us to Simoon Sound, one of two towns
along the coast that are afloat in the sea. The store, restaurant, bunkhouse, blacksmith shop, warehouse and owner's dwelling house, even a chicken house, rested on rafts
of cedar logs. Chains and cables moored these rafts to shore
and long boomsticks running from shore to the rafts held
them off and kept them from battering on the beach as the
community rose and fell with the big tides or was buffeted
by fierce winter gales. Outer boomsticks herded the buildings in line and also served as sidewalks.

Simoon Sound could change its town site with no more
formality than calling a tugboat. The village had shifted
several times. Once when the small daughter of its owner
had been ill and required sun, the community had been
moved across the bay and the weekly steamship bringing
mail and supplies had to go in search of the missing town.

We did not know we were arriving on "boat night."
Ordinarily only the owner, his family and a couple of
employees inhabit Simoon Sound, and for six days each
week almost no one comes to trade. But when the *Yakima*
entered the little cove beneath a sheer cliff, we found a
long row of gas boats moored nose-on to the boomsticks
and looking like tired horses at a cow town hitching rail.
We had to moor in the outskirts of the village. The town

98

was crowded. Handloggers from the entire district had gathered for the arrival of the weekly ship from Vancouver, their one contact with the outside world.

We walked to the store on the boomsticks, huge waterlogged larch logs worn flat on top by the steel-calked shoes of many men. Outside the store was a group of handloggers, each clad in white woolen undershirt, stagged khaki trousers and "corked" shoes. Robert deserted his family at once and Bobs and I entered to join the wives and children of the few married men. Mrs. Dunseith, postmistress and wife of the owner of Simoon Sound, was busy making up the outgoing mail. I looked at my shopping list and then in perplexity at the half-empty shelves. A fellow customer spoke.

"The ship will be here soon," she said, "and you can get everything you need."

When a whistle echoed from the cliff everyone went out to the huge landing float and soon the ship nosed cautiously into the cove. Lines were made fast, a door in the ship's hull was swung open and freight began to pour out. Large crates were trundled down the gangplank by the handloggers. Smaller boxes were thrown and caught in mid-air. Mr. Dunseith stood, like a general, checking manifests and directing the placing of cartons, bags, wooden cases and dozens of clanking boom chains. When I saw crates of lettuce, tomatoes, peaches, a side of beef and all sorts of luxuries set on the float I began to revise my list. Bobs reported she had spotted a crate of cantaloupe. The loggers were already tearing the wrappings off the green groceries. I had never seen such helpful customers.

Bobs and I hurried to the store to head what we surmised would be a long cue of shoppers. Mrs. Dunseith, sorting mail into rows of yeast foam boxes, showed no interest in us. The store seemed strangely empty. My excitement over fresh vegetables made me realize how I had missed them. I was almost drooling when Mr. Dunseith appeared with a handful of bills of lading. I began to read my list—lettuce, tomatoes, peaches, cantaloupe and steak. "A thick porterhouse," I added firmly.

"Sure," he said. "If there's any left."

"Left!" I yelped. "But I saw them! How do I—"

He nodded toward the wharf. "Help yourself like the rest, and give me a list of what you take."

We turned and ran. The crates on the landing float were empty. The last vegetables were disappearing into gas boats. One woman, carrying a half dozen heads of Iceland lettuce, saw my wistful face.

"Didn't you get any?" she asked.

Our tale of woe parted her from two heads. She thought a box of oranges was still unopened and warned me that the meat was being butchered.

"The restaurant will take most of the steak," she said. "All the single men will be staying over. Two jugs of liquor came in this week's freight."

I fled to save my porterhouse and met the restaurant cook departing with more beefsteak than I had known one quarter could produce. A handlogger was cutting meat while two assistants were wrapping chunks of beef in brown paper and writing names of the purchasers. I gratefully accepted an odd-looking portion which anywhere else would have passed as soup bone.

"You can weigh it in the store," the butcher said.

"What kind of a cut do I say it is?"

"Just beef. John'll know the price when he's had time to read the invoice."

We reported our purchases. A fellow customer wrote

the items in the daybook and said we could find out what we owed later. Rather forlornly Bobs and I carried our paltry loot to the *Yakima*. Bobs remarked plaintively that the restaurant might serve melons. I knew it would serve steak.

Dressed in shore clothes for a restaurant dinner, Bobs and I sat in the cabin and waited for Robert. He was not aware of our waiting or of our dinner plans but that didn't mitigate the crime of his non-appearance. We heard the sound of tramping feet and looked out to see a long file of handloggers disappearing into the restaurant. Robert came aboard a few moments later. He failed completely to understand the reason for his unpopularity, even when he reported that the cook said we must wait for second table.

I was silent when we dined on eggs because the steak had been eaten and had stewed prunes because there were no more melons. Robert didn't mind. He was much too elated over our luck in having arrived on "boat night." Two handloggers were celebrating the sale of a boom of logs and two gallon jugs of liquor on the counter had decided most of the men to remain.

Robert was among friends. He had encountered several handloggers who had been in logging camps he knew in Wisconsin and Minnesota and had been invited to their "shows," or timber limits. One new acquaintance who ate dinner with us offered to demonstrate handlogging if we would visit him.

I had heard the word before several times.

"What," I asked this man, "is a handlogger?"

"Just what it says, ma'am," he said. "A feller who logs by hand."

His eyes were twinkling, but he went on to explain.

Logging companies from California north use elaborate
and very powerful machinery to get the huge logs from
stump to water or railroad. But on the steep mountain
slopes of British Columbia a skilled man can so fall a tree
that it slides into the sea. If it stops sliding, he goes to
work on the many-ton timber with a tool that looks like
an overgrown automobile jack, and he will work a day or
two to get the tree into the water.

"You see, ma'am," the handlogger said, "a tree is never
a saw-log until it's in the salt chuck."

I knew the "salt chuck." We were using that word ourselves. It's a term from the Chinook jargon, invented by
early fur traders, in which "chuck" means water. Seldom
along the coast does a logger or fisherman use the words
sea, ocean or water. It is always "salt chuck," or simply
"the chuck." He also combines "chuck" with "skookum,"
Chinook for mighty, or strong. Thus a tidal rapids is a
"skookum chuck."

But Robert was fairly dripping with new handlogger
vernacular. The words "stumpers," "hang-ups" and
"slides" flowed from him. I unscrambled. A "stumper" was
a tree which never stopped from stump to sea. "Hang-up"
was a log which did stop. And a "slide" was one of the
handlogger's greatest dreads, an avalanche which in fall
and winter may denude a whole mountainside.

It was most evident that our skipper was looking forward to a large and happy evening, and that we were not
to share it. After supper we walked the length of the
boomstick sidewalk. Married handloggers were departing
with their families and when they cast off I saw them look
back wistfully. We passed groups of men, but in the store
found only Mrs. Dunseith. From a cedar shack equipped
with card tables came sounds of deep male laughter. When

Robert's glance strayed in that direction, Bobs and I bid him good evening.

I was reading at midnight when he came aboard. He reported a grand time. They had played poker, finished the two jugs and logged off at least three mountainsides. "Wasn't it a piece of luck we happened in on boat night?" he asked.

I agreed, and quite sincerely, that it was.

"We're coming here again next summer," he said.

I agreed to that with equal sincerity. But when he went on to exclaim about the magnificent array of fresh vegetables, the luxuries on the logger's menus, the fun of eating in a restaurant and the gaiety and good fellowship of the place, it was too much.

"Listen," I said. "Do you know what boat night meant to me? Two heads of lettuce, a half dozen oranges, a scrap of meat and an evening's imprisonment in this cabin. And if these gas boats continue to run around in circles I won't even be able to sleep."

He laughed, and my female martyrdom having been recognized, I laughed too.

That first evening in a float town led eventually to coast friendships which will never be forgotten. We found that handloggers, shy men perhaps because they toiled alone on mountainsides, did like to talk with women once they knew that a woman liked to listen to the things that they could talk about.

The next morning the last of the gas boats departed. Never before had I seen a gas boat travel in drunken staggers. I asked Billy Welsh, the only handlogger who remained, if he thought the departure wise.

"The inlet's wide where he is going," Billy said.

From Billy we learned much local history. He had a

capacity for graphic phrases and a nickname for everyone. The mildest was "skim milk," and the most colorful unprintable. He explained all phenomena in logging idiom. Of the pretentions of a remittance man he remarked, "In the old country they grade men like we grade cedar and that chap thinks he's number one. Old country grading ain't done by soundness of the timber. It's just a barkmark men carry."

Billy was seventy-three and famous for the logs he could put into the salt chuck. He almost drove his partners crazy with his slave driving, although he never saved money when he got it. Nor did he want to. His philosophy was very simple.

"The handlogger is the first man in the country and he walks over land that could make him a fortune. But he never stops. The second man makes the money, and a lot of grief along with it, like taxes and real estate troubles. At that, the handlogger has the best of it. Plenty to eat and he can always borrow until his boom's sold. I wouldn't do any different if I had to do it all over again."

Simoon Sound had existed since the coming of the first handloggers. It was their home, their club, their store, and when they returned from a city bust it was also their bank. The men wouldn't have traded elsewhere even at bargain prices. They helped with the unloading and waited on themselves. Much of the store's stock never reached the shelves but went directly from ship to gas boat.

We asked Mr. Dunseith how the self-serve custom started. He opened up the daybook and riffled through pages of entries written the previous night. They were in many different handwritings and no prices were entered.

"I'd be measuring out that stuff yet," he said. "Folks

started to wait on themselves naturally. How else would you manage when all the business is done in a few hours?"

"How do you know they are honest?" I asked.

He considered that a moment. "Most folks are honest if you trust them," he said. "If I didn't figure it that way, how could I give credit on a boom a year before it's in the water?"

His banking methods were as simple as his merchandising. A man would sit on the deacon seat and in half an hour talk himself into or out of credit. But Dunseith had slipped up once.

"That fellow rowed in here," he said, "filled up his boat with grub and tools and kept right on rowing to Alaska. I never laid eyes on him again."

August was half gone when we turned back from the head of Knight Inlet. It is the longest of the fiords, penetrating the very heart of the majestic coastal range, and the two-day run had been the most thrilling of the cruise.

"Have you been up Knight's?" men on the coast always asked us, for even to these people who spent their lives under the glow of the sea country's grandeur, there is something awesome about this giant of sea and mountain.

Peaks are higher and more varied, snow fields greater, reaches longer and more imposing, until at the head the solitude and remoteness, the chill that creeps down from the heights, have the effect of Arctic seas and Himalayan horizons.

The clear blue of our first glacier glittered in the sunlight. The glasses revealed a mountain goat far above timberline, but we thought he was a patch of snow until he moved. Turreted cliffs, like minarets, stood sentinel at the head of one long reach. Glistening battlements guarded others. Waterfalls thundered from precipices into the sea.

In the last half of the inlet we saw only one evidence of man's occupancy. The bright yellow of a handlogger's new cedar float cabin nestled at the foot of a great green-mantled mountain so vast the habitation seemed microscopic.

Only nature itself could mar those heights. Scars of avalanches cut sharply through forested slopes and laid bare the granite frames of mountains. The devastation was complete. We anchored at the base of a ridge swept bare the previous fall and went ashore to climb over thousands of cords of splinters that had been two-hundred-foot cedars.

A large river of snow water emptied into the inlet near that anchorage at the head and turned the sea to milky gray. The cold penetrated the hull of the *Yakima*, and a can of grapefruit hung outside was thoroughly iced.

We had thought the rose tints of sunset on the long stretch of snowy peaks were the high point of the summer, but that was before we had seen the dawn. We departed while night still lay on the sea and watched the heights turn from dull gray to warm gray and finally light up with gold.

Hours later we looked back at the ranks of snowy peaks sparkling beneath a midday sun. Not a breath of wind marred the clear mirror of the sea. It was beautiful, but for us it held an element of sadness. We were homeward bound, saying farewell to the mountains. A few days' salmon fishing at the Yucluetaws, a run south in convoy with the *Dawn*, and we'd gulp down the anchor. School would open and covers must come off the typewriters. Our vacation was ending.

"You talk as though it were your last one," Robert said.

"We can't take three months off every summer," I said. "And you can't work in the little *Yakima*."

Robert steered in silence. We knew what we wanted, but wanting and getting were quite different. Since our first blithe talk of regarding the *Yakima* as an experimental craft, our ideas on comfort and safety had changed, or perhaps had been formulated.

If we were to own a new boat it must have a galley, a bathroom, comfortable quarters for lounging, staterooms, an isolated place for a typewriter and a separate engine room. Most of all we wanted a sturdy ship that could take weather.

That was much more boat than we could afford. Writing hadn't provided an income which stretched to yachts. But I suggested that we might save up for one in future years.

"When you and I are too old to crawl around a deck," Robert jeered. "The time to play this game is now."

I admitted that was sound. Robert spoke of a royalty check due in mid-winter which we had planned to make the nest egg of a savings fund. (Of all our friends, we alone could not refer to "our investments.") Suddenly we found ourselves deep in a family conference on the whole subject of investments. It was not the usual talk of high and low yield and the advisability of safety. A banker wouldn't have considered our discussion a financial conference.

As we cruised between the mountain walls of Knight Inlet, our talk touched on such follies as taking the present and trusting to the future, of investing in experience and adventure, of buying years and memories instead of stocks and bonds. Our conclusions may have been folly, or great wisdom, but they were reached by our way of thinking and of doing. That was all that mattered.

I asked Bobs what she thought of spending her summers cruising.

"Of course she'd like it," Robert interjected. "What can a youngster do in a city?"

Bobs looked as worried as she always did when she knew grave matters must be put into words.

"Have you had a good time this summer?" I urged. "Do you like a boat?"

"If we buy a real one," she said, "I'll polish all the brass."

Robert grinned at me and we drank to the new boat before we sat down to dinner. Bobs clicked her glass of ginger beer against our two of Scotch. It was her investment too.

"We'll use the book royalties, and work like hell besides," Robert said. "Here's to the next ship. May she be a real one."

Fragment of the Sea Was Imprisoned

Henry's Boom Lay Beside the Yucluetaws

The Skipper Was Handy Around a Motor

The Triton

XI

THE "TRITON"

THE "TRITON" WAS A REAL
ship. She was designed by Winslow for the motor cruiser
race to Bermuda and built by day labor. The last is something more than the difference between custom tailoring
and ready-made. The cost may mount past all calculations,
but there is no scrimping on workmanship and materials.

Her owner had built six or seven boats and intended this
to be his last and most perfect. He said he couldn't afford
to keep her, and we knew we couldn't afford to buy her.
But we did, in February, when we heard she was on the
market. We bought her unseen. Her history was as far
above suspicion as Caesar's wife, and all good ships must
have spotless reputations.

The *Triton* had a straight bow, a wide transom stern and
was forty-three and a half feet long. Her beam was eleven
feet and she drew five feet, eight inches, which gave her
a grand hold on the water further helped by bilge keels.
Those deep lines also gave her full headroom throughout,
with seven feet forward. She had a raised deck forward
with a break well aft, and on the large afterdeck was a
trunk over the motor room. We had stipulated that our
new boat must have ample engine space, and our medium
duty Sterling occupied a baronial hall.

The builder was owner of a foundry and every fitting
was of solid bronze. The entire rudder assembly, even to

the quadrant, was cast from patterns he made. He even whittled out patterns for the port lights and made his own wildcat and windlass of bronze.

A mast carried a large mainsail and jib, largely for steadying purposes, though she would sail fairly well. We had no wheelhouse but an awning and windbreaker gave some protection for the helmsman. I thought we'd get very wet in a blow.

"When we rebuild her we can have a deckhouse," Robert said. "We'll make a lot of changes."

Several reasons had determined us to make none the first year. One was financial. I was partially responsible for that. I'd been rebuilt by surgery; and fees, hospital and nurses' bills, piled on the cost of the *Triton*, had put a dent in the royalty check. And we had not been able to sell the *Yakima*. We were reluctant owners of a second craft that was eating its head off at moorings.

But if we'd had the money, we wouldn't have rebuilt that first season. Only after we'd cruised in the *Triton* could we know what our peculiar needs demanded in the way of quarters below deck. The present arrangement was adequate but not one of the three could quite conceal his disappointment when we first descended the companionway to the main cabin. This was not our idea of a home afloat.

Her former owner had liked a crowd aboard. She was described as "sleeping eight." Our main cabin contained two transom berths with uppers and two single berths forward of them. The effect was that of a street car with lengthwise benches, though it was relieved somewhat by two handsome mahogany buffets. The stateroom at the foot of the companionway had a double berth. Bobs and I pre-empted it and the skipper had to continue making up his berth at night and stowing it in the morning.

The heavy mahogany dining table, which seemed to occupy the entire main cabin even when folded, was large enough to seat eight. The galley in the bow was on the same generous proportions. An ice box would take a hundred pounds of ice, something we couldn't buy in coastwise cruising. Two long galley dressers, a large stove, a very deep sink, locker space below each dresser and many racks for dishes above gave us a hotel air.

The bathroom amidships seemed ample after the midget of the *Yakima* and was equipped with bowl, toilet, medicine cabinets and three enormous drawers, apparently intended for linen. Our whole summer's supply filled only one.

I sometimes regretted the location of the galley when I tried to cook a meal in rough weather, and all three cursed the dining table when we barked our shins. But we accepted these inconveniences in our getting-acquainted summer.

The last and, oddly enough, most important reason for not wishing to make radical changes at once was the fact that the new boat did not seem as yet to be our ship. Robert's name was entered as owner and master of the nineteen-ton gasoline yacht *Triton*, but a boat, like a horse or a dog, does not change ownership with the mere payment of money. Ownership must be consummated. Only when the master has taken his craft through storm and fog, through tough times and happy sailing, does she become truly his.

We knew this the day the former owner came aboard to wish us luck. He and Robert went over the boat and then joined me in the cabin. Our visitor explained the

Triton's ways as though he were making a bid for understanding care.

"She'll roll," he said, "roll so far you'll think she's never coming back. But she always does, and without ever a snap. Couldn't want an easier motion. Once you've been out when the straits are smoking and have watched how she takes it, you'll feel the way—"

He broke off abruptly and walked up the companionway to the deck. When we reached it, he was stepping onto the pier.

"Good luck," he said, without turning toward us.

His voice was hoarse. We watched him walk away. At the ramp, he stopped, took one last glance at the *Triton* and tears were on his cheeks.

Six years later Robert and I understood better how he felt when we stood on a pier and watched the *Triton* move out into midstream with a stranger at the wheel. We too turned and walked quickly away and my last sight of her was blurred. The stranger's name was entered on the *Triton's* papers as master and owner. I had explained the galley gadgets to his wife. But the *Triton* seemed no more theirs than she was ours on the day we first cast off her lines and nosed out into the Lake Washington ship canal.

It was early in May, and we had stores aboard for six months. A larger boat and ample lockers permitted us to stow, not to eliminate, as we had in the *Yakima*. Our grocery list covered three typewritten pages, single spaced. The laundry question had been met with 2,000 paper napkins and as many paper towels. I regretted that paper sheets did not exist. It seemed almost prodigal to be able to fill an enormous underberth locker with paper for housekeeping use.

All our supplies could spread out. Under the main cabin

hatch were cases of butter, milk, jellies and canned meats. Behind the companionway steps were huge pushtop tins filled with preserved eggs. Canned goods, sugar and cereals crammed lockers under the berths. Ever since canned fruit has meant "starboard" and vegetables "port."

Even our personal possessions could be unscrambled. The skipper had a hanging locker of his own. The bo'sun and I could keep our clothing in our stateroom. Deep drawers under the berth permitted us to lay out dresses, and in an improvised corner closet we could even hang up coats. No longer could our "shore clothes" have an excuse for wrinkles.

The engine room pleased me as much as it did the skipper. The cook was no longer menaced by rocker arms and a revolving flywheel, and a meal would not be sidetracked by a motor crisis. Tanks holding 300 gallons of gasoline, a tank and cans of coal oil for the pressure burner in the galley, batteries, tools, bilge pump, everything mechanical, was in the engine room. This was shut off from the living quarters by a watertight bulkhead, and forward of that was a big fresh water tank the entire width of the boat.

We never caught smells from a hot motor when forward, the fire hazard was reduced, and the skipper had a playroom of his own. He even had space for his typewriter, and the engineer's berth, aft of the engine room, was converted into a desk.

We were more shipshape in many ways. We had a thirty-two volt electric system instead of the twelve of the *Yakima* and our living quarters were really lighted. Fifty-watt bulbs seemed sheer luxury after the Christmas tree lights of the first year. And a fresh water tank holding three hundred gallons, a month's supply, which could be replenished with a hose at a salmon cannery or a gas station, changed the skipper's viewpoint. Now that he was freed from the constant ferrying of water in a dinghy to maintain a comfortable balance in a sixty-gallon tank, he ceased counting pump strokes when Bobs and I washed our teeth. I was glad to know he was not by nature a water miser but had been made so by circumstances. Also we were free from the menace and inconvenience of a trailing dinghy, for now we carried our small boat in chocks on the foredeck, lifting it with the gaff of our boomless mainsail. And an outboard motor was lashed to the taffrail.

Our first summer had determined us never to cruise again with only one dinghy. It is often inconvenient and always unsafe to maroon one person aboard a gasoline-propelled vessel in cold water. But we made our second small boat the bo'sun's own personal craft and it came aboard in Bute Inlet before we reached the Yucluetaws. An Orkney Islander made splendid Norwegian praams and when we ordered one for Bobs he insisted on having her age and weight.

The result was a dinghy tailored for a girl of ten. When Bobs sat on the center seat it trimmed perfectly, though down by the head with an adult. Even light oars of cedar were adapted to her strength. It was beautifully built. Planking was of cedar, cut in the little water-powered sawmill the builder had erected, and it was copper-riveted. Knees were of natural bend, found after days of searching in the forest. The transom ends were mahogany.

The praam was shaped like a huge tablespoon with both ends cut off and Bobs could spin it on a dime. Its ability to move in any direction earned it the name, *Crab*, within an hour. Bobs never tired of rowing it and it was the most successful present we had ever given her. It was so light she could drag it off tidal beaches and so seaworthy we never worried when she was gone for a day. No one else used it without permission, which she gave readily enough if one could find the rare time when she wasn't planning a *Crab* expedition.

She used the praam for lengthy shore explorations. She taxied in it to visit other boats and her social contacts became extensive. The sight of a blond-haired youngster, dexterously spinning the *Crab*, never failed to bring an invitation to come aboard. She could have written a handbook on the history, personnel and below deck arrangements of the yachts and cruisers of the coast.

The Yucluetaws were no place for Bobs to try out her new boat and we sailed to a landlocked harbor in which, rumor said, was a bed of Olympia oysters. The bo'sun, the *Crab* and I started out at once on a voyage of exploration. We turned into a long bay to examine some deserted buildings and from a hill behind them saw a salt lagoon not shown on the chart.

By tracking the *Crab* through the entrance rapids we got inside to find a cabin and two charming Englishmen who were trying to make a living as handloggers. They stopped work and served us tea, remarkably good tea even in cups of thick enamel.

The chaps, both Oxford men, had been fellow officers in the War. Their fresh cedar shack was attractive, but the few logs lying in boom would have been considered pitiful by the Simoon Sound handloggers. Our hosts, however, were able to laugh about their hang-ups. Neither had lost his courage or sense of humor.

After tea we visited the oyster beds, all that remained of someone's dream of a fortune, and filled a sugar sack. It was high time that we were home but, like Cinderella, we had outstayed the magic hour and the entrance rapids were now a torrent. Bobs and I gave up the idea of tracking through and hunted a secluded cove where we could spend our enforced wait in swimming. We bathed and devoted an hour to exploring one of the most beautiful sea pools we'd ever seen. Small marine creatures scuttled among the thick fronds of olive-green kelp. Rich colors lined the pool and sea anemones trustingly thrust out their sunburst of colored feelers. They are timid creatures and at the slightest touch contracted into hard tight buttons.

The skipper found us at the pool and we remarked on the great convenience of two dinghies.

"Sure," he said bitterly. "One for you girls to get marooned in and the other for rescue."

He felt much better about the whole expedition when he tasted the Olympia oysters. To be at their best, these succulent tid-bits should be shucked on a deck and eaten without condiments. Hurling the shells to sea seems to add to the joy of eating. We sat on the *Triton's* foredeck and industriously ate oysters for an hour. We had started with the thought that a dozen or so would make a good first course for dinner. At dusk we reached the bottom of the sack.

Robert shook it regretfully. "I have to admit that my women bring in swell booty," he said.

Beautiful Mount Estero, clad in lovely blues, greeted us as we ran toward the Yucluetaws. That gorgeous peak was now our landmark, dividing the upper from the lower country. To see it meant too that we were close to Henry Maurin's float, which had come to be a home port.

It was strange to draw alongside the boom without the *Dawn*. It was at Henry's that we had first met Betty and Stewart White. We had spent days together beside the float. Convoy cruising had begun there. The friendship had continued during the winter in San Francisco. Stewart and Robert had played golf. Betty and I had explored the city when the men went to their weekly boxing shows. All four had shared an interest in boats, and Stewart and I had collaborated on a play, to the great amusement of the others.

Neither had ever written a play, as Robert often reminded us. Betty had tried to cheer us on, but she couldn't believe it was quite as fine a play as we did. Nor did anyone else. The comment of our literary agent, Carl Brandt, was masterly. He said it was an excellent reading play. But we'd had a lot of fun. The play was finished just before Stewart went hunting in Africa and Betty went to London.

Now the *Dawn* was spending a summer at her moorings.

"Seems funny to have only half the gang here," Henry said.

He admired our new boat. "Skookum," he called it. The Chinook word meant even more than "strong" and the skipper beamed his pleasure at the phrase.

We all trooped up the hill to say hello to Mrs. Maurin and to see Henry's latest pet, a baby seal.

"I heard it crying in the kelp one evening," Henry said. "Someone must have shot its mother."

Henry took its upbringing very seriously and didn't intend that it should grow up without learning to swim. An old dugout canoe was its private pool, and every morning and evening Henry carried a dozen pails of sea water up the steep hillside.

The seal was still bottle fed, but we'd never seen a more precocious infant. It knew its feeding hours and bathing hours and expected service from Henry, who was the only one from whom it would take its bottle until Bobs arrived. She was accepted as assistant nurse.

Henry had lost an old neighbor, the male bird of a pair of eagles which for years had nested in a nearby Douglas fir. Henry saw the tragic death when the male, diving for a salmon, imbedded its claws in the fish's back. The salmon was too large to lift. The eagle's mate went to his rescue, but she could only circle helplessly and watch the salmon draw her consort under in the heavy current.

After we paid our respects to the seal, Mr. Blair showed us his latest pets, a swarm of hornets he had trained to come at call. He maintained that people misunderstood his friendly insects. Their share of his daily fish money was a nickel's worth of candy. He placed it on the foredeck and announced the treat by ringing the ship's bell. Hornets came from every direction.

We staked them to a candy feed from our ship's stores. Mr. Blair thought Bobs should wait and receive their thanks.

"Little girl, my hornets will never hurt you," he insisted.

Until then Bobs had accepted as gospel every natural history fact Mr. Blair had told her. Now she hesitated. When she saw us poised for instant flight below hatches, she decided to watch the hornets from afar.

Fishing had been poor, the men reported, but nothing could have kept me off the salt chuck with my new salmon rod. I thought it would be invincible even when Mr. Blair saw us off with the warning, "Don't feel bad, Missus, if you get skunked."

All eighteen boats were skunked that evening. We were trailing our lines, awaiting the run, when we saw a school of more than forty blackfish coming through the rapids. The fishing fleet fled at once to the safety of the coves.

An enormous bull, nearly forty feet long and with a seven-foot dorsal fin splitting the water, was evidently the leader, and his defiance of the Yucluetaws was magnificent. He scorned the easier route near shore and fought the strongest current in midstream while cows with babies at their sides took advantage of the eddies. The spectacle was thrilling. The whole channel was filled with rolling, puffing, blowing whales bucking a ten-knot current. Huge black bodies rolled into view. The plumes of their breath adorned whirlpools and boils and the sound of their regular exhalations, a loud "shu-s-s-sh," broke against the steep-sided mountain and returned to us as echoes.

Rowboats have no propellers to drive whales away and the fishing craft clung to the beaches. We were delighted with the show but the fishermen didn't seem so happy. As the beasts disappeared, a chap near us dumped his can of herring bait overside.

"No fishing tonight," he said. "Those fellows scared every salmon this side o' Johnstone Straits."

The only other time we saw whale traffic interfere with the fishing fleet was just as the salmon run had ended. It was dark when we heard the first warning "shu-s-s-sh" and every fisherman started for shore. We were far out and the danger of getting mixed up with thirty-five feet of an acrobatic and intelligent, and perhaps even angry, torpedo made a college oarsman of the skipper. We couldn't see them but we could hear them coming. Not being able to judge their distance added to my terror. I was tense as a coxswain as I bent backward and forward in time with Robert's strokes. All I needed was a megaphone.

We won for alma mater and our own skins. As we raced to the boom the first big bull lunged past. When his loud exhalation broke about fifty feet astern, it was one time

I didn't consider the sound thrilling. I felt as though a fiery dragon were breathing on my neck.

After the blackfish had deferred the christening of my rod, Henry bet that my first strike would be from a dogfish. But he remarked that our ten-foot dinghy was a comfort. The previous summer everyone had feared lest we try to land a big salmon in the *Yakima's* tiny tender. Now Robert confessed that he'd had an open knife ready to cut the line.

Fishing prospects were bad when again I took out the rod. No salmon had been caught when daylight faded and for the first time we saw men quit fishing in the Yucluetaws. Even commercial fishermen gathered in a disgusted group in an eddy. Robert suggested that we go in too. Trailing a herring through empty water wasn't his idea of sport.

"But the water isn't empty," Bobs said. "I saw a big one roll over in that eddy."

We turned toward it, and a few moments later I thought I'd snagged the bottom of the Pacific. We stopped dead and then the line began to run out. That screech of the reel galvanized the salt chuck and I heard the clatter of oars as the despondent group along the shore started out. I heard them but I did not see them. I was much too busy. The salmon at the end of my line sounded, broke water, and somersaulted, circled, approached our boat, reconsidered and departed for distant places.

Robert begged me not to lose him. Advice as to how to land him came from all the boats, but that seemed a problem of the dim future. My immediate anxiety was how to check him before he bared the reel's spool.

But he was checked, and that salmon and I settled down

to a three-quarter-hour argument as to which controlled the line. At last, for the fifth time, he lay alongside.

Robert saw the pointed snout. "You've got a tyee!" he exclaimed. "For Pete's sake, be careful how you gaff him!"

I ducked that crisis. I said *he'd* better be careful about the gaffing, and if he lost him he'd better jump into the salt chuck. Then I sank back exhausted.

The sound of the salmon thrashing on the floor boards ended a tense moment. He was very much a family fish. Bobs had sighted him, I had played him and the skipper had lifted him aboard. But Mr. Blair, to whom we always gave our catch, pronounced the final tribute. He hurried over and took a quick look at the gills.

"By God! She's red!" he yelled.

That meant he'd get three times as much as for a white spring salmon.

For the first time I'd laid the largest fish of the evening catch on Henry's float. A forty-one pound tyee had christened my new rod. I thought him about the handsomest salmon ever caught in the Pacific, even though he was far from the record. Mr. Blair held tops for the Yucluetaws, with a seventy-three pound fish. Fifty-five pounders were not infrequent but commanded deep respect. The largest salmon recorded, caught in a trap, weighed one hundred and ten pounds. It was such a fish that we had seen rolling over in the current like a porpoise that first summer.

Our departure the next morning came very close to disaster. We were pulling out into the current and Bobs and I were waving our good-bys when the motor stopped. Robert leaped for the engine room. I ran to the wheel, where I stood helpless while a big surge put us over and the *Triton* started sternwise toward the granite shore.

Even should Robert get the motor started, we couldn't turn the propeller if we were in that bunch of rocks. Henry and Mr. Blair dashed to the end of the boomsticks but there was nothing they could do. In an instant gay departure had given way to threat of disaster.

It is amazing how much can pass through the mind in a split second. I remembered how great surges had moved boomsticks, floats and moored boats, setting them over fifteen feet as easily as though they were matchwood. I tried to imagine what it would be like when the tremendous force of the eddy crashed the *Triton* against the granite cliff.

We had ten feet to go when the motor started. We had six feet between us and shore when Robert catapulted from the engine room hatch. We were in go-ahead just as we were about to strike a rock. If that rock wore kelp, the propeller shaved it.

We didn't speak as we drew into the channel. I was ashamed of my trembling until I saw that Robert, too, was shaking. I'd never seen his face so white. Henry and Mr. Blair walked slowly back on the boomsticks. No one waved good-by.

"What happened?" I asked finally.

"Ignition," Robert said.

We were very silent until the rapids were behind us. I'd been doing a little thinking. So had Robert. Failure of ignition when a strong current demanded certain power had opened up a lot of questions.

Machinery can go wrong, as the loss of many ships has proved. Even good skippers have lost boats, and nowhere in the world can a boat be lost more quickly than on that rock strewn coastline. We had accepted that condition when we bought the *Triton*.

The wrecking of a ship is always sad. In addition to the monetary loss there is the matter of the skipper's self-respect as a navigator and his love for his craft. But while other yachtsmen buy a boat, we had invested in a home, and I suddenly realized what a home afloat involved. One can leave a house with a reasonable expectation of finding it safe on return. The odds against fire, earthquake or tornado are with the house owner.

Afloat, the odds were against us. Our home investment, financially and emotionally, was in constant hazard and demanded never ceasing vigilance. An uncharted rock, a storm, a fire on board, a fog, a leaky tank of gasoline, a neglected motor, an unwise anchorage, even a careless helmsman, could wipe us out. I said all this to Robert.

"Yes," he said. "We must stand a twenty-four hour watch."

Just how thoroughly the habit of watchfulness would be established I did not then realize. We accepted the need of it as naturally as one accepts a constant factor in any life. No detail of equipment was too small to bother with. Shipshape means more than cleanliness and order. It means a ship in readiness for instant operation. The last turn around deck is more than a pleasant evening custom. Wind, the lie at anchor, ground tackle, tide, all are factors of safety through the night. Anchorages must be made with caution in waters where an uncharted pinnacle rock may lie just off a steep-to shore. It is not enough to know the fathoms where a hook is dropped. The radius of the boat's swing in tide and wind must be dragged with a lead line.

Caution carried to the extreme of fearfulness would have destroyed the joy of cruising. But awareness of hazard became a fixed condition in our lives. We grew supersensitive to small noises. We knew how the boat felt at all times and in all places. That first faint shudder of a dragging anchor would bring Robert from a deep sleep while a similar rattle of the chain cable on rocks did not waken him. I knew a dragging anchor almost as soon as he. By the time he had reached the engine room I was at the wheel. My woolen anchor-watch trousers were kept within instant reach, for in those waters a boat didn't have far to go before it reached the rocks.

The few tense moments at the Yucluetaws had been revealing. We realized the conditions we had accepted in electing to live afloat. And we knew too what inroads the *Triton* had already made upon our affections. Each admitted that we had felt very differently than when we were threatened by disaster to the *Yakima*. We didn't know to what lengths our devotion would go in the years to come, when our record that the *Triton's* keel had never touched became a matter of deep importance to us. Had it done so, we would have felt that we had failed her. And masters don't fail ships any more than good ships fail masters.

XII

GREEN WATER OVER THE BOW

CHANNELS ARE NARROW AND tides swift in the long waterway from the Yucluetaws to the Pacific, and breezes often blow strong from the open sea. When the wind is against the tide a boat gets a dusting, and if she is a good boat her people are happy. The *Triton* was a good boat.

We swung through Whirlpool Rapids with the full strength of a big ebb. The *Triton* was deep in the water and the whirls got a firm grip of her and laid her over on one side and then the other while the motor groaned. But we only watched her and smiled as the shore line flashed past.

We didn't smile when the tide tossed us out past a point into the face of a stiff westerly and squarely into the midst of furious tide rips that stretched far ahead. The bow rose swiftly, swooped down with greater speed, and a sheet of spray came back to smack against our faces, oilskins and sou'westers.

"We're going to find out about things," the skipper said.

Bobs and I stood beside him, each with a firm grip on the pipe railing that held the weather cloth. That first swoop had brought an empty feeling somewhere that wasn't wholly physical. We were subjecting our ship to a test, and strangely our fear was not for ourselves but for her, and for the place she was already winning in our hearts.

We were running at regular cruising speed and when the bow rose the second time until it was higher than our heads, I saw the skipper's hand go to the throttle. I was glad he intended to ease her. But he didn't move the lever as we came down with a resounding crash that lifted a great sheet of spray for the wind to hurl at us.

In open, currentless water, waves have some regularity. At least they mount and fade according to certain physical laws, and they always move in the same direction. Tide rips are waves gone mad. They even get in each other's way and no man can predict them. They come from nowhere, rise in ridges or even in pyramids, fade into nothing. They strike the hull on both sides at once. They lift a boat and then melt beneath it, leaving the craft to tumble into a pit. There is something honest even in the malignity of heavy seas in open water. A tide rip is an erratic fiend.

Now they bothered the *Triton*, but they never touched her spirit. The skipper took his hand from the throttle, and I didn't mind. The *Triton* didn't need easing. She kept steadily on through a half mile of that senseless welter and then settled to the business of bucking the short heavy seas that pile up like walls when a strong tide meets the wind.

She climbed and she dived. Her bow was seven feet high, and the white crests of waves rolled onto the deck when she plunged into the trough. Once, in a furious gust, a wave lifted her so high that when her nose dropped to the next wave the solid water buried it and came rushing aft on the deck. But the *Triton* rose gallantly out of the smother and our stiff faces broke into smiles. We'd taken green water over the bow.

We kept on, the boat fighting every instant. We could feel the hull tremble when solid water battered it and Bobs and I clung to the rail as the *Triton* pitched.

The sea ahead was white, and out of the whiteness came a mast, and then a handkerchief of steadying sail, and finally the hull of a fishing craft. She was as large as the *Triton* and she was rolling her scuppers under. The tide tore at her from one direction and the wind from the other, and running before the seas she wore a harried look. Boats are never built to run. By spirit and design, they are at their best when fighting.

A hand flipped out of a wheelhouse window and I waved back as negligently. But I didn't feel that way. I could have hugged that fisherman. We too were sea people now, and we had a ship.

"Know enough about your ship?" the skipper asked after two hours of it, and he pointed at quiet water in the narrow entrance to a cove.

I called them "Surprise Harbors," one is waiting so often for you when you need it along that coast, and there's so little to indicate its presence. One moment you are pitching or rolling, and the next you've shot behind a point and the wind and spray have gone and the sun is warm and a steady deck is beneath your feet.

And then you get the hook fast in deep mud and look at the close shores and listen to the wind passing overhead, and you know that a good ship carries a little paradise of its own to spread for you wherever it goes. A sense of peace comes. We'd had it in the Canadian bush after a long day at the paddles, when a snug camp was made and the firelight made a haven in the wilderness. We'd known it under the low bright stars on a mesa in the Southwest, with the sagebrush campfire only another star. But in a boat it is best of all.

Our sense of peace in that quiet cove became elation when we could talk about the *Triton* without having words crammed back down our throats by the wind. We hurried below to look at lockers and buffets, to inspect galley and engine room, and we did not find that a thing had moved or been broken in all that pitching.

We were soaked despite our oilskins, and nearly frozen, but that will always remain as one of our happy anchorages. The *Triton* had proved herself to us. From that moment on she was truly our ship.

We waited for settled weather in a succession of small neighboring harbors. We discovered the succulent Minstrel Island clam. The bo'sun found an unusually beautiful nook which she christened the Grotto of the Ancient Cedar. She added it to her grotto book with a water color sketch that caught the Druidic mysticism of the natural amphitheater in which three moss-covered throne chairs stood against a high black wall.

We spent an afternoon with a despondent fisherman who mourned the old days. Once he had caught as many as six thousand salmon in a season and received as high as forty-five cents for each cohoe. Now he was trailing eight hooks and delivering scanty catches to the canneries for as little as five cents a fish. He reported that he had never caught a spring salmon in Knight Inlet but had caught many humpbacks, although he had only succeeded in landing twenty percent of the humpies because, though they were better fighters, they were soft mouthed.

He invited us to pick his raspberries which promised to be a bumper crop and added that he would accept as payment the shooting of a deer which had been molesting his potatoes.

"Game warden says that deer is a government ward," he complained. "A lot they care about my potatoes."

We advised him to bill the government for damages and left him composing a long letter. The correspondence would at least take his mind off his fishing troubles.

On the *Yakima* we had cleaned ship from a sense of duty. On the *Triton* we cleaned because we wanted her to be bright and shining. The skipper grew very zealous about the hull and was quite skipperish on the subject of throwing garbage to windward. He said so much about it that Bobs and I composed a ditty.

Songs had been sung on the *Triton* in her early days. She was that kind of a ship and happy voyages leave echoes in a hold. We'd inherited the *Triton's* song, a ballad of the cruise of the good ship *The Walloping Window Blind*. I'd thought we'd adopt it, but instead we wrote our own.

Our song had its debut when Bobs came above decks with the dinner refuse and unfortunately chose the windward side. But her mistake was forgotten in the din we made as we chanted at the skipper our little effort about "Throwing the Slops to Sea."

> *Oh, throw them to the wind, my dear,*
> *And throw them far and wide,*
> *That the incoming flood may catch them*
> *And carry them out on the tide.*
>
> *There be cukes and bobbing murphies,*
> *And carrots wild and free,*
> *There be coffee grounds and turnips mashed,*
> *Throwing the slops at sea.*

So throw them far and wide, my dear,
And throw them wild and free,
That they may not cling to my good ship's side,
Which is so dear to me.

The skipper grinned, brought the long-handled brush from the foredeck and cleaned off the evidence of Bobs' error. But she didn't make many, for she was as zealous as we of the *Triton's* trimness.

We hadn't taken too seriously Bobs' offer to polish brass and brass cleaning became a group orgy. After we had polished all the brass in the main cabin, skylight quadrants, berth chains and hooks and the large brass sheet at the threshold of the companionway, we cleaned paint from the bronze portholes and polished them. When Bobs and I ranged above decks and uncovered the big bronze cleats, the skipper warned us we would regret it some day. But he added proudly that the old girl looked very grand. Then I became ecstatic over what I could accomplish in freshening our living quarters with a can of white paint. The skipper countered with an equally enthusiastic calking of the afterdeck.

We were discovering the joy of grooming our own ship. Neither Robert nor I was a passionate devotee of house decoration. If hardwood floors required doing, a kitchen repainting or an automobile needed waxing, we called in a professional. And Bobs was really allergic to household tasks in town. But a boat is different. Gleaming fresh paint and shining brass repay one. Sailors maintain that a ship should always be white.

"They look awful pretty that way," an old salt will say in a fumbling effort to express that personification of a ship in the minds of men who sail them.

So the *Triton* became not only our home but our avocation, and instead of resenting the insistence of her demands we sometimes felt guilty over the amount of time we gave her. The skipper would confess, almost reluctantly, that he planned an afternoon of sanding or varnishing and then look so relieved by my enthusiastic agreement to join him and paint the deck.

The early morning run to Alert Bay was beautiful. The great snow-capped peaks rose glitteringly above shadowed planes of glorious blues and grays and purples. The glassy sea was island-studded and refracted light caused a strange mirage. Wooded islets appeared to stand high above the water, resting on pedestals of their own reflections. So we voyaged in a magic world.

Having seen community houses in native villages, we wanted to know the coast Indian in his industrial center. A cannery made it just that, and we found the town a strange merging of native and white culture. Community houses, gone citified, were very sad. A succession of old hags who looked like witches came and went out of the barnlike structures. The dignity and the beauty of the great cedar-columned buildings were lost above a doorway cluttered with shattered crockery, rusting stoves, and native disorder. In the only house we entered, decrepit victrolas, torn lace curtains and broken furniture competed with the thunder birds.

There is a difference of opinion as to what the white man has accomplished for the coast Indian. We heard both sides. One man spoke glowingly of the charitable men and women who have crossed the ocean to live in discomfort while they struggle to make the Indian more like the white man. Once the native didn't wear pants but tied a blanket around his middle. He danced heathen dances, rated his wealth in fictitious coinage, metal discs called coppers, and gave away his substance in giving dances, or potlatches. He erected strange heathen effigies, totem poles and oddly painted figures. But now every day the Indian was becoming more like the white man. The dances had been stopped. The coppers had been confiscated and the potlatch was illegal.

"Yes," a listener jeered, "the white man saw the Indian having so much leisure that he was envious. And ever since he's been trying to make the Indian want the things that he wants."

The Indian's year is divided between four homes, one for each season. In the summer, he fishes for the market and then rests. In the fall he fishes for himself in the rivers, gathers clams, and then rests. In the winter he rests all together and has time for carving and for dances. In the spring he fishes for eulachon, or candlefish, makes his oil and then rests again.

The potlatch and the coppers were economic devices. The copper, a small piece of soft native metal hammered with a design, represented wealth. An Indian could not carry a hundred trade blankets or twenty canoes about with him, so he exchanged these articles for a copper. It represented trade dollars and was easily transported. The value of the copper depended on its financial history. It doubled in value each time it was sold. This one hundred percent increase sometimes worked a disadvantage, for the value of a copper might outgrow market demands. One of the most expensive was worth $20,000!

This problem had been met without debasing the currency. A copper could be broken and the pieces sold at fractional value, but this entailed a certain humiliation.

That was avoided by a formality which everyone understood and which left all parties satisfied.

Two chiefs, each of whom owned an unsalable copper, would get into a fearful quarrel. Insults would be hurled and challenges given. To show what great fellows they were and how magnificent was their disdain for money, each chief would break his copper and throw the pieces on the ground. That gesture vindicated each one's honor and he could sell the pieces. The by-play helped the market for it was regarded an honor to buy a part of a copper destroyed under such heroic circumstances.

Coppers were inherited by the eldest son, but a memorial to the deceased carried a wooden replica of every copper he had owned. Similarly a woman's tombstone celebrated each copper which had been paid for her in marriage and which she had redeemed. An Indian bride is purchased but she and her family must pay back the purchase price doubled. To be an unredeemed wife is considered a great disgrace. The repaid price acts as a marriage dower and, as one Indian woman told me, "It is more respectable than a lot of your white marriages." But she did admit that the desire for many coppers on a tombstone might lead a woman into several marriages.

The potlatch, or giving dance, was an arrangement for old age savings. When a man gave a potlatch it was with the understanding that everyone who had received a gift would return twofold. One potlatch given during the productive years of a man's lifetime would provide for his old age. At one time every Indian gave a potlatch, but now that the custom had been forbidden by the government there is a division of native opinion. Old men who had given potlatches, and now had no hope of a return, were aggrieved. Young men who had received and were now freed from the debt were naturally delighted.

Even the Indians admitted that the potlatch had gotten out of hand. In the early days great piles of trade blankets, canoes, sacks of flour, cases of canned goods and hogsheads of colored glassware were given away. The gifts were distributed among many and there was hope of collection of the debts. But wealth from work in the canneries and a competitive spirit had raised the ante. When the Indians began to give away gas boats they defeated the purpose of the scheme. The game got out of hand as speedily as a Red Dog pot. Few recipients would ever be able to return two gas boats.

The women clung to their small potlatches. Gifts were small, odds and ends of china and glassware. They sang and made up funny little songs about each other.

"It's just a party and we all laugh a great deal," an Indian woman explained. "We give them in turns just like you white women give parties."

The real potlatches were conducted with ceremony and dances. The ban on potlatches resulted in a distinct cultural loss, for with the potlatch went all the color and dramatic material which accompanied them. Already younger natives could not do the dances or sing the songs. In a recent revival of the potlatch, permitted by the government in honor of the opening of the hospital, a Bishop of the Church of England had remarked that he had not dreamed anything so beautiful was connected with the ceremony.

The natives had sent to the reserves for their dancing regalia and wore masks of birds and animals and ceremonial blankets. A bright blue blanket of mountain goat hair was decorated with abalone shell and silver. One of vivid red was trimmed with shells. A black and yellow of lovely design and weave was fringed with beaks of sea parrots. The stage curtain carried the tribal design, a halibut on a turtle. In the male dance of the Flight of Birds each man danced solo. He entered the stage masked as a bird, was driven back to the underworld by the medicine man and uttered the sound of the dying bird as he made an exit. Women danced in groups while eagle down was thrown in the air and the music of the tom-tom merged with the chant of seventy male voices.

The more intelligent Indians felt a quite justified resentment of the white people's misunderstanding of the so-called cannibal dance in which the dancers pretended to eat the flesh of a chief.

"They don't really bite him," a mission-trained Indian explained. "They just want to become like him. You know," he added quickly, "it's the same thing as the sacrament in Church."

At a Hudson's Bay post in Ontario where we had spent a summer I had been amused and outraged to discover that each morning I had been dressing a tubercular breast for an Ojibwa woman who returned home to remove my dressing and apply a decayed beaver skin. She had concealed this straddling between white and red man's magic by replacing my dressing before she appeared in the post kitchen.

The cemetery of Alert Bay reminded me of the incident. The native burial custom is to put the body in a square tea box before rigor mortis and place it in a tree. Holes are made in the box to permit the spirit to escape and all other branches of the tree are cut away from the one holding the coffin, so that nothing can interfere with the escaping spirit. Then the estate of the deceased is spent in putting up replicas of coppers, redecorating totem poles and erecting wooden figures to commemorate the dead.

Alert Bay natives had accepted underground interment and marble tombstones, but these and coppers were used on the same graves. One family, unable to decide between a tombstone and a native figure, had a native figure done in black marble. Lips were carmined and eyes and cheeks white-encircled.

In midafternoon we watched the burial of a girl who had died three hours before. Her body had been carried out through a window. Paid mourners were still howling in her home while the family was installing a neat white marble slab decorated with clasped hands. That done, they hurried away to burn her clothes on a flat across the bay. The fire burned all night.

The natives had gone in enthusiastically for tombstones. These were white man's magic and so necessary that a drowning did not always relieve Indians from the duty. One family had met the problem by dumping an enormous carved marble shaft into the sea at the exact spot where the man went down.

Nowhere was the strange mingling of two cultures more pronounced than in the home of a famous carver of totem poles. Bobs and I called on him, expecting to meet an artist. He was. It was a joy to watch him handle the beautifully modeled surface of a feast dish shaped like the body of a seal, but he was much prouder of a row of highly colored enlarged portraits of his family. They gazed pallidly down at us through a thick greenish glass guaranteed to be unbreakable. He pounded on the surface with a stick of wood.

"See! No break," he said. "Last long time."

The durability of the glass did mark the pictures apart from the clutter of white man's products in the room—a victrola with dangling horn, a parlor lamp with raveling beaded shade, a chair with broken rocker, a bedside table leaning drunkenly while its drawers spilled out a collection of woman's ragged silk underwear.

No wonder the white man's magic of unbreakable glass had impressed him.

XIII

PURPLE LAGOON

W<small>E</small> STEERED A COMPASS
across Queen Charlotte Sound. It was an enchanted sail
upon an enchanted sea. A glittering phalanx of snowy
peaks encompassed us on three sides. Off our starboard
quarter lay the maze of islands we had threaded the previous summer. Off our port bow a thin black line against the
open Pacific marked the groups of Deserters, Walker and
Storm Islands. We hoped to see them astern the next year
voyaging north.

The sea was opalescent. An almost imperceptible ground
swell undulated the smooth surface and caused a gorgeous
play of jewel tones. Turquoise, amethyst and opal swirled
and circled and produced arrow darts of vivid ruby,
emerald and topaz. Mrs. Neptune was fingering her treasure chest.

A school of porpoises sighted the *Triton* and raced over
to frolic about our bow. This is considered a good omen
and it was the first time the *Triton* had been so honored.
The skipper looked very pleased. Bobs and I lay on the
foredeck and watched their bodies flash back and forth.
The definite coloring, black back and white belly, and
the swirling roll made a lovely pattern in the green water.
The sharp sound of their breathing reached us above the
gurgle of the bow wave. Often one of the eight-foot creatures leaped clear of the sea. Our speed of eight knots

gave them plenty of time for sporting events. To cross our
bows was child's play for animals which have been clocked
at thirty knots. We were deeply touched even to be
noticed by these gay greyhounds of the sea.

We were on our way to visit Dave Connel, one of the
early handloggers and the first logger to enter Seymour
Inlet. Handlogging fascinated me. A man, an ax, a saw and
gravity pitted against those enormous cedars three to five
feet across and from 150 to 250 feet tall! Logging by man-
power means nothing in eastern forests, but when one has
stood behind a seven-foot Douglas fir growing 300 feet up
a steep mountainside and watched a midget man on a
swaying springboard pecking at that forest giant, seen him
hurl that mighty tree straight on a selected route through
the forest below to its eventual plunge into the sea, one
knows the thrilling spectacle of handlogging.

Because Dave had come up the coast twenty years before and was rated as a skookum logger, we expected to
find a venerable and perhaps enormous man. It was like
tracking Paul Bunyan to his lair and we didn't believe
that the medium-sized, black-haired chap who came out to
take our lines could be Dave Connel. This man was young,
lithe and smiled easily.

We followed him to his float store and found him to be
as modest as he was genial. He explained his handlogging
operations in a remote inlet on the grounds of youth.

"I went up Seymour when I was the age to go up to
the head of any inlet just to see what I could see," he said.
"Logged to get the excuse to travel."

He had logged Seymour in the days of the roving license
when a man cruised the shore and cut any tree he wished.
Once in Seymour he had seventy-five successive "stumpers," trees which leaped from stump to salt chuck without

stopping. Robert asked what had been his total cut in Seymour Inlet.

Dave opened a little black book. "I got 889,000 feet out of there that winter," he said.

Robert had known small camps in Wisconsin where a crew didn't cut more than that all winter. For a one-man crew it was a skookum record.

"But I fed my crew well and kept 'em happy," Dave laughed.

Dave's background of school and a good family, his roving years and an alert mind, made him a delightful companion. A piquancy of phrase added punch to his stories. He gave us a firsthand account of early coast history. Often a hundred handloggers gathered in the Greenway Sound store and four or five poker games were going. A cedar rush had seen a whole inlet staked in a day.

Dave's subsequent work as a timber cruiser enabled him to give facts and figures about the logging industry. He was a mine of information and a lot of fun besides. He and the skipper were buddies after the first ten minutes.

In addition to logs Dave knew people, and he liked and understood the natives. The Indians must have liked him for they made him a Tyee. The celebration of his chiefship had required three weeks of feasting and dancing. The Indians worked themselves into a fenzy but Dave got very tired. He was beginning to wonder if he wanted to be a Tyee after all, when the natives finally led him off to sleep alone in a community house. Dave thought the party was over and fell asleep. He wakened to see two wild men, one painted red, the other black, peering down at him through the smoke hole. Stupefaction kept Dave calm, but the Indians were delighted with his courage.

The wild men were the final test and he had passed with honors. He was made a Tyee at once.

Dave's boomsticks held a community of floats, store, warehouse, dwelling and an emergency dressing station for the logging camps. Only the chickens used the shore, and then only when low tide exposed a beach. A dignified file of distraught hens walking a boomstick on their way to scratch gravel was most amusing. I remembered the crows and I asked Dave if the hens had tide tables.

"They've gotten smart since the day a whole row of them had to turn on a boomstick and walk back," he said. "The hens at the head of the procession couldn't find land and squawked and scolded and the ones on the float end wouldn't turn around. They had an awful to-do about it with both ends having different ideas about getting somewhere."

While we were moored alongside the store, village life went on about us. Two accident cases arrived from logging camps. The first, a crushed shoulder, was dressed at the emergency station and returned to camp. The second, a shredded arm and hand, with little hope of saving either, was sent to the hospital at Alert Bay. Queen Charlotte Sound was smoking and I didn't think the patient could survive the crossing. Even lashed in his berth, he was due for an awful rolling.

"Maybe it's better if he doesn't live," one of the men remarked.

A charter boat brought us a touch of the city. In it were four commercial salesmen calling on the coastwise stores. A boomman and a winchman and their families waited over a tide until they could be towed to a new camp. Handloggers drifted in. The local bootlegger appeared and was driven off the float. A provincial policeman, hot on a new trail of some mysterious racket, arrived and asked innumerable questions. When told about the bootlegger, he made large and glorious gestures and departed quickly in the opposite direction. I had been tremendously impressed by the officer's shining holster and military bearing and had imagined that we should soon hear shooting.

Dave advised us to carry on our search for handloggers in Alison, Belize and Seymour Inlet. These could be entered only through Nakwakto Rapids, which is possibly the fastest water in the world. The ebb runs at twenty-two knots. We were, I believe, the second pleasure boat to enter.

The inlets promised much, handloggers, gas donkey logging, an isolated district and spectacular scenery. These remote inlets had neither store nor postoffice. Some of the families had not been outside for two years, a few old handloggers for fifteen. The only mail and freight service was by means of a bi-monthly steamship which stopped in a harbor outside the rapids.

Dave suggested that we arrive on steamer day when every man in the three inlets would meet the ship and we would have a preliminary and wholesale introduction.

So we departed for the westward, but when we had passed through a narrow channel between two islands in the upper waters of Queen Charlotte Sound we had a "northward" feeling. This was the jumping-off place for the run to Alaska and for the first time there was no land between us and Siberia. A heavy ground-swell rolled in from the North Pacific and small islands were wind torn. Gales had twisted the branches of low cedars into tortured shapes. Vegetation began far back from tide mark, and rocky shorelines were scoured and scarred and beaten by mountainous seas.

North of us was the first of three open crossings on the route to Southeastern Alaska. I weighed the *Triton* against that unprotected water.

"Could we make it today?" I asked.

The skipper laughed. "When we try that next year, lady, we'll start at two o'clock some morning."

A light fog was drifting in. It caught us as we reached the Southgates. This island group had, as Dave promised, a charm of its own. We threaded narrow channels between granite rocks and wind-twisted cedars. Wispy trailing bits of fog moved like gray phantoms along green shores. It was terrifying and it was beautiful.

"If it doesn't get any thicker," the skipper added.

It didn't. In midafternoon we tied up at the float of a deserted logging camp, seventy-five thousand dollars' worth of idle offices, warehouses, bunkhouse, hospital and dwellings. Several handloggers had already arrived and were using the blacksmith shop. The caretaker told us that the *Prince John* was not expected until after midnight.

More loggers straggled in at supper time and we gathered in the office. Someone suggested poker. When Robert placed a chair for me, the men looked as astounded as though they had been invited to a game of tiddlywinks. I would have retreated, but Robert motioned me to stay. Having a sponsor put an added load on my shoulders, and I hated losing quite enough without that burden. When I concealed threes and got some raises from a two-pair logger, I saw Robert's eyes gleam. The men became very respectful. As my chips grew and the other piles diminished, a new respect permitted me to steal a sizable pot

with a bobtail flush. One of the men pawed over the
five cards.

"Missus," he said, "you got to come up to Seymour and
try that again."

At three in the morning a shout of "steamer" broke up
the poker game. I was the heavy winner, but the men's
approval of me seemed to grow with my stack of chips.
I'd never known such cheerful losers. We had invitations
to stop at every float cabin in three inlets. Robert looked
as pleased as a parent whose only offspring had just been
declared "Miss America" or something.

When we wakened late next morning not a gas boat was
in sight. I stared at the empty wharf and wondered if I'd
dreamed that crew of loggers. I hoped not because I'd
liked their hearty laughter and kindly eyes. And we had
missed early morning slack through Nakwakto. It had
swallowed our companions and already the rapids were
running. Their roar carried to us four miles away.

That sound topped all the descriptions of unleashed
fury we had heard and gave us a healthy dread of the passage. At the poker table one of the handloggers had told
a story of Turret Islet, a pillar of rock eighty feet high
which stands in the center of the rapids. Legend insisted
that the rock trembled from the terrific impact of the
water. A man doubted this and at dead slack his companions set him on the islet and left him for the six-hour
run of the ebb.

There he remained, without hope of escape, while the
tremendous might of the rapids battered at the slender
base of the rock. When his companions went for him at
the next slack they found him face down on the ground,
sobbing and clutching at grass and roots. He had gone
temporarily mad and later he reported that not only did

the islet shake but that it was only a matter of time before it would be carried away. The fact that Turret Islet has endured that onslaught for centuries could not dissuade him.

I sympathized with the man as we approached the pillar of rock that afternoon. Miscalculation and delay, both slight, had brought us to the rapids fifteen minutes after slack, but already the ebb was running swiftly. There were times when we barely held our own, even with the throttle wide open. My stomach did things as I watched that smooth sheet of water pouring downhill at us, and later the skipper admitted he had doubted if we'd make it.

But after we had managed to crawl past Turret Islet and catch an easier slant of current near shore, we reached the rocky point at the upper end. Here the tide was truly racing, a faster torrent than we could stem. Only by shooting across, gaining on the angle, getting a kick from an eddy, did we finally reach less turbulent water and pull free.

Nowhere on the coast is tidal fury displayed as in Nakwakto Rapids. They are short but narrow and shoal, and through this small shallow passage pour the tidal waters of three long inlets. The flood is not so bad, running ten or twelve knots on spring tides, but the ebb does not begin until three hours after high water by the shore in the open Pacific. Then it is literally running downhill and attains a maximum velocity of twenty-two knots.

But figures can't tell anything about it. The current attains such tremendous force and volume that water piles up against the shore and leaves a depression ten or twelve feet deep in the center. There are no whirlpools or boils. There is not even room for eddies as the ebb increases. It is just one 400-yard mass of mad resistless current sweeping everything before it.

Everything except Turret Islet. And I'll accept the legend and that lone investigator's report. Not even the core of the earth could stand in that torrent without shaking. So strong is the current it rushes through the five miles of Slingsby Channel and out into the open Pacific, where swells break against it several miles off shore. In the pass itself there is no slack in the sense that the current stops. The last dying swirl of one tide becomes the first movement of the torrent in the opposite direction.

After our breathless and, at times, dubious struggle to reach quiet water, our Seymour Inlet social season was on. It began with dinner at a logging camp in a beautiful lagoon not shown on the chart. We owed its discovery to the poker game in which the camp owner, Mr. A. P. Alison, had taken a hand. After dinner, at high tide, the crew helped us bring the *Triton* through the narrow shoal channel and we lay in a salt water pond.

Our host had started as a handlogger and knew the entire logging picture. His experience had made him an understanding boss and the camp was like one large family. From owner to flunkey, we gathered each evening, and the group produced some fine yarns. Everyone knew a few stories and told them well, for the narrative gift is sharpened when men must depend on each other for entertainment. A good tale was treated with respect and considered durable. We liked the frankness of the stooging.

"Tell about the time you bought a kicker, Charley," one of the group suggested.

Without further urging, Charley, an ancient handlogger, began the story of his first encounter with an outboard motor in the days when they were new. For thirty-five years Charley had depended on man power to get up the coast from Vancouver. He was a pushover for the first salesman and so pleased with the new gadget he invited a fellow handlogger to go along. For fifty miles out of Vancouver everything went so well that Charley's boasts increased in fervor.

"Damn fine little rig," he would shout above the noise of the exhaust. "Damn fine little rig. Save me a lot of rowing."

The guest was getting tired of hearing about it when the motor stopped. Charley fumbled with the strange contraption for an hour while the guest made his own comments on the "damn fine little rig." At last Charley began to row. He rowed silently for fifteen minutes, staring at that piece of useless equipment. Then in a burst of rage he arose, plucked that motor off the stern and heaved it overside.

"There, damn you!" he said as his new toy sank. "You needn't think after thirty-five years of rowing I'm going to start rowing you around."

The prompters laughed as heartily as we did.

One man's story of the handlogging partners who argued so fiercely over whether a seal had whiskers that they didn't speak all winter was capped by a half dozen yarns of cabin strife. Strains and stresses of marriage are nothing compared to partnership logging. It was heavy work and exasperating. A man might carry a sixty pound Gilchrist jack up a steep mountainside only to see it slide off a cliff. A hung tree meant days of labor, and at the end of every day there was communal male housekeeping. Weary men became so rasped they could not speak. Some talked to each other only while at work and one pair conversed solely through a cat.

"Well, Jerry," one would say, "I figure tomorrow we'll go up and cut that big fir."

And then the other would tell Jerry just how he figured that fir could best be felled and run. The arrangement worked perfectly. The partners were getting in a boom and the cat was getting an education in handlogging until he got into a mixup with a mountain lion. Unfortunately the story didn't have a fairy tale finish, for the death of the little cat failed to reunite the warring pair.

Machine logging was almost as exciting as handlogging. Somewhere out of sight up the mountainside the hook tender and rigging slingers placed the choker around a log five feet in diameter and forty feet long. The men scrambled to safety and the whistle punk tugged at his long wire. At once the donkey roared and shuddered and threatened to jump down the steep bank into the salt chuck as its drum and gears began to revolve. The donkey man, moving levers with both hands and feet, controlled that snorting power with the delicacy of a true artist.

I could hear the great steel cable thresh through brush far up the slash. A tree fifty feet high, and in the path of the oncoming log, swayed and fell as the great timber struck it. Moss and earth flew up, brush was flattened, another tree went down, as the captive log came seaward. Nothing, it seemed, could stop that all-crushing progress.

Suddenly all was silent. The donkey gave a final scream and shudder and was still. The chaser, whose job it was to fight hang-ups, ran to the scene of trouble. The mountain was quiet and men waited tensely.

"It hit a stump," a mesenger reported. "He'll have to roll the choker."

He meant that the cable must be reattached so that the

log would be made to roll sideways past the stump. A few moments later the chaser emerged from the thick brush and raised his arm.

The whistle punk pulled the wire and the shudder and clangor of the donkey began again. The cable whipped and threshed until at last the huge log, lifted now by the high lead cable, nosed out of the brush and swung and swayed down the steep bank, seeking the water like some harried monster.

Heat, dust, perspiring men, tension of the hang-up, and at last joy when the log came in!

"That's thirty dollars in the salt chuck," a man said as the unhooker threw off the choker.

I watched the crew for so many hours the skipper asked why I found it fascinating.

I considered for a moment. "Perhaps it's because I feel the log has got a chance," I said. "Like a salmon with a rod."

Robert repeated my speech to Mr. Alison that evening. For our host, the fascination of logging lay in the use of resistless power, in high leads and sky lines, and a vast system of overhead cables. He opened machinery catalogues and looked wistfully at pictures of 600-pound traveling pulleys, steel cable two inches thick and an array of huge compound donkey engines and winches as long as railway locomotives.

"This is the stuff which makes a fellow go crazy," he said. "Even Rockefeller couldn't finance the ideas that come into a man's head when he sees these things."

But he admitted that power alone was not the answer. It couldn't make up for inefficiency. A powerful donkey wasn't always the solution. Too much power would snap gear, and a broken cable took forty dollars out of profit.

The dream of every logger, "a bigger donkey than the other fellow's," may cost an operator a lot of smashed logs, broken gear and loss of mobility in spotty timber, where the donkey must be shifted frequently.

"A fellow's got to use his head," Mr. Alison said.

"That's exactly what I meant when I spoke of a salmon on a rod!" I cried. "Those trees can't be manhandled. You've got to figure on landing each one differently, as you do a fish."

Office logging gave me a tremendous number of notes to write each morning. I would think we'd exhausted the subject of donkeys, logs and loggers' viewpoints when we'd uncover a new golden vein of information. I wrote until I had writer's cramp and then pre-empted the skipper's engine room studio. Notes from our summer voyages were beginning to fill several books for we had gathered a vast amount of material, all invaluable fictional background.

Robert had suggested I write facts and figures indexed under different headings—fishing, logging, country, and boats. Finally when I became so fascinated by impressions which had no place under these headings or in the ship's log, I began a volume of my own. Robert jeered. He'd always maintained that a writer should carry the feel of a country and its people in his head and not in a notebook.

"Just write down facts I might forget," he said.

One evening, in a carping spirit, he flipped over the pages of what I called my personal log. Then he settled himself more comfortably, adjusted the light and began to read. When I was ready for bed he was still reading.

"This is stuff you'll always be glad to have," he said. "It doesn't make any difference if you never use it. You've put the fun of two summers in words."

Days sped in Purple Lagoon—visits to slashings, chats with the crew, swimming in the marvelously warm water, and always evenings spent in yarning. Bobs and I made a day's visit to a trout lake back among the mountains. The trail was lovely. It circled a mountainside and passed three waterfalls and half a dozen cedar grottos. We didn't catch any trout, but we ate our sandwiches beside sparkling blue water while we looked at white-clad peaks.

The camp had several visitors. Billy Welsh arrived with the two Finn partners he was driving mad by Simon Legree methods. They stayed all evening and Billy was the raconteur of the gathering. The partners didn't seem to care for Billy's stories, but were glad of the chance to sit and rest. Billy talked a great deal about his Indian wife who had died some years before. They had gone on many sprees together. Her eight-hundred-dollar funeral remained a monument to his devotion. He had hired every hack in Vancouver, conscripted every logger on the skidroad and personally seen that every man except the priest was joyfully and gloriously intoxicated.

"She'd have liked that," he said. "She wouldn't have wanted to be put away with a lot of weeping."

I had just started luncheon one day when Robert called that George Hunt was at the float. He was the man we wanted most to see for already we had heard something of his history. George lived in Fort Rupert, a discontinued Hudson's Bay Post where his father had been manager. His mother had been a Haida, a highly cultured people among the coast Indians. George's interest in recording the culture of his race, first awakened in field work with Dr. Franz Boas, had made him a valuable source of information.

We rushed to the float. George and his brother-in-law

had already unloaded supplies and pushed off in their gas
boat and we were introduced across an ever widening
stretch of water. Our only impressions were of a remarkably white mustache against a bronzed face, a musical
voice and a graciousness of manner.

Nobility was the word I used later in speaking of him
to Robert. And I felt that George had meant it when he
had called back that he wished we would visit him in
Fort Rupert.

XIV

WE GO SOCIAL

Our departure from Purple Lagoon was a leave-taking of friends. Almost the entire crew stood on the wharf and waved us off on our grand tour of the inlets. The butcher-paper wrapping of Mr. Alison's going-away present had aroused my hopes for a gift of meat, but when I saw the big prime rib roast I almost cried with joy. Rare roast beef after months without it! Our ecstatic plans for dinner got a rude jolt when we turned into Seymour Inlet. Robert looked down the long stretch of whitecaps.

"Isn't that hell?" he said. "A rib roast aboard on a day when there isn't a chance to cook it."

He didn't know what I'd go through for rare beef. No other food would have tempted me into that careening galley. Each basting was a crisis. I almost stood on my ear while I struggled to keep the precious roast from sliding onto the galley floor.

But we had rare roast beef for dinner and we ate it in a quiet cove with the *Triton* moored securely to a handlogger's float. That evening was the first of our float circuit. For seventeen nights we were tied alongside a different small cedar shack nestled beneath a mountain. We had not contemplated such wholesale visiting, but our engagements grew up on us. Before our mooring lines were cast off at one float we found ourselves dated up to visit another.

The tour became a succession of days of logging—hand-logging, gas-donkey logging, steam-donkey logging, Diesel-donkey logging. The skipper peered into the innards of donkeys, helped piece together a home-made donkey, tended logs in booms and, to the joy and amazement of all spectators, rode one big stick across the beach and into the salt chuck.

I thought he had concealed a rodeo past until he confessed to his family, "I damn near broke my back."

At every float talk fell into the same pattern—optimistic plans for a bigger and better set-up the next year. Hand-loggers intended to buy donkeys. The owner of a home-made gas donkey intended to scrap it for a factory product. Single donkeys were to be made to grow into a herd of donkeys.

"When my boom gets in," was the invariable preamble.

"Another Number One cedar in the salt chuck!" was the battle cry.

I thought we were touring through a logging Eldorado until I discovered they'd been making the same plans for ten years, while the only old-time handlogger who had expanded to a steam donkey and a small crew was wishing he could simplify things.

Steve was a completely disillusioned capitalist. He had sailed up the coast twenty years before and found Billy Welsh handlogging in Knight Inlet.

"I pitied the poor devil," he said. "Then I found out he was making more money 'n I'd ever owned."

That started Steve in handlogging and now he wished he'd remained. A handlogger had the best of it. A Gilchrist jack, saws and axes were the only tools needed. He had no labor troubles except his own and his partner's grouches. He had no pay roll to meet. He could always borrow and

hold his boom through a poor market. His only ambition
was to buy a donkey, and his unalterable belief was that
power logging would give him ease.

"And look at me!" Steve added. "Instead of the donkey
working for me, I'm working for the donkey. Investment,
pay roll of seven, fire regulations, and I got to have a show
big enough to pay to set up the rig. I got to sell my boom
no matter what the market is so I can meet expenses. I
saved to buy that critter over there, and it's eating me up."

Life had always been an adventure for Steve. He had
cruised the coast in a tiny steamboat, broke half the time.
He had rendered lubricating oil from dog- and rat-fish and
found his firewood on the beaches. No matter how tough
a hole he and his partner got into, they'd always found a
way out. When their steamboat had sunk in February off
the cannery at China Hat, they had stolen a cable from the
smokestack and raised the boat with two cedar logs, working through four tides. The nearest they had come to disaster was in a stiff southeaster in Milbank Sound when
the poker fell into the eccentric and broke the go-ahead.
They were off a lee shore. No boat repairs were ever made
faster, but they got going in time to nose out a shipwreck.

"Those were great days," Steve said. "It's still a great
country, mountains, big trees, fast water. No other place
in the world I'd rather live."

Six feet tall, deep-chested, he stood on his float, surrounded by mountains. Tide swirls gurgled and eddied in
the nearby narrows. Beside him stood his wife, slight, almost frail, but her quiet intensity matched his exuberance.

"And how I long to see an English countryside," she
said. "A smooth and quiet and civilized land. These mountains take me by the throat. Some days I hate them!"

To my relief, they both laughed. She looked up at him.

The top of her head came only to his shoulder. I knew his courtship had been as tempestuous as his steamboating and that she was thinking of it when she added, "But Steve's worth a couple of mountains."

Women in the float houses of that hybrid country of land and sea fascinated me. All revealed a yearning for contact with earth. Window boxes, pots of growing things around the float, did not satisfy. Women and hens—they must put their feet on land. Kinship with the earth is femaleness and as insistent as the male instinct for boats.

I had noticed the difference in our own cruising. The skipper considered land a place for action and spent his quiet hours in his home afloat. He read on the afterdeck. I invariably took my book ashore. He marveled at Bobs' and my elaborate preparations for an afternoon on land and would hand down to the dinghy all our impedimenta —towels, books, sewing, paints, notebooks and pencils— with the remark that girls made a lot of trouble for themselves. If he joined us later for exploring, it was from a desire to see the country and not because his feet, like mine, demanded the feel of earth. Every so often I had to smell the perfume of crushed sweet fern and to walk in open places.

Women of the float houses lacked the harbors in which Bobs and I found our outlets. Their homes, rising and falling with the tides, were fast to high mountains where land was inaccessible. A few climbed to the slashings, watched their men at work and shared the excitement over a growing boom. They were the happy ones, for they were defeating a country which frustrated femaleness.

Those who had not made this adjustment were often very lonely and very sorry for themselves. They spent their days marooned, bemoaning a sentence to life in a cedar shack which could neither travel like a boat nor be decently set on land. After listening to the lamentations of one woman for a whole morning, I could understand the logger's deep distrust of matrimony.

Marriage had become a timely topic in the inlets because of the recent innovation of "lady cooks." Arguments for and against them were still raging. Handloggers who had women cooks reported that good meals and comfort off-set having to clean up for supper and bring in wood and water and even wipe the dishes. Old-timers pointed out that the lady cooks usually married the loggers and became ladies and not cooks. After one recent marriage, a second lady cook had been imported to cook for the wife.

The whole problem of lady cooks was fraught with peril. One had achieved matrimony by taking a firm stand on the theory that a man had to marry the woman whose life he had saved. The logger had only intended to perform a neighborly kindness when he rescued her from a float house which was destroyed by an avalanche a few moments later. But he became a hero and just as inevitably a husband. Now cooks were in bad odor as rescuees.

Certainly matrimony was in the air of float houses ruled over by lady cooks. Usually the handlogger was completely unaware of his danger. We spent an evening listening to one boast how much a cook had increased his work time. He'd soon have a boom in the salt chuck and then he could buy a donkey. The cook said nothing, but a gleam in her eye convinced us that the next boom money would be spent on a honeymoon in Vancouver.

Each evening of our inlet tour was occupied. When we were not talking logs or playing cards, we were sitting up to all hours discussing an amazing range of subjects. No matter how determined had been our plans for an early

bed hour we always capitulated to the invariable, "Don't
go home. It's not often we get a chance for a good talk
like this."

Next to logs, and perhaps women, men in logging
camps like to discuss economics, politics and religion. I was
surprised how often religion cropped up in our talks. It
had been thoroughly discussed the evening we spent in the
float house of a logger who had started out in life as a
fencing master. His wife had been a textile worker. They,
their two grown sons, a daughter of fourteen, Robert and
I had all stated our personal beliefs. Bobs had listened.
Aboard the *Triton* she was thoughtful.

"I guess you've got to believe in either Gods or gases,"
she said as she went off to bed.

What these people called a "good talk" kept us on our
mental toes. We had been warned of the possibility of en-
countering those who had given thought and even study
to a subject by the incident of Dirty-Faced Smith.

No one knew his history. He was distinguished from
other Smiths by the reputation of being the most unwashed
man in a country where all loggers end a day's work black
from the admixture of bark dust and perspiration. Dirty-
Faced Smith was returning home on a coastwise steamship
when a radical began to harangue a group. No one bothered to answer. The handloggers had gone to Vancouver,
sold their booms and spent the money, and were now going back to earn themselves another bust. They felt free
men, despite the radical's insistence that they were industrial slaves.

Dirty-Faced Smith, who had been huddled in a corner,
straightened up and assumed charge of the meeting. He
took the haranguer back to the Fall of Rome, brought
him down through the history of the ages, went exhaus-

tively into the guild system, traced the rise of capitalism and the development of the entrepreneur and summed up the losses and gains of present conditions. He punctured the statements of the self-elected lecturer, tied his victim into knots, wrung him out and flapped the limp remains. Dirty-Face talked like a Cambridge man, and for all anyone knew he may have been one. When he had finished he pulled his dirt-encrusted hat over his eyes.

"Maybe that'll hold you till we get off this boat," he said.

"And that," a witness added, "was the only time we'd heard Dirty-Face say anything longer than, 'Here's how.'"

We did not encounter anyone so dismaying as Dirty-Faced Smith, but we uncovered logical and original thinking which we weren't able to handle with the tops of our minds. "Good talks" were absorbing, and fatiguing. I began to feel like a circuit conversationalist and it was time our family became re-acquainted.

I proposed a quiet night at anchor in a bay which had no handloggers. We chose our anchorage more for privacy than for protection. When the skipper went on deck for a last inspection he called me out.

"Come see your quiet night."

In the early darkness the bay had taken on a threatening aspect. The wolf-jaw silhouette of the high black shoreline added menace to the gray turmoil of the sea. I had no sense of being sheltered.

"We haven't very good protection," the skipper said.

He dropped the heavy anchor. Wide-fluked and weighing 130 pounds, it had never dragged but we didn't use it unless necessary. The skipper had to pay for his sense of security in having to bring it and thirty fathoms of heavy chain aboard with only a hand winch.

By midnight the wind was shrieking through the halyards. The *Triton* sailed up on her anchor cable, crossed over and brought up with a jerk that threatened to break the chain. She seemed to be alive and fighting to get free. Heavy gusts of wind laid her far over. It was more than wind. It was a solid push.

The skipper dressed and prowled the deck. When he came below he found me in the main cabin—prepared for trouble. He thought we'd hold, but he said the phosphorescence show was worth seeing.

I looked out on a bay strung with diamonds. Each wave was crested. Dark troughs were a black setting for lines of silver fire sweeping toward us. These broke against our bow and flowed out in long jeweled tongues. And as one broke, another rushed upon us. On and on they came, silver-helmeted troops of the storm.

I made up an upper berth, so that I might watch from a porthole. The wind increased. Its redoubled force snatched the gleaming crests of each wave and carried them in a glittering smother until the whole bay was afire.

I grew so ecstatic I forgot the gale and extolled the beauty of the night. The skipper was figuring how best to keep the *Triton* off the beach if our ground tackle failed.

"Think you're in a theater?" he asked.

When danger wears such jeweled trappings it loses its sense of threat. The first pre-dawn light drew down the curtain. I went to sleep. The skipper wakened me in full daylight. The gale had blown itself out and the *Triton* rested quietly at anchor. We drank coffee on the afterdeck and I marveled at that startling freshness of early morning after a storm. The skipper made comments on his crew. Bobs had not wakened and his mate's interest had been only in the phosphorescence.

On dark nights I'd seen oars drip jewels and the outboard motor leave a silver torrent in its wake. I had watched a school of herring become sparklets as they fled before a spangled salmon. A fisherman's story of a phosphorescent night in Rivers Inlet had made me envious. He'd fastened the dory end of his net to a cliff and wakened to see the net shining like a silver fence. Coming along it, all done up in tinsel, was a whale.

"Even his eyelashes glittered," the fisherman assured us.

A jeweled whale trying to find his way through a silver fence was quite as mad as anything in Lewis Carroll. I shrieked with delight.

The fisherman stared at me in an injured fashion. "But the cliff cut off the whale as well as me," he said. "If he came toward the dory, I was done for and if he went through the net, I lost my gear. What's so funny in that?"

Now I no longer begrudged the fisherman his tinseled whale. I had seen the sea bedecked with diamonds. And I insisted it had been a beautiful night.

"Quiet, too," the skipper added. "Your ideas always turn out so well. What's on for tonight?"

Until then I had forgotten the Saturday night dance. I had only a vague notion of the location of our host's float house and I could not recall his name. But I was sure we were invited and that I had accepted.

An afternoon nap set up the skipper so that hunting a party in a long inlet appealed to his sporting instinct. As we started in early evening his remarks about tracking the spoor of gas boats to a party were most entertaining. On a long reach we encountered a small craft. Its crew hailed us and asked if we were going to the party, so we fell in behind.

Our hosts were expecting us. Robert joined the group of

men and a girl of twelve led Bobs and me inside. I was grateful for the company of children. Their chatter was the only cheerful note as two lady cooks and I sat in a row of straight backed chairs. Occasionally one of the men would look in, pick out one of our trio and dance her solemnly around to the music of a victrola. Robert stayed outside and reneged completely on his duty to the lady cooks.

I had concluded that the affair was going to be rather dreadful, when we heard the shrill tooting of boat whistles and much shouting and laughter. The real party was arriving in a body. The lady cooks and I had been those nuisances, guests who arrive too early. The crowd trooped in. A violin and a banjo were unwrapped. The men came in, removed their coats and prepared to show what they could do in the way of the polka, the schottische and the twirling waltz.

When a handlogger swings his partner, he swings her. He dances as exuberantly as he logs. At three o'clock in the morning I had been danced off my feet. The party threatened to last until dawn but I didn't have another spin in me. I limped aboard the *Triton*. Bobs had gone off to bed at midnight. The skipper said he was exhausted, and had been for hours. He went below at once, but tired as I was, I could not leave the beauty of that night.

The moon was rising over a straight black cliff and sending a shaft of moonlight across dark water. Golden reflections from lighted windows of the float house met the silvered radiance of the moon. Down the shore the smooth granite scar of an avalanche became a huge shimmering gray mirror. I had never known that the path of an avalanche could be beautiful. The music of the violin and banjo drifted softly into my quiet world.

This was, I knew even then, one of those moments which would be forever unforgettable. Sea, mountains, friendly people, even the moon, had united to make it so.

We made a quick run up Belize Inlet and Alison Sound. One old grandfather of a cliff in Alison towered straight from the sea for three thousand feet. A waterfall accepted that challenge and jumped from its crest, a gleaming slender column of water that made all the other falls of a mere thousand feet or fifteen hundred feet look like sissies. We stopped to give it a hand, which was presumptuous, for it had been carrying on without applause for centuries.

As we nosed cautiously into uncharted Village Bay, the skipper remarked that we were undoubtedly the first cruiser to have done so. He stood on the foredeck and conned us in, and when he asked for slow speed I gave him a reluctant crawl. Charted rocks are hard enough.

The Indians had built a village for fall fishing and the river mouth was filled with salmon weirs. Rock walls laid in great "V's" led fish into narrow bottlenecks. The community houses were unattended by totem poles. Only a pair of thunder birds brooded solemnly over a collection of drying racks and cedar root baskets. There were no rusty pots and pans, torn lace curtains or broken crockery to remind us of the white man's culture.

The village was as primitive as if Columbus had never sailed. Within a stone's throw of the settlement the *Triton* swung at anchor. Just how great a contrast we presented I realized quite suddenly that evening as I looked around the main cabin. Books, upholstery, electric lights and gleaming white paint, Bobs deep in Conrad, Robert reading the "Confessions" of Rousseau. I had just put down a recent novel. Robert had spent the morning at work on a type-writer. We had explored a primitive native village in the afternoon. Our dinner had been much the same meal we would have eaten in San Francisco. That night we would sleep on springs and mattresses. A gasoline motor had brought us in and we would depart as easily.

"What's eating you?" Robert asked.

"I'm wondering if we haven't learned how to live at home while we travel," I said. "In every other outdoor game we've paid for adventure with discomfort or hard work. There must be something wrong with this. But I can't find it."

"There won't be anything wrong when we've rebuilt the *Triton*," Robert said.

It was a fine evening and a fine place to bring out the boat sketches. We'd been working at them all summer, planning, discarding and devising, and they were at last beginning to take shape. By lengthening the hull six feet we could improve the appearance of our stern, get an afterdeck and a stateroom for Bobs. A wheelhouse had been definitely decided upon one cold day in Seymour Inlet when a wind off the mountains drove Bobs and me below. Clad in oilskins and sou'wester, the skipper had stood a four-hour watch. Below decks was to be changed completely. We had designed a convenient galley, large main cabin, two staterooms, two bathrooms and places for two typewriters. We were amateurs as naval architects, but we spent space as preciously as life's blood.

We had reached the locker stage of planning. By some modeling in the bathroom-to-be forepeak, I found that a full-length hanging locker could be added to the plumb-ing features. I returned to announce this and Robert handed me a sketch. His tone was casual, but his manner was triumphant.

"Found a way to get a tub into the midship bathroom."

He had turned the neatest trick of the evening. And at once he was declared a hero and the tub was known thereafter as The Triumph of Village Bay.

XV

I AM NOT CONVERTED

The ensign drooped at the taffrail and the sea was glassy as we left the Southgate Group one morning. I was busy below with plans for a culinary orgy when Robert called me.

"Got to go to the engine room," he said shortly, and gave me the course.

I put the *Triton* on it and looked ahead to see the ocean lift in a long ridge and come rolling toward me. The *Triton* climbed with a swift soaring movement, swung dizzily at the crest and lunged into a deep wide hollow. The compass swung as dizzily as the boat and then we climbed again and pitched over with a corkscrew motion that put us forty-five degrees off course.

From the top of that crest I saw a succession of green ridges coming toward me, apparently untired by their long journey from the Aleutian Islands. How high they were, I don't know, but I have seen quarries not so deep. From crest to crest lay three or four hundred feet of valley, and it was valley, not vale.

It was a ground swell, the leisurely aftermath of a storm in the open Pacific. The crests did not break, but the mounting, inexorable sweep of those huge rollers made me look back longingly to the quiet of the Southgates. I looked even more anxiously to the engine room, where I heard the clank of tool on motor.

166

Despite my efforts, that infernal compass swung until it threatened to make a complete revolution. As we quartered into the swells they pushed the bow to port and then let it fall sickeningly to starboard. I planted both feet and wrestled with the wheel, but after ten minutes, when I wasn't getting anywhere at all, I looked despairingly around.

The skipper's grinning face looked over the hatch combing of the engine room. Until then I'd accepted that clanking metal as evidence of motor trouble. The dirty dog had planned to leave me on the bridge alone with my first real ground swell.

He took the wheel and I was pleased to see that he didn't hold the course any better than I had. I told him so.

"Wanted to find out whether you were a sailor or a sawlog," he said. "Did you see where that towboat crew painted her name and the dates on rocks?"

While in Seymour we'd heard the story of the tug with its boom of a million feet of logs, and now names and dates painted on rocks along the coast didn't seem like small-boy writing on blank walls. Such inscriptions were towboat totem poles.

The previous February a tug had spent twenty-eight days in the Southgate Islands waiting for winter gales to cease long enough for it to cross four miles of open ocean to the next shelter. The crew had painted evidence of their tribulation on a cliff, but they had waited in safety while the owner of that million feet of logs had no way of learning whether his property was in a snug harbor or being spilled all over the Pacific. A season's profit depended on the judgment of a man who couldn't be reached.

No wonder towboat skippers build reputations on their judgment of pace and weather. If a captain takes an unwise chance he may lose the boom, and if he is over-cautious and tows only in dead calm the market may fall out from under the helpless owner. One boom of a million feet from Seymour Inlet shrunk one third in value in a two months' journey to the mills.

Towing logs is much like an egg race, combining custody of a fragile object with a need for speed. A long tail of logs, made up of sections, can be broken up by a heavy ground swell. And if the boom isn't actually destroyed, enough logs can pop out in a breeze to destroy all profits. Some handloggers depended on the ability of towboat skippers rather than on insurance companies whose liability does not cover the minor loss of straying logs. One skipper who had the enviable record of never having lost a log was so jealous of his reputation that he carried a motor tender and would lower it to retrieve a single timber.

At first we'd pitied towboat skippers for their dreary existence, crawling at a two-knot speed. But after we'd met some and understood their problems we realized our sympathy was wasted. Always they are playing an absorbing game in which they pit their knowledge of tidal currents and weather against the sea. Ten miles? Five hours. Sky, feel of the air, barometer readings, instinct, a fund of wind lore gathered through many years, all are weighed. And once the start is made and the breeze strengthens, a race is on, as exciting for the skipper as if his speed were a hundred miles an hour.

We had known that if we continued to fool around in Queen Charlotte in August we would be caught in fog, but we never expected anything like the thick gray curtain which shut down suddenly in the narrow channels of the Deserters as soon as we got out of that ground swell. For all we could tell, our world ended one hundred feet ahead. I was sent to the bow as lookout and strained my eyes until I had "fog woollies." Sinister shapes appeared on all sides. They looked like rocks, cliffs, trees or headlands and melted as suddenly as they had come.

I cried "Rocks!" often, only to add a second later, "No! Gone now!" After that I wouldn't have expected the skipper to believe we were in danger until we struck.

The tide was racing. In the steamship channel we heard the whistle of one of the large boats on the Alaska run. Its periodic bellow was terrifying, for those ships maintain their speed, fog or no fog.

We crawled back into a narrow passage in a maze of islands and tried to discover just where we were. Whistle echoes, the usual method for determining the distance to shore, returned so instantly we knew the shore was close at hand. And long streamers of kelp lying all around warned us that we were in foul ground. It was up to us to find a way out, and quickly.

At last I saw a ghostly shape long enough to be sure it was land and before the fog shut us off we got a bearing. We checked calculations of current and running time, took compass readings on the chart, decided our position, lost faith in our calculations, reglimpsed the same ghostly point, renewed faith in our mathematics, and started all over again on a vicious circle of doubt, confidence, doubt, confidence, while we crawled through a labyrinth of channels.

During this fog wandering we passed a small cove evidently used by whales as a day-nursery. I don't know why those two youngsters, circling and ejecting baby-size jets of vapor, gave me such comfort, but they did. We didn't know where we were, but a couple of whale mothers were sufficiently sure of their bearings to have parked the off-spring.

The skipper decided that the most important rule for fog behavior was to figure out the course and then stick to it despite phantom shapes, mate's misgivings and his own inevitable doubts. A navigator could not be fluttery-minded. Robert is Scotch, and stubborn enough to try this. When I took the wheel and he gave the course, I understood from his tone that it was my job to keep it without planting any more uncertainties.

The theory, like that about blackfish behavior, would be good if it worked. Eventually we sighted Doyle Island, identified it past the shadow of a doubt and then began to applaud ourselves as navigators. A tight place successfully negotiated is a great bucker-up.

We were on our way to visit George Hunt at Fort Rupert. As we emerged from a thick bank of fog, the harbor lay ahead in dazzling sunshine. George and a bevy of nieces watched us drop anchor and met our dinghy at the shore.

"I am glad you came to see me," George said as we shook hands.

After a tour of the small native village we visited the remains of the old Hudson's Bay Post and the Indian graveyard. Nothing remained of the Company days except the dwelling house and wide expanse of tree-shaded lawn. George's sister, Mrs. Cadwallader, wife of the present owner of the store, still lived in the house in which she had been born when her father was company manager. In those days it had been guarded by a stockade and cannon.

She told us something of those early years when a thousand workmen received supplies on ration day and the dwelling house had been staffed with cook, nurse, house-maid and laundress. Those were happy days, she said. She and her ten brothers and sisters had played with native children and attended the mission school. They were dangerous days, too, for the Indians had been refractory. She had seen a man killed outside the stockade.

Legend reported that the Scotch manager had married an Indian princess and when Mrs. Cadwallader showed us her mother's picture we could understand the rumor. She had been a Haida, from a powerful family in Alaska, and there was dignity and nobility in her face. The girls showed us their grandmother's trousseau. Her dancing apron, woven of fine mountain goat wool, was trimmed with sea parrots' beaks and copper bells. A pair of ceremonial blankets was woven in the family's totem design. The eldest girls looked lovely when they modeled them for me. One looked astonishingly like her Haida grandmother.

Our comment on the resemblance pleased the girls and Mrs. Cadwallader. They were proud of this Alaskan woman who had left her people to be the mistress of a Hudson's Bay post. During her husband's lifetime, Mrs. Hunt had remained at Fort Rupert. After his death she made only one journey. She had not liked the traveling clothes her daughter had selected and said that the widow's black bonnet was ugly until she met a white woman, also wearing widow's weeds. Then the Indian woman recognized them as ceremonial garments of grief and admitted her error.

"Daughter," she said, "I am glad you dressed me in the right way to pay honor to my dead husband."

After a tour of Victoria, Vancouver and Seattle, where they visited hotels, theaters, and shops and the Haida woman saw for the first time buildings larger than a community house, she was content.

"Now take me home," she said. "I have seen the white man's cities and I can die happy."

Two months later they buried her in the native cemetery in Fort Rupert.

"I think she meant to die," Mrs. Cadwallader added. "She was very lonely for my father."

A photograph of the Haida woman explained why we had been so impressed by George Hunt in our first brief meeting. His face had the same strength and serenity as his mother's. He told of his work for the Smithsonian Institution which had taken him to Washington to prepare an exhibit of miniature fish traps. His wonder and delight at the honor scientists had paid his work were still with him after more than thirty years.

"Water was running through the traps and my little figures of men stood beside them," George said. "It was just as our people fished. Many white men came and looked and liked the things that I had made."

George invited us to meet his wife, who was preparing winter clams for Indians who were still away fishing. Mrs. Hunt was very large and very friendly and could not speak a word of English. She sat on the beach surrounded by clams. Hundreds were being smoked on racks. A washtubful was steamed and shucked.

She motioned me to sit beside her while she wove clams on three long sticks. The two outer sticks were thrust through the bodies or pillows of the clams, while the necks were interlaced around the center stick. One clam was strung on top of another. The plaiting was so beautifully regular that the finished product, a braid of clams two feet

The Seal Accepted Bobs as Nurse

Exterior of a Community House

The Triton *Rebuilt*

*Lua Was
a Sea-going
Dog*

long and six inches wide, looked like an elaborate piece of knitting.

I tried it but my plaited clams had great holes where I'd dropped clam stitches. We squatted there together, plaiting, smoking and stopping occasionally to eat a roasted clam. Talk was not necessary to establish a feeling of friendship and of understanding. I gave her several packets of cigarettes and she presented me with her best jewelry, nose ring and earrings she had worn when she danced the winter dances for Dr. Franz Boas. I felt I was being given the crown jewels.

"I can't take these," I protested to George.

"She wants you to have them because she likes you," George insisted.

George put on his dancing mask so we could take his picture. Its terrifying effect was weakened by the pair of gum boots protruding below his blanket.

I plaited clams all afternoon. Bobs and the younger Cadwallader children tended the low fires. George told stories that had been told around the fires of his people. It was a wonderful setting in which to hear legends—a huge, kindly-faced woman preparing winter foods for a village, roasting fires canopied with racks of clams, the sun-lit water of the bay before us, and George's soft voice in real prose poetry. His simple words fell naturally into musical cadence and the rich imagery of his phrases removed the gruesomeness from a description of the ceremony of carrying in the smoked corpse of the great-great-great-grandfather.

He told a story of the crossing of the great water when a whale had helped his people, the legend of the origin of the Queen Charlotte Indians.

"All the old storytellers know it," George said. "I think it truly happened."

Robert spoke of the theory of the Mongolian origin of American Indians and George became fired. He had traveled the west coast of Vancouver Island and learned all forms of this basic legend.

"It would be a great thing if I could prove this was true," he said.

We thought of George this year when Dr. Ales Hrdlicka brought back the long-head skull unearthed on the Asiatic mainland. For thirteen years Dr. Hrdlicka had worked on the theory that the long heads crossed from Asia to Alaska on a land bridge which has since crumbled to mere stepping stones, the Aleutian Islands. That skull was, to Dr. Hrdlicka, convincing proof.

George had made a map of these migrations based on the folklore of his people and we went into the house to see it. Map and notes were in a roll-top desk and above was a picture of Dr. Boas. Otherwise the house was like that of any native. Mrs. Hunt looked at this student's corner with great respect and prompted something in their native tongue. George laughed in embarrassment.

"She wants me to show you the cookbook I am writing," he said.

He had visited the old women and had written their native recipes. We read how to make sweets of salal berries, how to cook seals and even the details of the ceremony of the West Coast Indians when they ate whale meat and wished to absorb the whale's brave spirit. The missionaries had not approved of George's research. They felt that it was only working harm among a people who might much better forget their ways and learn those of the white man.

"But this is valuable!" we cried. "Soon all this will be forgotten. Don't let anyone stop you."

George sighed. "Last winter I worked very hard. But now since June when my son died I only want to hunt and fish and go on trips. The Indians have a word for my sickness. It is called running-away-from-the-sorrow-of-your-love."

Robert made an engagement to spend the following day with George. Bobs and I accepted an invitation to go crabbing with the two oldest Cadwallader girls. We met on the beach at five o'clock for the early morning tide. They carried three enormous cedar root baskets and showed us the simple native method of walking over the flat and testing each hummock of seaweed with our feet. A hard one meant a crab. In less than two hours we had filled three baskets.

We carried our sea harvest to the dwelling house where Mrs. Cadwallader told the small boy to build a fire in the outdoor hearth and to put on the kettles. Bobs and I made a polite gesture of going home.

"But you'll stay and eat them with us!" Mrs. Cadwallader protested.

Crab so early in the morning sounded startling. I still had misgivings when a hot boiled crab and two stones were set before me on the lawn. My attacks on crab armor had always been made with knives, forks and hammers. One of the girls saw my hesitation and neatly detached my crab from its breastplate, tore the body and legs from the shell and handed the undressed crab to me. From there we proceeded with stones for cracking and fingers for forks.

A faint yearning for lemon or mayonnaise died with my first taste of hot fresh crab. Never before had I known this crustacean's full flavor. We sat in a semicircle in front of big kettles and cracked and gorged and talked. I'd forgotten there were such things as meal hours, condiments or plates and forks. When Mr. Cadwallader passed I called to him to grab a crab. He shook his head.

"He eats only at a table at regular meals," his wife said, as though explaining a quaint custom. "White men cool their crabs to lose the flavor and then put on mayonnaise to make up for the flavor they have lost. He says it's civilized to do it that way."

I felt as sorry for him as she did. Elaborations had never seemed quite so idiotic. As I started on the second crab of my morning snack I seemed to remember some other self in a comment on the native's irregular meal hours. "It's either a feast or a famine, and they eat when game is caught." Now having sloughed off layers of tradition, I wondered vaguely why this had seemed so reprehensible.

Filled with crab, we lay on our backs in the sunshine. I'd never felt more content and happy. The morning had been perfect and the afternoon promised to be.

"I like this kind of party," Mrs. Cadwallader said. "It's fun to sit in the sun and talk."

While Bobs and the youngest Cadwallader boy held a climbing contest in the ancient apple trees overhead, our talk ranged through women's topics—marriage, children, families and, inevitably, recipes. I asked how native women cooked venison and discovered that coast Indians did not eat it because they were afraid it would make them forgetful.

"You know how a deer looks all the time," Mrs. Cadwallader said.

I'd always attributed the deer's flighty manner to a constant state of fear, but the Indians had decided a deer couldn't keep his mind on one subject.

Before we could go further into this interesting subject of taboos our peaceful afternoon was shattered by an announcement that a missionary boat had dropped anchor. A few moments later we were facing a missionary and two women assistants. They had come to hold a meeting and most evidently expected us to be grateful. One of the children was dispatched to summon the men, but Mr. Cadwallader couldn't leave the store and Robert and George Hunt refused to come. The missionary's manner suggested that this was just as well. George did not stand well in mission circles.

Mrs. Cadwallader proposed rather wistfully that we hold the meeting out of doors, but that idea was vetoed instantly. As we were herded into the parlor, my hostess seemed as helpless about the situation as was I. The meeting was opened with a hymn and I like to sing hymns, for they offer one of the few justifications to raise my voice in song. The missionary began and I was preparing to add my tuneless monotone when the silence of the two assistants and their rapt look of admiration told me I would be crashing in on a solo. The missionary liked to sing hymns, too, and apparently for the same reason I did. But he preferred to sing alone.

The hymn was followed by prayer. I had been taught that prayer should be a humble declaration of gratitude or an intercession for aid and, while I prefer the poetry of ritual prayers, I am always moved by a heartfelt expression of an individual. But this man asked me to kneel through ten minutes of personal sales talk to God. He thanked his Maker for sending him among us. He forwarded our thanks for the comfort of his presence. He expressed gratitude that he had been made to realize our need of him as a missionary and he thanked, again, in advance, for all the good his coming would accomplish.

By the time the sermon began we were restless, for a stiff westerly was blowing into the harbor. I was anxious about the *Triton* and I noticed that our hostess often glanced out of the window. The sermon promised to be about as helpful as I had expected, for while the small boy was inviting the men to the meeting I had discovered that this was the missionary who had visited Seymour Inlet. I had heard about his sermon, preached in each float house, on the iniquity of wasting love and devotion upon lap dogs. As there was no dog, midget or full size, in the entire inlet, the theme had left his listeners baffled.

Now the missionary had abandoned his crusade on lap dogs and was extolling individual passivity. But he had scarcely established his point when a particularly hard gust made us all look out of the window.

"My boat!" he cried. "It's dragging."

He dashed out of the house and down to the beach with the entire meeting at his heels. Once there, Bobs and I lost all interest in the missionary's boat. The *Triton* was gone. We stared at an empty stretch of water where our home had been anchored.

Not until Mr. Cadwallader came, did we learn that our boat was safe in a sheltered cove across the bay with Robert and George aboard. The *Triton* had gone through one of her major perils. George and Robert had seen her start to drag, had run half a mile, launched a dinghy in the breakers and gotten aboard when she was only a hundred feet from a reef. Had she struck it there would have been no hope of saving her.

But we were left stranded with the missionaries.

Mrs. Cadwallader invited everyone to tea. Time and talk dragged on while we sat in the parlor and ate dainty triangles of sandwiches. Everyone was waiting for something, Bobs and I for the *Triton* to come back, Mrs. Cadwallader for her guests to go, and no one knew what the missionaries were waiting for until the man asked abruptly, "Are you not expecting us for supper?"

I hoped she would say no. I would have been quite willing to have said it for her, but her manners never slipped. While the lady missionaries sat at ease, the girls and I went to the kitchen to wash tea dishes and prepare a meal for ten. There, at least, we could talk the situation over. The girls felt they were paying a bit high for spiritual solace. I, for the first time on the receiving end of missionary endeavor, was belligerent. I apologized for my race. I wanted to believe that this was an isolated case of bad manners.

"But some missionary comes to us each summer," one of the girls said.

After supper the missionary invited me for a walk, evidently intending to do something about my soul. I was planning a bit of spade work myself. He supplied the opening with his comment on a beautifully carved feast dish in a community house.

"People wouldn't believe that such barbaric things exist on this continent," he said.

I asked if he knew anything about the culture of the coast Indians and he answered that he'd hardly call it culture.

My instantaneous sounding off was purely a safety valve measure for I knew before I started that I would accomplish nothing. I suggested that he at least learn how well a system of mores fitted a society before he undertook extensive changes. I questioned the right of the missions to impose a set of economic, esthetic and social laws upon a people who had worked out a practical one of their own.

From our complete disagreement on this question we worked into the topic of coastwise visiting among the white families. I spoke of our recent Seymour Inlet tour and asked him how much he knew about those people. He answered that he had carried out the Biblical command, Go ye into all the world and be a friend.

"Friend" was as quick a fuse as "culture." I had a satisfying half hour while I discussed the hunger of those remote people for books, conversation, outside contacts, laughter and understanding and expressed my opinion of his inept attempt to meet that want. I added that above all things this "friend" should have a sensitivity which would make it impossible for him to commit the impertinence of an intrusion into a home. Then he knew that I was slightly mad.

We walked back in silence. He maintained a wary distance between us. Robert watched us come down the path.

"What kind of a scare did you throw into that missionary?" he demanded later.

"That's just the hell of it!" I fumed. "His complacency was unshaken."

The *Triton* was again at anchor. George and Robert wanted food and, while I fried bacon and eggs, I gave them an account of the afternoon. George laughed and told us a story of his boyhood.

"Long ago the first missionary came. He wore a long black dress and sat on the point and played an accordion. The Indians have always known there is some great spirit. Maybe the sun or the moon or the stars. But they knew it was a big god. They thought he was speaking to them in the music and they all gave themselves to the priest. A hundred of them were baptized and given papers.

"Afterwards another man came. He said he was God's man, too. The Indians were very glad and they all carried their papers to him to show that they were saved. But this man grew very angry. He threw the papers in the fire and said they were not God's papers and that the Indians must be baptized again. The Indians were very glad to know this. They were sorry that they had made a mistake. So they got new papers.

"After a while the first man came back. The Indians showed their papers and told him what had happened. And he got very angry and said that the new papers were no good. He would have to baptize them again. Then the Indians talked it over. They said these people who say they are God's men don't understand which papers are good papers and which of the men can save us. So the Indians sent back word that they didn't want any more papers. When the white men agreed about their own medicine, the Indians might try it. And ever since not many of our people have gone to the missionaries."

There wasn't much to be added to the subject after that.

George left early, though we urged him to stay. There were many questions we wanted to ask. He hesitated for a moment and then explained in his gentle voice that Indian friends had come to his house and had brought wine.

"And my wife will be very happy," he said. "She will sing and dance and she will make me sing and dance. And I will be very happy and we will have a good time together."

XVI

IT WAS DELIGHTFUL TO CRUISE
again in protected waters. Behind us lay Queen Charlotte
Sound where fog and gales were a constant threat, where
trees were bent and tortured by the wind and even underbrush could not gain a foothold. Now we sailed through
quiet channels. Mountains were clothed by forests. The
sun shone. Harbors were warm, intimate and inviting.

We spent our mornings at anchor. Bobs rowed the *Crab*,
explored the shore, sailed her boat and went in swimming
off the *Triton*. I wrote notes. Our weeks of visiting had
left me far behind on my job. Each noon, when the skipper had finished his daily fiction stint, we lifted anchor
and changed our homesite from one bay to another as
lovely. We stopped to call on friends, old friends now. We
revisited favorite streams and trails. Our days slipped into
pattern.

Evenings were times of enchantment. We three gathered on the foredeck, our favorite lounging place. Sometimes we read. More often we sat and watched the last
molten shafts of sunset fade on the peaks surrounding us
while shadows deepened along the shores. Always we had
waterfowl for neighbors. Innumerable gulls and terns settled for the evening, with the neat little Bonaparte gulls
remaining slightly aloof from the general assembly. Scoters
cocked their tails jauntily and scudded about, apparently

merely for the fun of aquaplaning. Myriads of jellyfish
rose to the surface and gently undulated gossamer parasols
as they moved tranquilly with the tide. And after the peace
of the twilight hush a moon might rise over a mountaintop
to silver our world.

August is an enchanted month for cruising.

We visited a real pioneering family at Dave Connel's insistence. Fishermen and loggers often called themselves
pioneers and boasted of the largess of their sea country.
"Every time the tide goes out it sets a table." But fishermen and loggers supplement this generosity of the sea by
marketing natural resources, fish and logs. The Hallidays,
Dave's pet pioneers, were wholly agricultural.

We intended a one-day call and remained for three. Our
own pioneering venture, when we had spent five years in
a northern wilderness, paled into insignificance compared
with that of the Hallidays. Thirty years before, Mr. Halliday had discovered a valley of natural grazing land
tucked away in the mountains. It was almost treeless, in a
country of such quick growth that the wilderness reclaims
almost as fast as man can clear. Against the miracle of a
ready-made ranch was the disadvantage of remoteness. The
nearest settlement, the Indian village of Alert Bay, was a
two-day rowboat journey, even in good weather; and in
winter the weather of Queen Charlotte Sound is seldom
good.

Mr. Halliday built a log cabin and brought in his wife
and two children. Their assets were a rowboat, a cabin,
six head of cattle and fifty-five dollars' worth of groceries.
That meager beginning had now grown to a gas boat, a
large house and a herd of cattle which produced a comfortable income. The house looked like an English country
home and was equipped with plumbing and electricity.

Five grown children had attended schools and colleges. The thirty years were a saga of indomitable courage, but those years had not left scars. Neither Mr. nor Mrs. Halliday was aged or toilworn. Our hostess served tea in a firelit library lined with books. We discussed a volume of recent plays. I could not imagine her in a setting which did not include an old silver tea service, thin china cups and a low tea table set before an open fire. Yet I knew she had borne children in an isolated log cabin, attended only by her husband. At seven o'clock dinner our host, looking like a county squire, carved the roast and told us of efforts to improve his herd by importations of thoroughbred stock. Yet for seventeen years he had made the four-day journey by rowboat to Alert Bay and back to sell beef to the natives for ten cents a pound.

They laughed as they recounted those early days of barter when Indians had no money, and neither had the Hallidays. Often they lacked the quarter to give a native who brought their mail and the postman had to take his pay in vegetables. Mr. Halliday showed me their financial record, the beef and butter book. Seventeen years passed before it recorded its first surplus, twenty-eight dollars.

Seventeen years of unfaltering struggle. It brought a catch to my throat and I felt very humble. But remembering our first editorial check, I wanted to know how they had spent their velvet.

Mr. Halliday chuckled. "I bought a kitchen cabinet and loaded it in the rowboat. A sou'easter came up and that cabinet and I camped ashore for three days. My wife didn't know what I was bringing and she knew that ordinarily I'd have returned in that weather. She'd spent three days thinking I was drowned before I came rowing in with that six-foot piece of furniture."

The skipper howled with glee. He, too, had experimented with surprise presents which had gone so terribly wrong.

The Hallidays' recent years had been easier. A nearby pulpwood camp had supplied a steady market.

"But we'd have made it through without the camp," he added quickly.

Of course they would. That sort of courage doesn't know when it is licked.

We spent an afternoon at the old log cabin. They brought a tea basket and we had a garden party under an ancient apple tree with old-fashioned flowers running riot among tall grass. A woman who had pioneered, made tons of butter, taught her children and still found time and energy for a garden, explained much. Mr. Halliday led me through their first log home. He confessed that he still slept there occasionally.

"The family doesn't understand why I cling to this place," he said. "Births and deaths, good times and bad—sounds queer to cherish a reminder of those first hard years."

It didn't sound queer to me. Robert and I had owned a log cabin, gone through some first hard years and knew the keenness of despair and joy. And we, too, made our pilgrimages of the spirit.

We voyaged south reluctantly, for now instead of greeting familiar landmarks across our bow we watched them fall astern. When a jutting headland shut off a last glimpse of a beloved white-clad peak we said good-by to another friend.

As we crossed Knight Inlet we watched for whales. They seemed to hold regattas in these waters. We had be-.

come definitely whale-minded since that first terrified encounter with a school of blackfish and now we knew the difference between a finback and a humpback. The finback's spout is a thin, high column and his speed has won him the name of racing greyhound of the sea. The humpback's spout spreads to form a low bushy cloud, and when he sounds, his great flukes look like a huge black butterfly which has alighted momentarily on the water.

We encountered whales, mostly humpbacks which sounded in a prompt and spectacular manner. I'd almost relinquished my pet bogey, a deaf whale, when suddenly a large humpback appeared off our port beam. I was at the wheel and as in all my crises the skipper was in the engine room. I expected the whale to sound according to good whale behavior, but he kept coming closer. He was sixty feet long, but to me he looked as large as the *Leviathan*. I knew I should do something. That whale apparently didn't know propellers or even traffic signals. If I turned I had no assurance that he wouldn't. As it was, we promised to arrive at the identical spot of ocean at the same moment.

I froze to the wheel and did nothing until he spouted fifty feet away. I could see his knobby head and the white blotches on his black body. Then I screamed to Bobs to come on deck and scuttled to the afterhatch.

"A deaf whale!" I yelled. "He's going to sink us."

Robert's head popped up. He thought it was a joke, and he didn't think the joke was funny. I pointed, but there was only that smooth circular patch of water which marks the spot where a whale has sounded. It was less than thirty feet away. Robert stared.

"Wow!" he said. "Why didn't you call us sooner?"

Apparently the whale wasn't deaf, but he was certainly

hard of hearing. He missed us, but the margin was too close for comfort.

The next morning we were lying at anchor when a sudden outbreak of artillery fire beyond a point brought Robert boiling out of his studio-engine room and Bobs and me erupting from the cabin. Explosions convinced us a small war had broken out and we leaped into the dinghy to investigate. As we rounded the point Robert warned us that he would not be prodded into a hero's role. If armed forces were shooting it out they could continue to do so for all of him.

The cannonading came from a smother of foam and geysers of water a mile down the channel. Curiosity overcame discretion and we speeded up the outboard motor. But as we drew closer we saw we had been lucky enough to happen upon three large humpbacks engaged in lobtailing. We had read of this but had scarcely hoped to see it. Whales previously encountered were always traveling and had no time to disport themselves.

These three whales were practically standing on their heads with the posterior part of their bodies in the air. Their enormous flukes described great semicircles, thrashing the water first on one side and then on the other. Spray and foam, water shooting high, lashing tails and cannonfire—whale calisthenics provide an exciting spectacle.

Bobs was tense, her eyes as large as saucers. We sat in the dinghy, and very close to shore. If that mighty thrashing should come nearer, we wanted trees to climb.

The theory that lobtailing is a de-barnacling performance has been questioned. Scientists maintain that it is a form of play. I thought it might be some sort of competition to determine which whale could stand on his head the longest and thrash up the greatest sea. If that were so, the game was a draw, for they all stopped simultaneously and swam quietly away. The game may have set them up, but it left me weak from the excitement of watching a hundred and fifty tons of whale whip up a flock of geysers and churn the sea to foam.

Two months' mail awaited us at the Yucluetaws. It is odd how one's attitude toward mail changes as weeks pass without it. At first one is certain that momentous events have occurred and then, as day after day slips by without letters, papers or periodicals, interest dwindles. Events in the world outside become less and less important until at last they lose significance. I'd almost forgotten that Robert had mailed several stories, the fate of which we would learn in the next mail bag.

So instead of rushing to Henry Maurin's we turned aside to watch a forest fire where two hundred men were attempting to limit the blaze to one mountainside. A forestry boat with a wireless set stood by. This was new equipment on small boats and we were intrigued by the idea of wirelessing an invitation to dinner to the superintendent of the forestry maintenance shop. We had dined with him and his wife on our way north.

A four-hour run and two tidal rapids lay between us and our potential guests. The skipper consulted current tables and agreed that we could make it if we ran Greenpoint and Whirlpool Rapids on the same slack. We sent our invitation and departed.

A few teas had been given aboard and we'd had the odd dinner guest, but this was to be our first real affair. I planned to make it quite impressive. As soon as our anchor was aboard I signed off as an able-bodied seaman and became an anxious housewife. A hen which had grown refractory about laying eggs in a float chicken house had been presented to us by her disgusted owner. Fricasseed, she was to be the pièce de résistance and automatically called for red huckleberry jelly, baking powder biscuits and a corn soufflé. Homemade cake was to enliven a dessert of canned fruit. The entree was to be my triumph—canned artichoke hearts stuffed with caviar, hardboiled egg whites stuffed with capers, tomato aspic and the whole garnished with ripe olives and julienne carrots which I hung in a wet bag on deck to be chilled by evaporation.

All this magnificent preparation required time, and galley duties were more important than navigation. When we ran through the last of the flood in Whirlpool Rapids, I didn't even glance out a porthole. I gave all my attention to keeping the party foods from landing on the floor. Later I ignored Robert's calls until his skipperish tone brought me abovedeck on the run.

"I smell smoke," he said. "Fire forward. Take the wheel."

He disappeared below without even telling me where we were. Bobs was on the trunk behind me and she looked as terrified as I felt. The thought of fire in a gasoline-powered craft is unnerving at any time, and now ours was complicated by Greenpoint Rapids which lay just ahead. In a few moments we'd be in them and the ebb was already strong and growing stronger. I didn't dare take the *Triton* through, and if I didn't run it at once, we couldn't get through at all.

I hadn't settled this problem when the skipper reappeared. He looked frightened as he reported that smoke was all through the cabin and even in the engine room. Everywhere he went he smelled smoke.

The first heavy current of the rapids hit our bow.

"We've got to get through Greenpoint," he said as he grabbed the wheel. "Hunt the fire afterwards."

A fire which required hunting was doubly terrifying. A boat is two-walled like a home, but the space between the planking and the ceiling is designed for ventilation. Any fire starting between those walls would have ample draft. The real hazard lay in two big tanks of gasoline, tanks of lubricating oil and kerosene and an oily bilge to carry the fire from one end to another. Somewhere in one of those hidden holes a fire was smoldering and might at any moment burst into a blaze.

"One of your damn cigarettes," the skipper said. "It's slipped down behind the ceiling. Soon as we get through the rapids we chop out woodwork."

He'd often held me up as a fire menace. Because I tried to be careful I ascribed his warnings to the emotional disapproval moderate smokers have for one who smokes too much. To be condemned without evidence was manifestly unfair, but I was too scared to argue. I dashed below in such a panic that I couldn't smell at all. I set Bobs to smelling and she couldn't detect smoke. But she was as frightened as I was, with her parents dashing about searching for fire. Nevertheless, I went up to report our failure to find smoke.

The skipper was swinging the wheel hard over to negotiate a sharp turn to port. He had an island, a few rocks and a swift current before him. He had a fire below. My announcement was the final straw.

"Anybody could smell it," he snapped in his best skipperish manner. "I can smell it up here."

I stared at him in amazement and saw what the blindness of panic had made me miss before. A thin wisp of smoke curled from the pocket of his heavy woolen shirt in which he carried the cloth sack of Bull Durham. I looked at it until I was certain.

"I'm going below and finish cooking dinner," I said.

Halfway down the companionway I looked back at his astonished face.

"Anybody can smell smoke if he carries his fire with him," I added. "Go jump overboard and put out the fire from your own cigarette."

It was ten years before he ever mentioned cigarettes to me again. Even that first evening the incident paid dividends. Without any urging, he dolled himself up in yachting whites on our way into harbor. A resplendent host greeted a dinner party whereas usually he began to dress about the time the guests arrived. I felt almost sorry for him, he was so eager to square himself.

XVII

WE LIVE HALF ASHORE

THE YUCLUETAWS MAIL BAG brought news of the sale of three short stories. That helped a lot. Midwinter book royalties would need nourishment to cover the cost of rebuilding the *Triton*. We had much to learn about both royalties and boat building. "Estimated Cost" is a sum which must be doubled before the job is finished. The boat builder doesn't understand this either. He is always as surprised as the owner.

The mail opened other questions as to our fall program. A real estate agent wrote she had found just the house for us in San Francisco. Bobs' school reported several new and desirable extras. One, a daily period of nature talks, cost more than the art course. This left Bobs wholly disinterested. Robert was equally cool to the house. He bundled the letters together.

"We don't have to answer now," he said. "Couldn't catch a mail steamer anyway."

Ideas develop simultaneously in our family. They must breed in the air. I had been thinking with growing distaste of that school, of that house, of that winter's routine. Then Robert turned to me quite suddenly as we cruised down the Gulf of Georgia.

"How serious were you about that English boarding school in Victoria?" he asked.

The previous winter we had talked with parents who had sent a daughter there.

"It's too late for Bobs to enter this fall," I said. "But she could make it by midwinter."

"A semester under our supervision wouldn't do her any harm," he added.

Then I knew we had the same idea. Two homes, one afloat and one on land, were beyond us. We could swing one. That evening we held a family conference. Bobs' reaction to a winter in the north was positively joyful. She brought out an arithmetic she was supposed to study that summer and spent at least five minutes in intense application. Her school operated on the individual instruction theory, a good one if the subject appeals. But it seemed to break down before the rigors of arithmetic.

The present *Triton* wasn't arranged for a fall home, study hours and fiction-writing. So we planned to rent a base on land, a small cabin which would enlarge our orbit.

"We'll find something down the Gulf of Georgia," the skipper said. "And we can live in the house later while the boat is being rebuilt."

Within a week we had found a three-room log cabin. It even had a piano. Also it had charm, a fireplace and a float where the *Triton* could lie and serve as a studio. As a family we could now spread out.

We became bona fide dwellers in our sea country. We lived both afloat and on land. We called at the store and post office in our dinghy. From beaches we gathered wood for the cabin fireplace and towed rafts of huge fir logs with the *Triton*. These were logs which had popped out of booms and which tides and gale had lifted high. Fishermen came to see us. An old ship's master told us stories of early sailing days and taught us sea chanteys. We walked trails to inland lakes. We came to know everyone in the harbor. We made short cruises in the *Triton*. And we worked to supplement midwinter royalties for rebuilding.

If Bobs' interrupted education had caused misgiving we were completely reassured. She was far more occupied than we. She disappeared for day-long explorations in the *Crab*, and with a compass made a detailed chart of our large harbor and its deeply indented arms and bays.

The daily arithmetic hour was not too successful, but Bobs wrote an amazing number of English themes. She wrote and illustrated a volume on clipper ships, in which she had a passionate interest. She began a novel, written in a very modern manner, and with a heroine who whirled through a breathtaking series of sea adventures. Intimate knowledge had not cramped her imagination. Free verse poured from her that fall, and astonished us with its deep feeling for the beauty of a sea pool, of a sunset in the harbor, of the ocean's unending assault on granite shores.

Robert and Bobs spent hours investigating the manners and morals of gulls and cormorants and embarked upon a fervent crusade in behalf of cormorants. Their indignation was the more diverting because even thought of gull reform was futile. They estimated that at least a thousand gulls roosted along the shores, preening their feathers and talking over fishing prospects. But they did no fishing. They would sit there for hours. Then six cormorants would come flying into the harbor. The first gull to see them sounded the alarm and instantly a thousand gulls were in the air.

It was the time of the herring run, but those millions of small fish were too deep for the gulls. The cormorants dived many fathoms and drove the herring to the surface, whereupon the lazy gulls acquired a meal. That might have been all right with Robert and Bobs. But a cormorant cannot eat a fish under water. He must grasp it amidships and come to the surface to give it that sideways flip which routes the herring down his gullet. But twenty gulls were always ready to snatch when he flipped. That was the only time Robert or Bobs ever developed a sense of social injustice.

Cruises, walks, chats with sea folk, harbor life, rows in the *Crab*, unlimited composition and reading—there just wasn't any time for the formal education of a ten-year-old. Sometimes I wondered if our delight over her themes and free verse was wishful thinking; I only knew she was fully occupied and happy.

Midwinter was upon us before we knew it. And if the *Triton* were to be finished for an early spring sailing it was time that the work should start. The skipper begged Bobs off for another month of grace from the boarding school. She'd enjoy the two-day run to Seattle and she had a city bust coming as well as we.

"When the *Triton's* rebuilding is started, and we've settled down here again, is plenty of time for you girls to look into schools," he said.

Bobs' education was deferred for the time and at four o'clock of what we thought was only a very dark, cold morning in January, we started for Seattle. We faced two long days of North Pacific winter weather. Out in the gulf we discovered that dense fog hung fifty feet above the water, and when belatedly the daylight came the fog settled down. We saw the shores for a brief hour that day and never saw land again until we reached Seattle.

All during those two days it was so cold that half-hour tricks at the wheel were all Robert or I could stand. The second morning the entire boat was sheathed in ice. The fog was even more dense. But we never touched the whistle cord. We did not ask for echoes, did not "Siwash" or beachcomb our way. We ran courses like a big ship, and we made good our course and speed.

We knew that we had done so when the entrance to the ship canal locks opened before us. It was a grand feeling to pull up alongside the mooring in Lake Union when our friends had not expected we could make it. They had pictured us cowering in some harbor a hundred miles away. As a crew we felt we were worthy of a new *Triton*.

For a week we held conferences with shipbuilders. Robert fairly lived at the shipways where the *Triton* was hauled out and we could see the lines and depth of her hull. It was astonishing how much space we had to work with.

"She'll be the biggest fifty-footer on the sound," the shipbuilder said.

I spent my days selecting marine housekeeping equipment, galley stove, sink and pumps, electric light fixtures, upholstery and paint colors. The shipbuilder suggested that we live in Seattle while he rebuilt the *Triton*, but we knew that neither Robert nor I would write a word of fiction if our boat were within visiting range. Already our city bust had become a buying orgy on the waterfront. So we declared it over and returned to our British Columbia harbor cabin, counting the weeks and the months before we could take possession of our home afloat.

XVIII

A SHIP MUST HAVE A SHEER

MUCH HAD HAPPENED BEFORE we again saw the *Triton*. We had been back in our small log cabin up the coast less than a week when we discovered that publishers' glowing reports do not always bloom into fat royalty checks. This blow fell the day after we received a photograph of the demolished *Triton* which the boat builder had sent as proof of his speedy progress. He had torn off the *Triton's* stern and ripped out the interior from the engine room forward. I looked from the picture of the skeletonized *Triton* to the figures on the check.

"Now we've got to finish her," Robert said.

The order of events was lucky. We didn't have to rationalize a bigger, better *Triton*.

The next crisis was not so well-timed. Bobs wakened with acute appendicitis on a morning when the Gulf of Georgia was lashed by the worst southeaster of the winter and no steamship was due for two days. Isolation is wonderful when all goes well. Now we had to get to a hospital. There was no chance of bucking that gale to Vancouver, but we knew that a paper mill town five hours' run up the coast had a hospital and a skilled surgeon.

Robert went to the store to find a fishing boat while I got out blankets, packed bags and tried to remember what one did for appendicitis.

197

When we carried Bobs aboard that little craft its owner didn't think we could get through.

"But when a kid's sick you got to take some chances," he said.

The chances were divided. We didn't dare not try to reach a surgeon and nothing less than a matter of life and death would have taken us into that welter. When we left the last sheltering point I learned the difference between a "good blow" and a winter gale in the North Pacific.

We ran before it, a dangerous procedure for a small boat in heavy seas, and once started there could be no thought of heaving to. We had to go on, and if we broached to or were pooped, it would be all over.

For four hours we lived through that second-to-second suspense. Robert remained on duty in the wheelhouse. I watched Bobs lying in a berth and stared at mountains of gray-green water rushing up astern. Each one that left us safe was a milestone. The boat's seams were opened by the wrenching and water trickled across the planking behind Bobs.

Robert came down to warn me that the worst was yet to come.

"Got to take these seas broadside when we turn in behind the breakwater," he said.

I put on a life preserver and lashed another about Bobs. Then I clung to Bobs' berth and waited. Once I was sure we were going over when the motion suddenly changed and we rolled our keel out. We had wired the hospital to prepare for an emergency operation and the staff watched from an upper window. Not one in the watching group expected us to make it. When we reached the hospital the nurses were almost as shaky as I was from momentarily expecting to see our boat capsize.

The operation, followed by peritonitis, resulted in a two months' stay while Bobs slowly crawled back on the road to health. No one thought about the *Triton*. During Bobs' spring convalescence I was almost surprised when a shower of boat bills began.

It was then we discovered that a builder's estimate is only the ante.

So, to reach Seattle at last and find the *Triton* complete, down to the smallest locker, was something of a miracle. We made a formal inspection with the builder, a tour of mutual admiration. We admired him for making our plans come true and he admired us as naval architects. He'd never worked with plans which fitted so accurately. They should have. We'd measured to the sixteenth of an inch inside the *Triton's* hull. The interior hadn't been designed; it had been molded.

The skipper's and my forepeak bathroom had toilet, bowl, medicine cabinets and a large clothes locker. My modeling in Village Bay had been accurate. Aft of that was our stateroom with berths, dressing table, a full length mirror on the door and lockers everywhere. My typewriter table disappeared under the skipper's high berth. The color scheme, daffodil yellow with a soft green trim, which the builder had accepted with much misgiving, was declared an unqualified success.

But neither the attractive color scheme nor the large compartmented lockers under each berth was so important as having a stateroom and adjoining bath. Never again aboard the *Triton* would the bathroom line have to form of a morning.

The main cabin was large enough to hold a chair, two buffets, berths and still have plenty of floor space. The

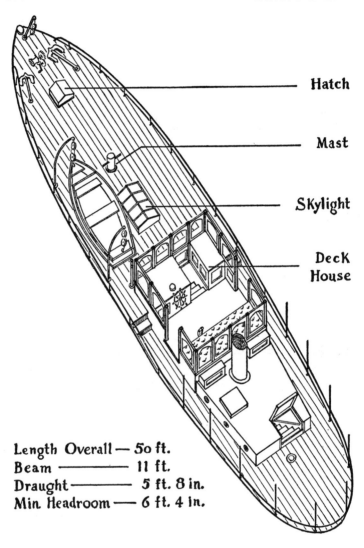

Hatch

Mast

Skylight

Deck
House

Length Overall — 5o ft.
Beam ————— 11 ft.
Draught————— 5 ft. 8 in.
Min. Headroom — 6 ft. 4 in.

Deck of the Rebuilt Triton

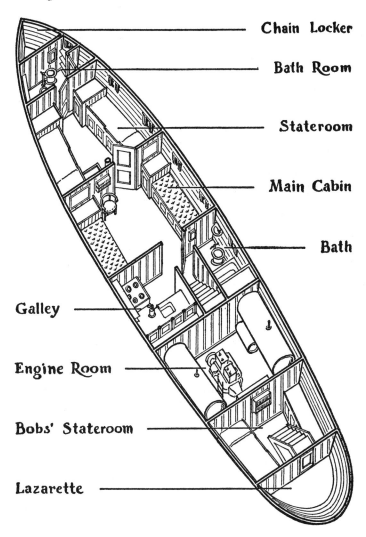

Chain Locker

Bath Room

Stateroom

Main Cabin

Bath

Galley

Engine Room

Bobs' Stateroom

Lazarette

Below Decks

dining table spent its leisure hours folded neatly against
a bulkhead and slipped out and down on a runway. We
had departed from good marine usage by making the two
sides of the cabin different. (Amateur naval architects are
not limited by tradition.) On the port side was a conven-
tional transom berth but on the starboard was a low couch.
That was to be my own corner and I had already ordered
a special lighting fixture.

The skipper decided that he could read comfortably
when stretched out on the port berth. Bobs experimented
with the chair and found it fitted her. We were taking
possession of a living room, and not a Pullman compartment, nor a long bare corridor such as the *Triton* had been.
We had thought the rebuilding would improve our main
cabin, but we had not expected the miracle it had worked.

The galley was our greatest achievement. Every space-
saving, labor-saving scheme which had occurred to us had
been carried out. It had its own hatch for ventilation. A
metal dresser-table, six feet long and four feet deep, held
a centered sink, and ran back under the deckhouse. The
builder had protested that this might be wasted space, but
I'd wanted a garage for all the odds and ends that accumu-
late in meal preparation. The stove burned kerosene under
pressure and was as flexible in heat control as gas. It was
placed at a right angle to the table and on a level with the
metal top. Racks for dishes were overhead, lockers for food
beneath. I had one tier of eight-inch drawers for spices
and condiments and small articles. I could stand in that
galley and prepare a meal for ten people without moving
a step.

Across from the galley was the amidships bathroom. The
tub had fitted, but the allotted space wouldn't have taken
one an eighth of an inch larger.

"We put it in with a shoe horn," the builder said.

But it was in! And a shower, with either fresh or salt water, provided flexible bathing. The tub was emptied by an electric pump, a real luxury, as anyone knows who has ever worked a hand pump to empty a tub below the water line. By the time the tub is empty the tubee is in such a lather that another bath is indicated.

The machinist who installed our ship's plumbing had become inspired. An innocent-looking switch on the after bulkhead started machinery which could bring salt water to the shower, empty the tub, pump the bilge or flush the decks. It was weeks before I dared turn that button without expert advice. I never lost my fear of what I might start after the morning that I intended to empty the tub and brought down a shower of glacial water from the sea. My leap landed me in the middle of the main cabin and my howl of anguish could have been heard ashore.

The companionway led to a deckhouse. A chart table would hold even as many charts as Robert bought. A berth was set high so that kibitzers could take their minds off navigating by looking out the windows at the view. The deckhouse became our sun porch and extra room. As it was heated by the galley fire, skippering would be comfortable in fall and winter cruising. Only the engineer had to step outside. I could go through a southeaster without putting on a sweater. Deckhouse, galley, main cabin, stateroom and bath were in one communicating unit.

I exclaimed about the convenience and the comfort while the skipper admired sturdiness and craftsmanship. At this point the builder began to break the news on costs.

"Here's where the money went," he said. "The fellow who built this deckhouse put it on to stay. There isn't

enough water in the Pacific Ocean to jar it loose. I told
him to build it right and let you folks worry about costs.
You can't afford to cruise in a cracker box."

The engine room, amidships, lay between two airtight,
watertight, and gastight bulkheads. In addition to the
motor and tanks of fuel oil, it contained an electric plant.
Our batteries were no longer charged by the main engine.
I looked at the new equipment with deep affection for I
could now use juice in a free, wide and handsome fashion.
We celebrated this innovation with electric iron, vacuum
cleaner and sewing machine.

Increasing the length to fifty feet gave us something far
more than a longer afterdeck and a stateroom for Bobs.
It gave us grace of line. Transom stern vessels, no matter
how beautiful the bow, always look as if they had been
built by the mile and sawed off to the desired length. They
resemble boxes, and ships must have a sheer.

The *Triton's* sheer was not achieved on a drawing
board. The semi-elliptical stern was sketched on paper by
a navy yard workman who felt as we did, but the sheer,
the sweeping line from bow to taffrail, came from the
sense of beauty in a man's eye as he stood a hundred feet
away and had a carpenter lower and raise and bend a
scantling until his eye was satisfied.

Bobs liked her detached quarters aft. We suspected they
permitted reading in her berth, for she often slept late
in the morning. That factor was of no importance compared with the real value of her isolated room. Bobs, like
us, now had a place of her own. We could always get
away from each other in the *Triton*, and privacy ranked
higher than comfort in our family.

An awning over the afterdeck gave us a fine place for

lounging and shaded an enormous fresh vegetable locker aft of the deckhouse.

First inspection of a new ship is the glorious part of becoming owners of a home afloat. Less pleasant was the skipper's report when he had seen cost sheets. He looked rather shaken when he came aboard.

"Everything ran higher than we expected," he said. "But it had to be done right. It would have been a shame to botch it."

Home ownership had always been held up to us as proof of reliability and ambition. Friends who had involved themselves with finance companies spoke of their future payments through ten and even fifteen years as though these agreements proclaimed worth. We, mere renters, had been at some sort of moral disadvantage. I had never understood why the fellow who writes a rent check promptly on the first of every month should be considered a worthless creature. But I had detected an implied criticism when others drew themselves up primly and said that they were toiling to pay for a home.

Now we were among the ranks of the respectable.

"And we can take our home adventuring," I added.

The skipper looked relieved. "I was afraid you might be worried when you knew what we'd let ourselves in for."

Worried! I was ecstatic. I set up the portable sewing machine on the table in the cabin and made doll-size port curtains and pillow and berth covers. Not since we had left our log cabin had we had an outlet for home-making instincts. I selected china, painted food containers in matching colors, and added dashes of the blue and tile red of the china to the galley lockers. Discovery of after-dinner cups decorated with a sailboat in the same colors was a major event which the whole family shared. Bobs began at once to paint table mats with motifs of trailing kelp and exotic fish which peered goggle-eyed from underwater forests. It was an orgy of ship decoration.

While the skipper arranged the engine room, Bobs took charge of her quarters. She ordered book shelves and devised an elaborate compartmenting of lockers which baffled the ship's carpenter. Evidently he was not a parent for he did not understand the odd assortment prized by an eleven-year-old. She spent as long stowing her stateroom as we did to stow the entire ship and called us to see the completed job. The heterogeneous possessions were sorted and she had, indeed, found a place for everything, clothes, books, writing materials, paints, crayons, charcoal, drawing pads, odds and ends of marine collections, queerly shaped stones, tinfoil, colored paper, molding clay, a model yacht, and a set of cutting tools. Kelp carving was our latest shipboard hazard. A remnant of wet kelp on a deck is much more effective than a banana peel.

We looked at the stateroom and wondered whether it harbored a girl, a boy or an acquisitive crow. Then we saw a large cardboard box jammed into the opening of the lazarette.

"You can't keep that there!" the skipper protested. "I might have to get at the steering gear in a hurry."

"And why do you drag an empty box around?" I demanded.

"But that's my theater!" she cried. "I'm going to put on marionette plays."

The skipper began an exhortation on the folly of junk and the joys of being ship-shape. I took him by the arm and led him on deck.

"It's her stateroom," I said. "The first good sea will make a frightful mess down there, but let her untangle it."

On our way forward we stopped for a peek at the other playroom. The two were so similar it was ludicrous. Twenty-one wrenches, each living in a separate loop, stretched across a bulkhead of the engine room. A long shelf held tins of assorted nuts, bolts, screws and odds and ends of marine hardware. No motor could ever need that many, but the skipper showed them as proudly as a housewife displays preserves. The ship's painters had been recalled to do what Robert had described as "freshening the engine room." Now a shining gray motor sat on a tile red floor in a room of dazzling white. I peered down.

"Good heavens! This place is dressy!" I said.

He retorted that it was merely efficient.

I'd thought of those weeks of stowing and performing odd jobs about the boat as the completion of a home afloat. A new house is a finished job. I didn't know then that a boat means constant grooming, constant care and never-ending improvements. Nor did I know how a boat grows in the owner's affection through the very demands she makes upon him.

It was so with the *Triton*. There was never a time when we were without some scheme for her improvement. And, as we carried them out, our pride grew, and our love. We had thought that a home afloat would be only an instrument for comfortable living while we wandered. But we built far more than that. And then I knew why all good sailors speak of a boat as "she." For a ship comes to dwell in the hearts of the men who serve her, and for them she becomes alive. When that has happened, man and boat possess one another, and sacrifice and service are the expressions of that love.

XIX

AN IRISH GENTLEMAN

BUT WHEN YOU LOVE A SHIP
you must suffer for and with it. On our trial run on a
windy day in Lake Washington, we burned out a con rod
bearing. At least, that's all we thought we had done when
the ominous clatter sounded through the *Triton* and ended
the gaiety of our guests. The motor was stopped, the anchor dropped, and we rolled and tossed until our ignomini-
ous return to our mooring astern a tug.

It was a sad trip home. No one cared to eat the party
food. The skipper tried not to show how anxious he was
about the damage and the men at the mooring made a fine
pretense that trial runs always ended in a tow. The mechanic who had been hired for duty in the engine room
so that the skipper would be free was deeply regretful.
He had become seasick. The oil pump had lost its prime,
he had not watched the gauge and far more damage than a
burned-out bearing had resulted.

The cylinders had been so badly scored that new
cylinder blocks were necessary. Robert reported the full
disaster the next day.

"Alaska is out this year," he said. "I wouldn't take
chances on a long run. And we can't get new cylinder
blocks from the East in time to go."

The motor could be put into shape to run, but the spark
plugs would foul quickly. After repairs were made we

departed, but fresh paint and bright work and bath tubs and vacuum cleaners do not make a ship. The power plant is its heart, and the most handsome male doesn't attract the girls if a defective vascular system keeps him in a wheel chair. But we didn't love the *Triton* less. We just felt terribly sorry for her.

On our way north we stopped to pick up the fourth member of our crew, an Irish terrier who had joined the family early in the spring. When Bobs had first asked for a dog the skipper objected. A dog didn't belong in a boat. He would be both unhappy and a nuisance, having to be taken ashore night and morning. Bobs could do that in good weather, but who'd row that dog ashore when it rained? Robert offered a kitten, or even a pair of them, a last despairing gesture, for he knew that a dog and a child belonged together.

During Bobs' spring convalescence we carried our dog problem to a kennel man.

"An Irish terrier would fit anywhere," the breeder said. "He's smart and as intuitive as a woman. After two days aboard you'd think he was born on the water."

We selected an Irish gentleman. One cannot buy a dog any more than one buys a boat. We paid a sum of money and asked Lua to try us as a family. He was registered as Luagh, Gaelic for swift, but answered to the kennel name of Lua. His ancestry was impressive. Eleven champions, English, Canadian and American, appeared in the last three generations. He was a grandson of the famous "Turf Commander."

Lua made Bobs' convalescence happy. He was already a part of our family when we sent him to board at his puppyhood home while we went south to get the *Triton*.

But I alone believed the breeder's claims for Lua's adaptability. While the skipper jeered, I ordered a large flat galvanized receptacle fitted into a varnished wood shell and the whole contrivance set in a rack on the foredeck. This expensive canine comfort station brought forth many humorous comments from the skipper and boat visitors. One suggested a papier-mâché hydrant for the center. Everyone viewed the pan with skepticism and when the skipper filled it with sand as a pre-departure task he did it merely to indulge me. He knew who'd row that dog ashore.

He rowed Lua ashore the first evening. On their return aboard we three went to the foredeck and extolled the virtues of Lua's plumbing. Lua listened attentively. Bobs, recognizing a crisis, lifted him inside and explained the proper procedure in great detail.

"A lot of good that will do," the skipper jeered. "We might as well throw that outfit overside."

He apologized profusely the next morning when Lua marched up to the foredeck as though he'd never heard of a tree or lamppost. No act of Lua's had ever won so much applause. Bobs spent the morning with an arm around his neck, assuring him that he'd done something quite spectacular. And Lua basked in her approval.

From then on the *Triton's* decks were sacred. So were the decks of the *Dawn* when the Whites joined us. But Lua, most ceremoniously, expressed disdain for all other craft immediately upon boarding. That, too, was his right as a good sailorman.

He worked out other adaptations as a sea-going dog. He buried biscuit under a coil of rope on the foredeck. Occasionally he retrieved a piece for a between-meal snack but ordinarily he only verified its presence, as a dog will sometimes dig up a bone to reassure himself about his stores.

When the skipper, in an excess of ship-cleaning zeal, shook bits of biscuit from the rope, Lua went forward and reproachfully nosed them back in place. That rebuke rendered his ship's cache as sacred as our decks.

Immediately he became a constant passenger in the *Crab*. Bobs called the hours of rowing "taking Lua for his exercise." We feared he might upset the boat, but if Lua had known of our misgivings he couldn't have conducted himself more circumspectly. He never entered the *Crab* until Bobs was seated and gave the command. Then with all the dignity of an Admiral he took his place at the stern and sat gravely while he was rowed about. Disembarking was as orderly. He left the *Crab* first, and scrambled up the accommodation ladder while Bobs steadied the craft. He never seemed to tire of his daily rides. One by one, Lua disproved all predictions. Bobs was ecstatic and I felt a bit smirky. A dog in a boat was working out well.

But the skipper clung to his suspicions concerning Lua's shore conduct. A lively year-old Irish terrier must inevitably get into trouble. He'd be sure to chase game. Bobs would search for him and both would be lost. Or he'd disappear and we would be held in harbor while we carried on an agonized search.

"And you know what chance we'd have of getting Bobs to leave without him," Robert added.

Bobs insisted that Lua never left her while ashore but her reliability as a witness had been weakened. She had also reported that he slept quietly at the foot of her berth, although in the morning we were apt to find Lua's head on Bobs' pillow and Bobs' on Lua's blanket. They had established that equality which can exist between dog and child. Bobs regarded Lua as another person and he undoubtedly thought of her as a dog.

The skipper was always restless during the pair's shore expeditions. The afternoon we rowed in to investigate we found them carrying on a mutual project of digging out a chipmunk. The *Crab*, on a long painter, was swinging in the tide and its movement carried the boat against a rock. At the first sound of grating Lua stopped digging, rushed to the shore and with his nose traced the painter to the boulder to which it was made fast. Reassured, he went back to the chipmunk.

I looked at the skipper.

"Well, I'll be damned!" was all he said.

By some canine mental process, Lua had recognized the importance of a dinghy in his life afloat, but we had not expected him to know he would be marooned without it. He demonstrated his funny doggy thinking a few days later.

The *Dawn*, with Betty and Stewart aboard, arrived in the harbor where we eagerly awaited their coming. Excited over the reunion, we three jumped into the dinghy. At the time we didn't know that the *Dawn's* decks would be held as sacred as our own and the skipper did not want our greetings to be spoiled by a contretemps. He told Bobs she could not bring her dog.

Lua sat forlornly on the afterdeck and watched us board the *Dawn*. As the two boats lay only a hundred yards apart and Lua could swim the distance easily, we expected he might jump overside and join us. Instead Lua walked to the foredeck where the *Crab* was held in chocks, climbed into the craft, seated himself in the stern, and waited. There was no telling if he thought the *Crab* would waft itself over like a magic carpet or was calling for service.

The Whites knew dogs and loved them as we did. Stewart got into his dinghy.

"That deserves a water taxi," he said. "Come along, Bobs, and introduce your dog."

From then on, Lua, like Bobs, had two homes afloat.

We couldn't go to Alaska, but there were compensations. The Whites had warned us this might be their last year of cruising and we could be together the whole summer. As both skippers were planning to work every day, they agreed on a comparatively leisurely season with mornings of writing, afternoon runs, water golf, swimming and playing about in the warm harbors of lower British Columbia, which we called the banana belt. While the skippers studied charts, Betty, Bobs and I caught up on twelve months' news.

For a year I had been aware of missing Betty White, but I had not known how great a hole her absence made until her coming filled it. She had a gift for two-dimensional friendship. Her friend-making roots spread both wide and deep. She held up the world for many people, but an instinctive valuation of things which really matter never lessened her capacity for laughter or dimmed the rarest whimsy I have ever known. Integrity and gaiety hand in hand—such a little person had no right to scale so high in human-being count.

"How come a mere five-footer can make such a difference in my summer?" I demanded.

And then we did a sailor's hornpipe on the deck and made magnificent plans.

In convoy or temporarily separated for family jaunts, the *Dawn* and the *Triton* pursued a summer home existence. It was not adventure, unless contentment and halcyon days give adventure. They did so for us. A ship so new that we still admired it openly, a gorgeous playground, and dear and close friends to share it—these came close to perfection.

Convoy cruising takes all responsibilities of "guesting" or "hosting" from the companionship of fellow sailormen. Each family has its own home, yet the other is within megaphone call. The arrangement permits both independence and the joy of doing things with people who like to do the same things.

We converted dozens of bays into golf courses by the simple process of determining the limits of the fairway with trees or rocks on the opposite shore. We drove from a cocoa doormat on the beach, using for a tee an inch of rubber hose anchored by a string. Accuracy and distance determined scores. The balls were floaters and were gathered up with a dip net. Collecting three dozen white bobbing golf balls, which resemble gull's feathers, bits of foam and flotsam, was as fascinating a game as the driving. The fellow wielding a dip net from the bow of a dinghy powered by an outboard motor had all the excitement of riding a bucking horse as the boat spun, circled and swerved swiftly from one ball to another.

Gulls took a hand in the game and added suspense, for balls had to be retrieved before a bird absconded with one. One gull mistook a ball for a clam and tried to open it by dropping it on a rock. He refused to be shaken in his conviction that he had gathered food. Never before had he coped with a bouncing clam, but he kept trying again and again, each time from a greater height.

Probably he was no more baffled than fishermen who encountered our lost balls floating in the Pacific Ocean hundreds of miles from any golf course. Such a discovery had all the makings of a mystery yarn. And whoever came upon our elaborate golf club must have been considerably puzzled.

The crew of the *Triton* built it as a surprise for the *Dawn* when we arrived at a designated meeting place a day ahead of schedule. A large painted sign announced it to be the "El Loco Chuck Golf Club," and the green conformed to appointments in the best clubs. We built a bench for players and wrote membership rules in a booklet. Beside the cocoa mat was a box with sand, water and a dangling towel. A sign asked members to please replace splashes. The fairway was even more ambitious. Anchored buoys marked the limits and stated yardage, and their colored pennants gave the bay a festive air.

When the *Dawn* arrived, Stewart used binoculars and then a megaphone.

"For Pete's sake, what's going on?" he called.

We appeared on deck in sports clothes. Even Bobs was out of overalls and in a dress for the first time that summer.

We heard Betty laugh. She took the megaphone.

"We'll meet you at the Country Club," she said. "And no one but the Pinks would go to so much trouble for a laugh."

August's date lines in the log startled me. The summer was slipping by so fast with mornings of work, voyages in convoy, temporary partings when either the *Dawn* or *Triton* departed for a one-boat cruise, reunions, golf, fishing, shore expeditions, guests aboard, clam bakes ashore and swimming.

Lua took part in all our activities. He didn't understand some but he joined us nevertheless. He watched in amazement the first time Stewart and Robert dug for clams.

Chipmunks, the only game he knew which required digging, did not live below tide mark. Finally as though
saying, "The Lord knows this looks foolish, but I'll play
along," he began to dig.

When we shouted with laughter, he looked up with
gleaming eyes. "It's funny, is it?" he seemed to ask. "I'll
show you fellows how to dig," and sand flew as he dug
himself out of sight.

Bobs vainly searched her sea books for a title for Lua.
He was a member of the crew, but no one knew his rating.
He took on several duties. If the motor faltered he was as
instantly alert as was the skipper. He knew that a kelp-
and rock-strewn passage called for slow speed and caution and he would stand on the forepeak, look anxiously
overside and then back at the wheelsman as much as to
say, "Don't you see this kelp? What kind of a sailor are
you?"

Dolphin baiting was his favorite sport. At the sound of
the first spatter as they leaped about our bow, he would
dash to the foredeck. With frenzied barking he threatened
to jump into the sea and annihilate them, all the while taking excellent care not to go too near the rail. But the gesture permitted him to swagger off, once the dolphins had
departed. Like his ancestors, he had dared the other fellow
to step on the tail of his coat.

Dogs are proverbially bad sailors, but Lua modeled his
conduct on that of the Admiral in "Pinafore." When the
winds did blow, he not *generally* but *always* went below.
He took no chances of becoming really seasick. One or
two uneasy gulps were the signal for a retreat to the floor
of the main cabin, lowest and least active place in the
boat. On the companionway he always halted for one re-

proachful glance at the skipper for not making the boat behave.

But even the floor of the cabin failed him the night we were caught by a qualicum in the Gulf of Georgia. It had been my idea to make a moonlight run and like most of my brilliant suggestions, it went terribly wrong.

We were snugged down in a quiet harbor. At dinner Robert and I reminisced for Bobs on how we had often paddled through the night on big northern lakes to avoid wind by day. It might have been her admiration which led me suddenly to propose that we make the Gulf of Georgia run that night.

"We've been sissies, always snugging down by dark," I said.

We were off by nine o'clock. As we watched the sea turn from opalescence to shimmering gray and then to quicksilver, I gave myself a lot of credit. Bobs and Lua and I sat on the long seat in the deckhouse, the skipper stood at the wheel, and all were filled with a sense of adventure.

"What do we have running lights for?" I demanded. "We ought to do this often."

The skipper agreed even when small cat's-paws moved the water, but later when Bobs started off to bed the halyards played a rat-a-tat against the mast and the skipper suggested it would be a good idea to have the whole crew forward.

That was sound. Ten minutes later I couldn't have gone aft to Bobs' stateroom. The qualicum hit just after I had berthed her and Lua in the main cabin.

We had heard about this strong local night wind which came up with little or no warning. Soon we were rolling our bilge keels out and the smack as they struck the water added to the confusion of the night.

I heard the crash of falling objects below and as I dashed down for emergency stowing the skipper called a warning not to stay too long. In the cabin books were popping out of racks like projectiles whenever a big wave hit the hull. Bobs was fast asleep, but Lua at the foot of her berth looked most unhappy. I put books and trays and all loose gear on the floor before they could be thrown there.

Back in the deckhouse I clung to a handhold and asked the skipper what we could do about it.

"Marble Bay is the only harbor," he said. "And we can't find it in the dark."

We were off an island which had only one haven in twenty-seven miles of precipitous shoreline. And that haven was only a black notch under a mountain. The moon had set. The scudding clouds, the heavy beam sea, the noise and confusion of wind in the darkness had quite cured me of any desire for night cruising.

The skipper said the *Triton* was taking the sea all right. But like a good ship she recovered slowly and in those moments when she lay far over with the deck trying to be a side of the house, and water hissed along her rails, I wondered if she always did come back as her former owner had assured us. And while she was making up her mind, my stomach slipped its moorings and got mixed up with my throat.

"Nothing to be scared about," the skipper said. "If it doesn't get any worse."

Just then a big boy hit us. Everything in the ship went to port, including a girl and a dog. I clawed my way to the main cabin. Bobs, Lua, blankets and pillows were all on the floor. Bobs went right on sleeping, but Lua extricated himself and gave me an accusing look. He seemed to think I was in some way responsible. And maybe I was.

I made the floor as safe as possible by throwing blankets down for padding and left them to wash back and forth. Bobs was better there than awake and frightened.

Folly and adventure are close partners. On occasions like these I knew it was folly for a man and a woman to crew a boat, for lives to be dependent on mechanism, and for a woman to face the possibility of having to take the wheel in that welter in case of motor trouble. Always in those moments I determined to have a second man aboard. But always afterwards, safe in harbor, folly again became adventure and I would forget my resolve to have a two-man crew.

When the sea was at its worst and we had no hope of finding Marble Bay, we opened a light on the island. Its bearing and appearance told us it was within the entrance to the bay, but we knew at once we couldn't count on it for it was only a lamp in a dwelling house.

To me that lighted shore home only made our plight seem worse. I didn't murmur, like a good sailor, "God help all landsmen on a night like this." It was the other way around.

"Do you suppose that fellow will stay up long enough for us to crawl into Marble Bay?" the skipper asked.

I had no hope, but I began to implore the man to stay awake. The suspense increased as we wallowed on. When eight bells struck we were sure the light would disappear. I could imagine our unconscious benefactor as he looked at the clock, yawned, closed his book and remarked that midnight was too late for reading. But he didn't, and twelve-thirty was another zero hour.

The shore was now a huge black shadow under a mountain. That light was our only chance to make the harbor and we couldn't take a bearing on it from the careening ship. That fellow just had to go on reading. We were fairly begging him to begin only one more page when we slid into the narrow entrance and past the lighted window.

But we were only half rescued. Reefs from both shores interlocked in the channel. With the skipper at the bow and the mate at the wheel we skirted one long reef under a slow bell, turned abruptly, executed a perfect "S," and were inside. Never an anchor made a more joyous splash.

I led a sleepy bo'sun and a reproachful dog aft to their quarters, and went to bed without mentioning the delights of moonlight cruising or the advisability of making long runs in large waterways on windless nights.

But I did make a call ashore in the morning. I was so sure I'd find an avid reader that I carried books and magazines as a thank offering, only to discover that a lamp in the window burned all night, every night. It was tended by the widow of a missionary who had made his circuit in a boat. She had first lighted it for her husband and now, knowing that others had come to depend on her beacon, she never failed to keep it burning.

XX

THE VELVET GLOVE

EVENTS MOVED SWIFTLY WHEN the *Triton* and the *Dawn* reached Seattle at the end of summer. Stewart and Betty had decided to build a new boat and cruise Alaska with us the next season. Friends' boat plans are almost as exciting as one's own. The *Simba* was ordered, named and on paper before the Whites left for their winter home in California.

The *Triton* moored at the yacht club, although our trio did not feel that we were yachtsmen. We had played the game as cruisers, and as cruisers we remained. A yachtsman's cap in the skipper's locker, the club burgee aloft, a convenient and pleasant mooring and occasional dinners at the club were our only concessions.

The *Triton* lay in a club slip while Bobs and I spent hours shopping for a school outfit. She was entered in an English school a few miles outside Victoria. When Bobs and I had visited the school I had thought it looked a bit severe. I glanced around the huge living room with a scanty assortment of upholstered chairs and asked Bobs how she imagined a girl ever got to them first.

Bobs wasn't interested in the easy chairs. She was delighted with the low work tables.

"Who wants to swing her legs from overstuffed furniture?" she said. "I'd a lot rather paint at a table."

So her name was entered and long black woolen stock-

ings, tailored shirts, school ties, school blazers and an odd
appearing blue pleated garment called a tunic, were purchased. We were warned by the school matron to buy
the tailored suit for church attendance "large enough to
grow in."

In Seattle the sewing machine was set up in the main
cabin and worked overtime attaching name tapes to garments. We labeled everything but the girl herself. Fortunately we had eaten up ship's stores and had locker space
for the dozens and half dozens of stockings, shirts, bloom-
ers, handkerchiefs, linen and uniforms.

Several times a day Bobs went into our forward stateroom for an ecstatic inspection of her school trousseau.

I looked at that growing pile of garments, too. And
when no one was about I grew a bit tearful. For two summers and a winter Bobs and I had scarcely been apart. We
three had shared life very completely, and now that close
companionship was to be ended. One phase of parenthood
was gone forever. Even had I been able to, I would not
have held back time, but I mourned the passing.

The skipper mourned it too, but man-like, he devised a
camouflage. He called her more frequently by her pet
name, "Old Sox," which had clung since babyhood. But
he said it with more than usual heartiness of tone and
grumbled about the imminence of the Thanksgiving holidays when she'd be back to be a nuisance.

Leaving Bobs at school, duly enrolled as a third former,
gave me a strange feeling. The English system of abrupt
dismissal of parental anxieties is kind but disturbing. The
manner of the mistresses implied that for generations English schools had been taking charge of the very young
and making a successful affair of their upbringing. But as
I said good-by to an unfamiliar child, proudly wearing an

odd blue tunic and school tie, whose main interest was
that I carry on as calmly as the other well-trained parents,
I felt as though I had casually handed in a package at the
proper wicket.

It was a relief to reach the *Triton* again and find Lua as
disconsolate as myself. His world had crashed. He missed
his comrade. He missed airings in the *Crab* and runs on
shore. Sedate walks across the club lawn on a leash bored
him as much as they did Robert.

We departed at once for our season of real fall cruising.
As we dropped anchor in our first small harbor in Puget
Sound, I had an odd dislocated feeling. Perhaps it was a
fall nostalgia for the land, or the human instinct to conform to the behavior pattern of others.

Betty had gone south to her home and garden. Bobs
had gone to school. At the club, boats were being berthed
for winter. I was ridiculously delighted to discover that a
neighboring fishing craft was going to be the home of its
owner through the winter.

"I'm a lot more comfortable afloat," the fisherman said.

"Sure," the skipper agreed. "That's the way we figure."

We did. I was at home in what was practically an apartment. I was surrounded by my own things. I was fully
occupied and very comfortable. And we had not swung
at anchor more than a day before the strangeness of a fall
home at sea left me completely.

"It must have been an atavistic female instinct," I said.
"That first autumn chill makes a woman think of leaving
water for the land, even when there's no rhyme nor reason
to it."

There was less rhyme or reason for retreat to land every
day that passed. We liked the sharpness of the early morn-

ings, the vivid coloring of fall foliage on the hills, the warm October sun at noon when we lounged on the fore-deck, the afternoon walks ashore with Lua and, most of all, the evenings aboard the *Triton*. Then we were indeed a home afloat, tight, snug, warm and comfortable. The blackness of cold fall nights only added to our sense of well-being.

It was the challenge of the world outside that made me insist on lighting the deckhouse every evening although the skipper protested. The extra illumination used up juice and made the *Triton* look gaudy. A well behaved boat should show only porthole gleams. But one of our fisher-men neighbors settled the argument about my porch lights.

"I like to lie alongside the *Triton*," he said. "You folks always look so cheerful. Makes a fellow feel he'd be wel-come."

Neighborliness was a part of fall cruising. Salmon trol-lers were home from Cape Flattery and beginning their winter rest. They gathered in their houses ashore for after-noons of beer, smoked fish and yarns. We gathered with them.

Those big slow-spoken men talked casually of a hazard-ous calling. As in all outdoor trades, shop talk was pregnant with surprises. We might think we were beginning to hear why a man wasn't high boat that season and find that we had been carried into a tale of a sou'easter, a boat swept clean of gear and days and nights of mountainous seas. Just when I'd given up the men and boats as lost and was wondering stupidly how the narrator happened to be there, some incredibly ingenious feat of seamanship would bring everyone safely home.

The stories were told without emphasis, as something in

the day's work. They set a mark to shoot at and have made me a bit choosey in sea tales ever since.

We had long afternoon fishing sessions, and a longer one the day I thought to return hospitality. I invited a pair of good fishermen friends aboard for afternoon refreshment. I'd made a batch of doughnuts and had a pot of coffee ready when they arrived promptly on the hour, dressed in city suits and gleaming celluloid collars. We chatted from four until dark. Suppertime was in the offing. I opened cans and fried a half gallon of smelts which a purse seiner had given us that day. Talk went on. After midnight I realized that our guests were hungry. The other half gallon of smelts was fried, more cans opened and I cut a cake.

Fueled, we began to fish again. We fished the entire north Pacific Ocean and went through every famous blow which has harried a fishing craft. It was four in the morning, just twelve hours since they'd come aboard, when they rose to go.

"Missus, we've had the best time we've had for years," one said. "There's nothing better than a good talk."

And Robert and I had had a good time, too. Fall is the proper season for storytelling.

"Bring your storytellers home," became my motto as a wife.

A former sealing captain came aboard one morning at ten. He was old and not well and he lay on the couch. He lay there until six at night and did not rise. Nor did he stop talking.

Never have I known such prolonged tension and excitement. He crowded a dozen "Sea Wolfs" into that day, and then another dozen volumes of material of which Jack London had no inkling. Captain Jacobson was one of the first pelagic sealers in the eighties, one of the last to quit when three governments ended the slaughter, and there was nothing connected with the deaths of those millions of animals, or the men who killed them, that he did not know.

He was a giant of a man with bigger hands than I'd ever seen. His fingers were broken and bent and each was twice the size of Robert's. He thrust those great hooks into my face when telling how he'd grasped a man by the throat, and I imagined the vertebrae in my neck snapping like peanut shells.

We moved from one snug anchorage to another in a succession of tight little harbors. We stayed a week and often longer at each anchorage and grew very well acquainted with our fall neighbors. Some lived in boats, and some ashore. We had time to know them, for when summer cruising is over there is a sense of leisure. We ourselves became old settlers and established friendships with an amazing variety of people, fishermen, ranchers, loggers, retired seamen and all sorts of world wanderers who had tucked themselves off in odd holes along the coast, because a man who has once known the sea is never again quite happy unless there is a tide mark at his front door.

Until we had rebuilt the *Triton* for fall and winter life I had not known that each season of the year afloat had its distinctive charms. Even more than a house on land, a boat reflects and brings an awareness of seasonal change. Instead of monotony our days slipped by too quickly.

We were working very hard to finish a novel which was to be a major effort to take ourselves out of the paying-for-our-home ranks. Robert wrote every day until midafternoon. Sometimes I wrote and usually we talked the story over in the evening. Nothing broke in on our jobs—no telephones, no interruptions, no unexpected guests, no contacts except those we chose to make. In that respect there is an odd difference between a boat and a house. A boat swinging at anchor has detachment which repels invasions. "Won't you come aboard?" means more, is not given so lightly, nor is it expected so readily as a hospitable gesture at the front door of a land home.

One afternoon Robert came up from work and handed me two chapters of the novel as I sat on the afterdeck. He departed to take Lua for a run on shore.

"Best job I've done so far," he called back from the dinghy. "When you've read them, row in with the *Crab* and tell me how swell they are."

I grew so fired with admiration that when I'd finished I departed immediately to pay my tribute as his "best friend and severest critic." He beamed his pleasure while I raved. We decided the occasion rated an extra special drink, a hot rum concoction of honey, butter and lemon which sounded dreadful but was amazing in smoothness and authority. Although it had a name, I'd christened it "the iron hand in the velvet glove."

Robert had set the ingredients on the galley table and was measuring out the makings when he asked where I'd put the manuscript. My look of horror and quick dash aft broke the news. He abandoned bar tendering and reached the afterdeck as soon as I. Not a page of manuscript was in the deck chair where I distinctly remembered having laid it.

Neither spoke as we climbed into the dinghies. A breeze, ruffling the water, stirred silvery gleams which we hoped might be sheets of paper. Because the tide was setting in, we made a circuit of the harbor. I found nothing. He returned with one dripping sheet.

He laid it on the chart table. Nothing short of a magnificent gesture of self-destruction could make amends so I asked instead if he were going to have a drink.

"Two," he said. "Maybe three."

XXI

UPHOLSTERERS ARE CHEATED

The "Simba," Betty and Stewart's new boat, made an impressive entrance in our rendezvous harbor late in May. Stewart struck a pose on the forepeak, ostentatiously moved a lever and an electric winch released the anchor. Then he sauntered aft. Man-powered ground tackle was a closed chapter in his life. We applauded from the *Triton*. At least one skipper in our crowd wasn't going to pull his heart out in the deep anchorages of Alaska.

Furnished and peopled, the sturdy fifty-eight foot Diesel-powered boat looked even grander than when we had last seen it under construction. Betty and I considered its most desirable feature to be a foc's'le which housed a cook, and she made an immediate declaration of the *Triton's* vested interest in this luxury.

Robert considered an engineer for a week far more important than a cook for all summer. Charlie Drumm had been sent by the engine factory for a week of final adjustments, and after a few hours in the *Simba's* engine room, Robert became Charlie's confirmed admirer.

Not only was he an exceptional mechanic but he knew boats and the North Pacific. He had been engineer in "halibuters" on trips to the westward, worked in steam vessels, taken a yacht from New York to Seattle, and had engaged in various, and diverse, sea adventures up and down the coast.

"Besides all which, he's a swell fellow," Robert said.

I was prepared for some sort of Paul Bunyan of the motor world when Charlie pulled over to us against a stiff northwest wind.

"Hey, Pink!" he shouted from a dinghy. "Can you get your motor going before this crate of ours climbs a pile of bricks? I've just pulled a piston and that patent hook don't like B. C. mud."

The *Simba* had added her bit to Stewart's little by-play with the electric winch by picking up her anchor and starting for the beach. The *Triton* went in pursuit, but our towing was like lending a capitalist a nickel for his carfare home. This time we all jeered when Stewart called upon his electric servant and Stewart laughed as hard as we. Charlie's big shoulders shook at the unskipperly exchange of advice and comment. He turned to me.

"I sure like the way those fellows kid each other," he said.

During the two days the *Simba* remained in harbor our vocabularies were freshened by many more terms than "bricks" and "crates," but Charlie's greatest contribution was a robust zest for life and a gift for narrative. We were sorry he wasn't to spend his whole week near us, but the *Simba* planned to cruise while we waited for our bo'sun. School authorities had agreed that Bobs might waive examinations for the advantages of travel, and as soon as she had joined us the two boats would meet in Queen Charlotte Sound for the run to Alaska.

The *Triton* was ready except for a complete crew. And this year we felt certain of our motor. In late winter Robert, who had been working very hard, decided that he needed a vacation. This took the strange form of fourteen hours a day in the engine room where he began a complete overhaul before the installation of the new cylinder blocks. "There won't be two pieces of that engine attached to each other," he said, and there weren't a few days later. When the motor was completely dismantled Robert searched for a mechanic. Vic Thurlow had the reputation of being one of the finest gas engine men in the city, and he lived up to his reputation. A passion for infinitesimal adjustment, for that remorseless care which insures performance, burned to white heat in him. So Vic came to share six weeks of what I believe were the happiest moments of Robert's life. They sat in grease, washed their hands in gasoline when I called them to meals, and chattered and debated and cursed joyously.

They gave the *Triton* a dry exhaust and a stack. They installed a second Bosch magneto and a third set of plugs so we'd have three sparks in each cylinder. They attached a lubricating oil cooler. Each bearing was made perfect. They did a lot of things that I couldn't understand, and never will understand, but which were vastly important to them. I only knew that a wet exhaust which had caused back pressure and sticking valves, and fouled plugs and all other ills of motors were a past chapter in our lives. Never again came that old familiar stutter or hesitancy which had aroused Lua and me. So long as we owned the *Triton*, the motor never again failed us in any way.

The two men ranged over the foredeck and installed davits for the small boats so that even Bobs and I could lower them. And now that there was no longer need of the mast, we had it cut away.

When Robert's motor job began to stretch indefinitely, I too plunged into boat work. If a skipper immersed himself in carbon, oil and engine grease, and talked combustion, explosion and timing even in his sleep, a mate was justified in becoming absorbed with turpentine, pigments and paint brushes. I donned a suit of painter's overalls, but they didn't help much. Before I had finished a complete repainting of the *Triton* my skin and hair rivaled Joseph's coat. Paint, turpentine and paint remover became my cosmetics.

My painting orgy, like the skipper's overhaul of the motor, grew up on me. I intended only to surprise Bobs with a stateroom in warm tints which would glow in sunlight with the sheen of an opalescent sea. Her quarters needed redoing because a lazy painter had added flat white to enamel. The man had cost ten dollars a day plus twenty percent to the shop and when I protested that he was no painter the union answered that he had a card. I didn't have one, but I thought I couldn't be any more disastrous than he.

"Go to it," Robert urged.

I explained my color scheme in various paint shops, but clerks shook their heads and suggested that I bring in a sample. Since I'd never seen the shade I wanted, that was impossible. So I started at scratch with white lead and an array of tubes of color. The elusive shade I sought, neither gray nor lavender nor pink, was finally achieved in one of those high moments of creative effort.

"I've got it!" I shouted to Robert in the engine room.

He looked up from an assortment of engine parts and asked what I'd got.

"What I've been trying to get for days. Come see how it glows in sunlight."

He didn't come, but he admired the completed job, walls of a soft shade accentuated by a rosy red trim inside the lockers. Everyone who came aboard admired it. I was asked for painting formulas and thought I'd given the precise ingredients until other amateur painters began complaining that they'd only spoiled paint.

"The mate paints, as she cooks, by ear," the skipper said. "Even she can't reproduce that shade."

He was right, as I discovered by secret experimentation. But I had learned how to lay on enamel. When I had gotten its tendency to curtain under control, my painting fervor was aroused. I attacked the forward quarters. Wet paint became a menace in galley, companionways and bathrooms. The skipper developed a habit of sidling like a crab.

When I had achieved a professional swing with a brush I dared work in public, on the outside of the *Triton*. Hull, decks, bright work and deck gear fell under my onslaught. My painting hours broke every union rule, and my behavior didn't conform to good yacht manners. I learned this from a comment which floated back to me from a pier visitor. I was chipping iron on the foredeck when a woman walked past the *Triton*.

"Isn't that terrible?" she said to a companion. "If I had money enough to own a boat like that, you wouldn't catch me making such a sight of myself."

She didn't know that half the joy of boat ownership lies in the grooming and the care. I was having quite as much fun as was the skipper in the engine room. I told him about it when we ate our sandwiches that noon. We didn't look much like yachtsmen. He was smeared with grease, I with paint.

"And neither of us has ever had a better time aboard this boat," I added.

"The kick you got out of it is worth the mess I figured

you'd make," he said. After he looked around he added, "And we didn't get the mess."

Coverage of wood and metal on a boat is far more than decoration. It means protection against weather and must be thorough. Nowhere else does messy paint or varnish show up more badly. I had made a professional job of the *Triton*. When the skipper added that not only had I done several hundred dollars' worth of work that spring but had proved that we could do our own spring and fall painting, I'm sure I purred.

I should have been content, but I ruined my standing as a marine decorator while we waited for Bobs. One evening at dinner the skipper said he was sorry we had not had the transom berth re-upholstered before we left Seattle.

"We can do it ourselves," I said. "I watched the upholstery man work in the *Simba*. Seventeen dollars a day! And anyone could do it."

Robert was skeptical. Seventeen dollars a day meant special skill. I was insistent. He need only take off the cover. I would fluff up the hair stuffing as I'd seen the upholsterer do. He could tie the sagging springs in place.

"Sure you know how this job's done?" Robert asked when he had taken out the berth and laid it athwartship in the cabin.

"We'll have the whole thing finished in two hours," I said.

As the cover came off I began to extract hair and fluff it. Robert started on a round of tacks and nails and tape and reinforcements. He found seven more rounds, all imbedded in hard wood, and it was past midnight before he'd even reached the springs.

And all that time I'd fluffed hair. What had started as a small pile of innocent-looking stuff now filled the cabin. It piled high in the corners, overflowed into the stateroom and invaded the galley. It was everywhere. No one could walk or sit or move below decks until that mass of hair was under control.

Robert, looking up from his job to suggest that we finish upholstering in the morning, saw what I had accomplished.

"For Pete's sake!" he yelled. "Now we've got to get this stuff back where it belongs before we can go to bed."

We began to work in earnest. It was two o'clock before we reached the springs and tied them into place. Robert's humor grew more caustic as the night wore on. Between laughter and sheer weariness I grew hysterical as I stuffed armsful of fluffed hair.

It was four-thirty in the morning when Robert tacked down the last corner of the cover. I brought a tray of food as a peace offering and for a minute I thought he was going to refuse it just to show he was through with me forever. Then we began to laugh. It was daylight. We'd been working on that berth for ten hours.

"And now I'll tell you something about upholsterers," he said. "If those fellows get only seventeen dollars, they're cheated."

We rechristened Bobs on our way north. Bo'sun didn't fit the self-reliant young person we met at the railroad station in Nanaimo. We had observed the beginning of the change during the Christmas and Easter holidays. But the change had set now. She still committed the depredations of a twelve-year-old. She borrowed our books, and lost our places, and left the volumes in the sun or rain. But now she murmured "Sorry" like a grown-up. I found myself less a mother than a hostess.

"We've got a young woman with us this summer," Robert confided to me that evening.

He liked the new companionship. So did I, but I missed the child.

When she took the wheel of the *Triton* through the Yucluetaws and Whirlpool Rapids, the skipper ceremoniously declared her to be quartermaster. Her stateroom too was different. The old collections of odd objects disappeared and a microscope and slides and notebooks took their places. The microscope was brought out in the evening and specimens of hair and skin and sea water and diatoms were examined, while Lua sat beside her and jealously tried to see what absorbed her. He resented excitement which he could not share. The evening she watched an amoeba dividing brought triumph to her and agony to poor Lua.

That fast run north to join the *Simba* in Alert Bay bewildered Lua. Neither dinghy was off the foredeck. The reunion was to be a double celebration, my birthday and the beginning of the cruise to Alaska. Standing on the deck and waving as wildly as Stewart and Betty was Charlie Drumm.

"My week stretched," he said as we went aboard.

Charlie was now engineer in the *Simba* and that was the first of many times we were glad to see Charlie Drumm. The celebration began at once. We caught up on three weeks' news. Stewart and Betty marveled at Bobs' new stature and grown-up air. We drank birthday cocktails. Stewart read a poem he had written in my honor. Betty showed me my cake which I cut later at the birthday dinner.

Bobs was led through the *Simba* and admired it profusely, but confided to us later that she was still loyal to

Lua Always Waited for Orders

Early Morning Mist

The Second Year We Removed the Mast

the *Triton*. We had expected that. The previous winter we had been much disturbed because a friend had arranged to take Bobs to tea on the Bordens' big schooner, *The Northern Light,* which was on its maiden voyage to the Arctic. We thought the *Triton* would be spoiled for her and we awaited the weekly school letter with some dread. Her comment was that the bathrooms of the schooner were not as nice as were the *Triton's.*

When the news, the returned daughter and the new boat had all been discussed, the skippers got out the charts.

Charlie regarded the *Triton's* one-man crew with considerable misgiving. He had run north winter and summer in halibut schooners with a big tough crew which stopped at nothing, and a man, woman and child didn't strike him as enough crew for the Alaska run.

"I hope you folks know it can get awful tough crossing Dixon Entrance," he said. "Twelve hours is some trick for Pink to take."

XXII

ALASKA

Everyone had told us Alaska was different. We had known we would find higher mountains, larger waterways, a more intricate maze of islands, arms and straits, and a greater number of uncharted reefs and rocks. The coast of Southeastern Alaska is regarded as one of the world's worst steamship routes.

Nothing had led us to expect an international boundary to change the flavor of a country, yet we sensed this soon after crossing the line. In Ketchikan we found an instant sense of fellowship. Even physical features of the town were significant of the spirit of its people. A narrow strip of land between mountain and sea had been made a townsite by putting the town on stilts. Dwelling houses clung to a steep hillside and the main street was of planks supported by piling. Over these planks rattled a continuous stream of traffic.

As Ketchikan was mostly one street wide, it had to stretch out lengthwise and the town was several miles long. Everyone used taxis and nearly everyone riding in them waved to us. Before a day was over half the population called us by name.

The warmth of this friendliness was the more pleasant since we came into it from a twelve-hour slog across Dixon Entrance, last of the open waterways. As with the others, we'd had good weather-luck. Only once, as we ducked behind Watch Island to cut off Milbank Sound, had I understood Charlie's misgiving about our slender crew. The great ocean swell had followed us up a narrow rock-cluttered passage and I knew what Charlie meant when he had said that the Pacific could throw a boat around. Had that swell slapped us down on one of those rocks, we'd have quit cruising right there. The *Triton* was ahead, and stepped carefully indeed.

After the three crossings were behind us, I found my dread of them was gone. A healthy respect remained, and we never lost that. We always chose our weather for jumping off. But the *Triton* and its crew of three made them afterwards, both alone and in convoy. They became merely a job, long hard days of cruising, which we accepted as part of summers in Alaska.

On our first voyage to the north we had stopped to explore many harbors, but I never again saw the country between Queen Charlotte Sound and Alaska except from the deck of the *Triton*. Only when rough weather compelled a halt did we make more than a brief overnight anchorage. We were a non-stop boat, with Ketchikan as our first port. Usually on the run south I didn't even see the country. I spent that time below with the sewing machine letting down hems and attaching name tapes so that Bobs could leap off the *Triton* for boarding school.

The first cruise in Alaska was exploratory and we covered more waterways than in any other. After that we skimmed the cream. But Southeastern Alaska cannot be learned in one summer. A season affords only a swift glimpsing of the vastness, the stupendousness and the prodigality of the land.

Robert's first errand in Ketchikan was to ask at the post office for our pet pioneer, C. R. Johnston. We had never seen him, but his trail had run like a thread through our cruising years. We had come across it first in Princess Louise when we'd found the remains of an old cabin and wondered who had lived there. Two years later we found the answer. A chap who knew the family made C. R. Johnston a real person to us.

We were fascinated by the story of the tall eagle-eyed Kentuckian who had ridden into a Colorado town, and four days later had ridden out with the schoolteacher, now his wife, behind the saddle. We knew the names of his sons and daughters and all about the boys' wild-man hunts. They had gone into the mountains behind Princess Louise with rifles but no food, and barefooted they traveled above timber line. The rules provided that a boy could not carry or share his kill. Each killed or went hungry, while his brothers ate.

The country had become too settled for this modern Daniel Boone when a logging camp was built within thirty miles of Princess Louise. He had taken his family and moved to Alaska. Robert's effort to locate his pet pioneer in so large a territory amused me, especially after the postmaster reported that Mr. Johnston called at Ketchikan for mail twice a year. Any man who required only a semi-annual mail service must live far from the beaten track.

As the *Simba* and the *Triton* cruised in Behm Canal, Alaska smiled on our northern venture. We saw the land first in bright sunshine. Glistening snow peaks were cloud patterned. A blue sea sparkled. Forested slopes were in lovely tones of green merging into dull olives at timber line. Masses of naked cliffs glowed in warm shades of rose, violet, deep blues and dusky purples. The coloring was as exciting as the bigness of the land.

Alaska is not always so gracious. We discovered later that its heavens can pour rain with the same intensity as they smile. Through weeks of downpour or drizzle we have worn hip boots and slickers until the squeak of rubber and the rustle of oilskins seemed to be the normal sound of humans.

Our first anchorage brought an exciting day in a new country. The land was hospitable. We could walk. After summers in British Columbia where steep mountainsides offer impenetrable barriers of underbrush, we were as thrilled by a river running through an open valley as are fresh-air children by their first sight of a green field. We splashed up shallow riffles with the current tearing at our legs. We explored a valley and found a new type of muskeg, dry and spongy. We saw signs of beavers, wolves, bears and many deer. We came upon a brood of goslings and it was the first time we had been in a land where the wild goose nested. We visited a lake, a blue jewel encircled by high mountains. We followed game trails through thick forests which opened suddenly into parks where our feet trod on deep beds of spruce needles.

Even the river mouth was different. It was broad and flat. Grass grew almost waist high and the blue of lupin was a wide splash of a painter's brush. When we came out again to the sea the tide was pushing up the river and our dinghies rode far out on long mooring lines. The late sun of the north was still high and burnished the greens and bronzes on timbered slopes behind us.

Betty White announced that it was one of those occasions when the *Triton* should take advantage of vested rights in the *Simba's* cook, an invitation which was the final touch in a perfect day.

Bobs and Robert and I went aboard the *Triton* to freshen up for dinner. Now Bobs wore white slacks each evening and cared about the color of shirts and sweaters. Also she cared what the skipper wore. I thought her return to the family had made him a bit more dressy. He was actually putting on a tie this evening when Bobs appeared in our stateroom on an errand.

"Dad's getting all dolled up," Bobs said.

"Have to with two women aboard," he said. "How about it, Sox? Like the *Triton* better than school?"

"Sure," Bobs said.

But the skipper's elation over the day demanded a real expression of opinion.

"I mean it," he insisted. "Do you really like this sort of thing?"

Bobs stared at him a moment. They were alike in their dread of emotional speeches.

"At school I was never homesick like some of the girls," she said. "But now that I'm back with you people and Lua and Betty and Stewart, and having such a good time, I'm wondering why I wasn't homesick."

It was an unusually long speech for Bobs. When she'd gone aft to her stateroom, Robert turned to me.

"Damn decent to tell us how she feels about coming home," he said.

She hadn't had to tell me. I'd known it from the grin she wore when the skipper asked her to take the wheel and the way she had plunged into boat work. She was as fervent a brass polisher as Robert. I knew she loved cruising in the *Triton*.

Later as we were all sitting on the *Simba's* deck drinking cocktails, someone commented that only a few hours before we had been standing beside a mountain lake which had been visited by very few. We were all excited over our day. Alaska had already paid us dividends.

"Hell, Stewart!" Robert said. "We can't even touch the fringe of this country in one summer."

And then as always when land was even mentioned, the two men got out charts, straddled distances with dividers and made lists of bays with rivers. They spoke of this as their nightly chore, but it was really their vice.

A week later we were still exploring Behm Canal. A country with snowbanks at sea level, mineral springs bubbling out of the sea like broken water mains, scalding springs which contained living plants and steamed beside a snowbank pink with microscopic vegetation, was too fascinating to be hurried past.

As we lay at anchor one morning Betty and Stewart called on their way to investigate a shoreline snowbank. Bobs decided that Lua should have his picture taken standing in a snow cavern and the *Crab* joined the *Simba's* dinghy. A pumpkin pie in the oven kept me at home, and Robert remained to finish his writing stint.

I was in the galley when I heard the sound of oarlocks and then Robert's voice on the afterdeck.

"You're C. R. Johnston."

I tumbled up the companionway in my excitement. A tall, thick-chested, black-haired man was in a rowboat staring at Robert in amazement.

"How'd you know that?" he asked.

Robert insisted he could recognize a Kentuckian on sight, although I suspected that the skipper might have spent the summer accusing people of being C. R. Johnston.

The explanation convinced our guest when we asked

about the children, calling each by name. He laughed and told us that the youngest girl, fourteen years old, had shot her first bear the previous day, and he was much more proud of this than of his oldest boy shooting a mountain lion at the age of eight. He was probably relieved to know that the family wasn't petering out in the softness of modern life.

He invited us to visit his handlogging show in the next arm and, as we dropped anchor off the group of new cedar shake cabins nestling under high spruce trees, I was almost sorry we had come to the end of the Johnston trail. A legend of courage is very precious. If the girl who rode away with the tall Kentuckian had regretted her impulsive sharing of life with a man who had to have a whole inlet to himself, I didn't want to know it.

But with my first glance at the fine strong face of Mrs. Johnston, I knew she had found happiness. The look of pride in her eyes when she introduced her childen was inescapable. Four cabins housed the family. One sheltered grandchildren. In the boys' cabin were guns, traps, snowshoes and outdoor paraphernalia. In the girls' were books, pictures, pretty clothes—and also guns.

That afternoon the two girls led us to their favorite mountain lake. The trail ascended steeply and we came suddenly upon a blue mirror set in crystalled snowbanks and encircled by a phalanx of white spires. I wondered how many people had stood beside that lake.

"Pioneering is still possible," I proclaimed to Robert that night as we were getting ready for bed. "You never met a happier or more competent family in your life."

My favorite theory had been fired to crusading fervor since we'd discovered Alaska. Here the water, the air and the forests were filled with life. It pulsed all about us. Waterfowl flew in clouds from beaches. A shovelful of sand brought up not one clam but a dozen. Eight- and ten-inch crabs were so thick that we rowed over a score with a dip net poised, choosing only perfect specimens. Rivers were filled with trout. Thousands of deer roamed the forests. Berries and flowers grew in tropical abundance. Huckleberries barred passage and the blue, red and yellow of flowers were solid swatches of color on the river flats.

Nature had set so lavish a table that I had mourned the emptiness of the land. Now I had found a family who had partaken of the country's bounty.

And, as I went on to say, they were not imprisoned or toilworn. One boy was an engineer. Two others were handlogging with their father. Ruth, the oldest girl, was as poised and charming as any young woman we knew. The youngest, a beauty, was a thoroughly happy girl. She had come aboard that evening in a vivid red dress which had made her black hair fairly crinkle and her clear skin glow, and she sat for hours talking with Bobs about things all girls discuss—books, movies and clothes.

Every winter the entire family visited Ketchikan where even C. R. Johnston attended movies. He liked especially pictures of foreign lands. His body might have halted, but his spirit still wandered. None of the family felt their lot was hard or even especially romantic.

The mother had summed up the early years when she learned that we too had built our own log cabin.

"Then you know how it is," she said. "Maybe you've had to scrimp or go without. But a bit of contriving for your man and your children never brought any real unhappiness to a woman."

I quoted this to Robert.

"And that pair started," I said, "with only what one horse could carry."

"But the most important thing they had didn't add to the load," Robert said. "You forgot to mention that those two had guts."

Cruising weeks sped by. We voyaged on sunlit straits of glassy calm with a gorgeous stretch of the majestic peaks of high mainland mountains lying off our beam. We made equally exciting runs in stiff southeast winds when the *Triton* rolled her bilge keels out. And we cruised in steady drizzles and marveled that any sky could rain so continuously.

We stopped for days of explorations of bays and rivers, snow fields and hot sulphur springs. We had community hot boiled crab feasts ashore with crabs served native fashion. Betty and Stewart agreed with Mrs. Cadwallader. And we also followed the native custom afterwards, of lying on our backs in the sunshine while the tautness of the skin across our tummies relaxed to a point of comfort.

We spent days up rivers. Each was beautiful and each was different, but all were silver threads leading into the mountains. We made day-long expeditions, setting off early in the dinghies, abandoning them when the river proved unnavigable and splashed on afoot. Hip boots were the regulation equipment. Each wore or carried a nose-bag lunch. The rest of river impedimenta varied with the individual. Stewart always had trout tackle and usually a movie camera. Betty carried a book and tackle. I merely took a book which usually I didn't open. Bobs took Lua for a diversion and Lua took his nose, which worked overtime. Sometimes I suspected that he had a more intimate knowledge of the stream at the end of the day than any of the rest. Robert relied on his legs for entertainment and ranged off on side canters through spruce forests.

Straggling along by twos or threes, by families or by sexes, depending on the character of the river or the inclination of that day, we met on some sandy bar at lunch time. There we munched sandwiches and exchanged gossip of the river.

These river trips were a new complication of our cruising life and so fascinating that I could not bear to miss them. But they kept the crew of the *Triton* hustling. On the *Simba* life went on whether the owner was aboard or not. Boat work was done and dinner was ready. On the *Triton* cabins had to be put in order, berths made, breakfast dishes washed, lunches packed and the evening meal at least planned. Bobs and Robert and I divided jobs and managed to be ready, but there were times when I felt breathless.

Laundry days ashore were out. I was much too busy exploring, and no one wanted to drag a family washing up river. Laundry service of the Alaska towns gave us at least three lifts through a summer, but stockings and underwear and shirts piled up quickly. We had already begun to polish brass, wax floors, and do the major cooking while we ran. Now, to the skipper's horror, I added laundry to cruising hours and hung the washing on the afterdeck.

He cringed the first day he saw a row of stockings dangling from the awning. When he became hardened to this sight I added other garments. The scheme worked, for when Stewart produced his laundry song, the *Triton's* skipper laughed. It was a good song, the best of many produced in convoy cruising. Stewart sang it one evening to the tune of "Comrades."

Laundry, laundry, ever since they left home,
Rubbing and scrubbing, eternally tubbing,
Wherever the Pinkertons roam.
It floats in the breeze in the morning,
It's in sight throughout the day's run,
Till you wonder, by thunder, what she can have under
When it's all hanging out in the sun.

We found the old trading town of Wrangel a great contrast to the bustling activity of Ketchikan where halibuters and salmon trollers fitted out for long trips and shipped fish from filled holds. Wrangel dozed peacefully in the sun. Its population was partly white and partly native. On our first evening in town we discovered movies. Until then they had played no part in cruising life. The theater was filled very early and the first ten rows were taken by native children who regarded the play's action seriously. When the hero rode to the rescue of the endangered maiden just in the nick of time he was greeted with deafening stamps and cheers. The excitement was too much even for the film. It parted with a snap which only added to suspense. We all sat in darkness and debated whether the gal would be saved after all.

It was dark when we left the theater and we were surprised when our Wrangel friends suggested a walk to the point to see the sunset. To top off an evening movie with an eleven o'clock sunset was something new in programs. Apparently it was a town custom, and I understood why when we reached the wharfs.

Above the mountains across the channel the sky was ablaze. Rose deepening into scarlet extended to the zenith.

And all this color was reflected in the calm water of Stikine Strait. A flaming sky and a flaming sea, with one blending into the other, we were bathed in color. It stretched before us as though another world had opened. I stood there, dizzy from it, transported by this glory. And then I suddenly knew that of all the sunsets I had seen or ever would see, this would be the most unforgettable.

XXIII

ICE—DEAD AND ALIVE

As we turned a point into Wrangel Narrows we three burst out laughing. After our fear lest the twenty miles of narrow, twisting, rock-filled channel might not be plainly marked, the forest of lights, beacons, spar buoys and nun buoys was more dismaying than no navigation aids whatever. We weren't accustomed to such sea guidance. For years we had cruised on a coast where a lighthouse was a rarity and a buoy a subject of wonder. This superabundance was an embarrassment.

The intricate channel lies between dangerous ledges and flats. Tidal currents are strong and the streams enter at both ends and meet in the middle. Steamships find difficulty in making the hairpin turns and any vessel drawing more than ten feet is advised to have a pilot.

The *Triton's* six-foot draft presented no difficulty, but the confusion ahead made me dizzy. When the skipper said my job was to check off the numbers of buoys and spars and keep our position on the chart, I moaned.

"It's easy," he said. "We leave red buoys and even numbers to starboard."

Red, black and white dotted the channel. There appeared to be no system to it, unless it were by a punchboard method. Bobs came to the chart table.

"I see how it goes, dad," she said.

It was the first time that I encountered that attitude

which was to become known in our family as "taking care of mother." I found myself both liking and resenting it. Bobs and I checked off buoys together as we zigzagged our way through the maze. Suddenly it became easy to find the channel and I admitted with surprise that Uncle Sam did have a system after all.

"Mother thought they stuck them in like she cooks, by ear," Bobs said. "Can't you see the wild way she'd mark these narrows?"

We were on our way to visit glaciers. The tour began modestly, for we tackled dead glaciers first. When we were within striking distance of two of them, Baird and Patterson, I brought out my non-turn freezer. I had prepared for icebergs with a patented contrivance which was warranted to produce ice cream in an hour and I carried the descriptive pamphlet when we went for the evening domino game aboard the *Simba*.

The booklet was convincing. Betty admired my foresight and showed proper gratitude when I announced the freezer large enough to service both boats. The ice cream dessert for tomorrow's dinner was discussed in detail and I made the mixture the next morning before we went to visit a glacier.

There was plenty of ice in the dead glacier. A dreary gray expanse extended far back among the mountains. The desolate land on either side was without vegetation. Clouds of terns rose into the air as we approached and scores of seals slid into the water. A cold wind came off the ice. Even before we had left the dinghies and crossed a strip of muddy pulverized granite between sea and ice cap, my body was frozen and my spirits were chilled by that pitiless encroachment of ice on the land.

We walked on the dirty gray carcass of the glacier and

stared down into a fissure. It was a minor crack, but wind, cold, emptiness and desolation had so stimulated my imagination that I found myself shrinking from it as though it were a dangerous crevasse.

I was relieved when we started back. Robert carried a chunk of ice. Right then there was nothing I wanted less than ice cream. At the sea Robert immersed the ice to wash it. To my relief, the piece sank promptly. One moment it was there and then it wasn't. Soil, and perhaps old age, had destroyed its buoyancy. He didn't believe it, but went back for another piece.

He hung onto the second piece while it was laundered and, back aboard the *Triton* he packed it in the patent freezer, remarking that probably no one had ever frozen a dessert in antique ice. Two hours proved that he was right. The dead ice had turned to muddy water and the ice cream mixture was barely chilled. We megaphoned regrets to the *Simba*.

"That ice has been dead a long time," Betty called. "Tell Bobs to come over in the *Crab* and collect some hot gingerbread."

In the evening domino game I didn't mention patent freezers, but everyone else did. The nightly gathering was the time when untoward incidents were taken out and shaken.

We met ostensibly for a domino tournament, which began in Alaska, the *Triton* playing the *Simba*. Bobs declined to play. She and Lua curled up in a corner where Bobs read every volume on both boats. Betty, Stewart and Charlie took turns on their two-man team, and I often caught a wistful gleam in Betty's eyes as she looked at Bobs comfortably established under a reading light.

"Nowadays the young have learned to be firm about things," she remarked.

Le Conte was our first live glacier, very much alive and spawning bergs. We made the run to Le Conte Bay in the *Simba*, left her in Charlie's care outside and finished the voyage in two dinghies powered by outboard motors. As we approached, a long procession, hundreds of bergs, streamed out of the bay on the ebb tide. Like great white chariots they came on and on, until they struck shoal water where they grounded. When the tide turned they lifted and streamed back.

We lunched in a cove while the bergs marched past us on their return to the mother glacier. We joined them in the two dinghies. It was the first time I'd seen bergs except from the deck of ships and even from that height a berg looks formidable. Now we were at water level. Pieces as large as an apartment house floated by. Knowing that only one-eighth of a berg is out of water, we computed that some were as large as a city block. I was conscious of a traffic problem. These great masses had no skippers, whistles, motors, knew no rules of the road, and had a habit of suddenly rolling over.

We may have been in dangerous proximity, but that was forgotten because of the beauty. Bobs was ecstatic. Bergs conformed to her idea of what sculpture should be. Their shapes were varied and exciting. Some were majestic. Others were great masses molded with strength and beauty and one's eye followed with pleasure the rounded surfaces, sculptured by sun and water. Some were slender spires with an exquisite purity of line, and still others looked as though they had been carved by an artist with his tongue in his cheek. The young have a natural appreciation of modern art and Bobs exclaimed and pointed and was as intoxicated as I had ever seen her at an art show.

The color was as amazing as were the shapes. It ranged from sparkling white through every possible shade of sapphire, turquoise and peacock blue to a deep indigo. Each hue was alive and glistening. The whole effect was breathtaking.

Bobs and I could have spent a day rushing from one berg to another, but the skippers were conscious of swirling tides in which the bergs milled. Stewart's motor had broken down and we were towing the *Simba's* dinghy. It was not a flexible arrangement and a barricade of bergs was forming at the mouth of the bay.

"We'd better make it while we can," the skippers shouted at each other above the noise of our exhaust.

We were all silent as we ran back. Hours of such beauty leave one tired and very happy inside. I was still lost in it when I heard Robert's ejaculation and looked up at the *Simba*.

The house, rails and most of the hull were covered with a strange dull black. I thought of fire or some strange paint disaster. Stewart was staring in amazement and Betty's tone was horrified.

"Charlie!" she demanded. "What has happened to my beautiful new boat?"

Charlie made a weary gesture with his hat and brushed off a thousand flies from one square foot of bright work.

"I've been spending the afternoon doing this," he said. "About ten million of these birds have come aboard us."

We never knew what kind of flies they were, or why they came. We never saw anything like them in Alaska again. They might have been a visitation from ancient times, long buried in an ancient glacier.

XXIV

Betty and I concluded that heaven must watch over the world's nicest people. We evolved the theory as the *Simba* and the *Triton* followed Dr. De Vighne's little cruiser into Juneau. Stewart and Dr. De Vighne had known each other when fellow officers in France, and now, in hospitality as expansive as the mountains of his country, he had dashed out to escort us in.

He had brought his wife and daughter, who was Bobs' age, and met us two days' run from Juneau. Betty and I watched his navigating with wonder. We had been trained under skippers with convictions about rocks and reefs and the inevitable consequences thereof. But Doc's carefree piloting brought his *Chirikof* off scatheless.

Everyone in Alaska called him Doc. There were other physicians but only one "Doc." Twenty-five years before he had stepped off a steamship with total assets of a very new diploma, an equally new wife, a scanty kit of instruments, five cents in cash and a friend-making smile. Now he was health commissioner of the territory and its 60,000 inhabitants, 60,000 of whom were his friends. When his babies, and he was beginning the second generation, reached three thousand, Juneau expressed its affection and esteem. Any other city in the world would have given Doc a gold watch. Juneau dedicated the telephone directory to him.

The three boats anchored overnight in a harbor. While we waited aboard the *Simba* for Doc and Mrs. Doc and their daughter Dana to appear at cocktail time, Betty and I defended our theory that Doc was underwritten by heaven.

That afternoon as the three boats had cruised a coast with foul ground extending a half mile from shore we had looked back to see the *Chirikof* tranquilly wending its way toward a reef. Robert looked startled and studied the chart. The *Simba* edged toward us and Stewart called that Doc was going to get into trouble.

The *Chirikof* was beyond call. Both boats started toward her. Robert began to make motions of getting a dinghy overside. Doc saw that he was the center of attention and waved a friendly greeting. There was plenty of tension aboard the *Simba* and the *Triton* and none at all aboard Doc's boat. He didn't honor the reef with a glance as the *Chirikof*, apparently of her own volition, picked out the one place which was safely below her keel.

To see such hairbreadth piloting was much like learning that one's every-day companion had been granted the gift of miracles. Stewart and Robert scoffed at our theory and contended that after twenty-five years in Alaskan waters Doc probably knew the silhouette of every reef. When the crew of the *Chirikof* joined us Stewart began an inquiry. He managed to sound casual.

"Doc," he said, "you had us a bit bothered when you skimmed across that reef."

"Reef!" said Doc. "What reef?"

Charlie Drumm staggered aft. "Doc travels with his hand in God's pocket," he muttered as he passed me.

When we berthed alongside Juneau's municipal float we found that being a friend of Doc's carried club privileges.

Townspeople stopped to shake hands. Sourdoughs addressed us by first names. Taxi men refused payment. Citizens didn't bother with the keys to the city. They gave us the city.

Our boats lay under Alaska's largest gold mine, which day and night masticated a mountain and spewed a continuous stream of tailings into the sea. Our way to the town lay through a district in which the least respectable of the women lived in rows of small houses. A nice spirit of neighborliness existed. Women sat in doorways gossiping and crocheting doilies. Occasionally one could be seen bearing a napkin-covered dish to a neighbor. Vice, crocheting and bearing presents of homemade cookies looked astonishingly suburban.

Our first days in Juneau were spent doing the usual things. We visited Mendenhall Glacier, attended movies and spent an afternoon at the museum, where Father Kashiverof showed us an absorbing Aleut and Eskimo collection. Father Kashiverof was born on Kodiak Island, trained for the priesthood in Russia and returned to take charge of the church in Sitka, a favorite of the Czar's. Now he was curator of the museum and a fascinating authority on native cultures.

We had planned a day at Taku Glacier to watch the big bergs break from the face. It was a tourist stunt. Most of the steamships stop there and the ship's whistle is often sufficient to loosen a berg. Smaller craft must wait for Taku herself to put on a show, but the glacier rarely fails her public.

It is exciting to see a piece of ice the size of a city skyscraper break from the face of a glacier. It is not at all like a brick falling from a chimney. There is a majesty, a slow motion effect, as the great piece severs the bonds of ages and slowly sinks into the sea. A cloud of ice dust rises from the cleavage. Spray goes high into the air and a tidal wave is thrown across the inlet.

I was torn between counterattractions when Doc came aboard and proposed that we all run up Taku River to his log lodge. He had to take supplies to his caretaker and bring out a disabled motor. By leaving at three o'clock in the morning we could catch high tide in the shallow river, lunch at the lodge and visit the rarely seen Twin Glaciers. He added that Father Kashiverof was going and that Dana was hoping to have a whole day with Bobs.

I accepted at once for Bobs and me. The *Triton* gave her so few opportunities to be with girls her own age. Stewart, Betty and Robert declined. A long day in a gas boat couldn't compete with Taku Glacier. When Doc had gone, Robert made some objection to our going. If Doc operated a gas boat as he piloted a cruiser, Taku Inlet with countless swirling bergs and Taku River with swift currents were no places to be his guests.

Stewart assured him there was no danger we would ever reach the river. We'd never get off at three in the morning and catch high tide.

"Doc probably treats tides as he does rocks," Stewart said.

Instead of expecting tides to wait for us, we usually waited for the tide. So no one took the expedition seriously even when I set the alarm.

At exactly three in the morning Doc's gas boat pulled alongside the float where Bobs and I were waiting. I knew the skippers had their ears cocked and Doc's promptness seemed some sort of personal triumph.

As we ran down Gastineau Channel, a long narrow gut between mountains, sunrise was a rosy glow on snow-covered peaks. Doc turned toward a beach and said we would have to pick up ballast.

One spring, after due thought had been given to the trim of the *Triton* and the cost of lead, we had reballasted. Men had come aboard and tenderly laid hundred-pound pigs along our keel. That had been a momentous occasion. Now we six made a merry occasion of extemporaneous ballast. No one was in any hurry. Mrs. Doc served hot coffee from a thermos bottle. The girls competed to see who could carry the largest rocks aboard and the growing pile of ballast in the boat became more a matter of personal prowess than proper trim.

Out of habit, I spoke of the tide in Taku River.

"We've never made it yet," Mrs. Doc said. "We just shove the boat through the mud. But there isn't a rock in Taku River to go aground on."

Aboard again, we all examined some oddities about the motor, a converted automobile engine. During the inspection we heard a metallic tinkle and Bobs and Dana backed away. Bobs looked rather stricken for she had been taught that any mechanism is sacred.

"Why, the girls have dropped the top of the cooling system into the bilge!" Mrs. Doc exclaimed. "Isn't that what you call the piece that's gone?"

Doc remarked that something did seem to be lacking, but it probably wasn't important.

Evidently the missing piece wasn't important for the motor started. When it continued to run, Mr. and Mrs. Doc agreed that the girls had improved its operation. Never before had it gone a full hour without balking. But a little later someone noticed that the engine was smoking.

"Must be getting hot," Father Kashiverof remarked sagely.

Doc agreed with the diagnosis. He was about to dump a pail of water over the smoking motor when I let out a cry of protest.

"You'll crack the cylinders!" I warned.

That speech established me as a motor expert. Doc thanked me. Tributes to my intelligence became almost heady, for in the *Triton* I was not rated a mechanical genius. But when Doc's motor stopped and my opinion was consulted, I saw that I had stuck my neck out. Fortunately Doc discovered that by jiggling everything movable he could start it again. Laughter over this demonstration made everyone forget an expert's presence.

The motor tired of the joke before we did. After a half dozen polite responses it stopped with decision. And, moreover, it had halted when we needed power. The tide had turned and a fleet of bergs was coming toward us from Taku Glacier. If we were to keep out of their way, something must be done quickly.

Doc turned to me.

"When an engine quits suddenly, it's the ignition," I said.

As the gas had already been checked, my remark wasn't exactly inspired. But it impressed my audience. Everyone nodded and waited for me to go on. I asked about the coil and distributor. In the hours and hours of talk between Vic and Robert I'd heard those terms and learned they were connected with ignition. Apparently I was the only one aboard who did, for Doc called me to help probe for them. We recognized the coil. We identified the distributor by deduction. The vibrator attracted our attention because obviously it was a vital spot.

"The spark should jump across here," I guessed.

The cheers which greeted this remark went to my head

completely. Applause in a field in which one has been rated
a moron is intoxicating. After that I wouldn't have been
human if I had admitted an inability to fix it. Since then
I have been told that adjustment of vibrator tension is delicate and requires skill and time, and I have not been able
even to understand the explanations of why this is so.

Fortunately, I was not then inhibited with too much
knowledge, for I turned down the screw as calmly and as
vigorously as I would adjust tension of a sewing machine.
Doc, his boat and everyone aboard must surely have been
under divine protection.

The motor fairly purred. I sat back, the center of admiration, but I caught a suspicious gleam in Bobs' eyes. She
wasn't going to tell on me, but I hadn't fooled her. For
years she had been watching Robert grab the simplest
mechanism from my hands. Sometimes I wasn't even
trusted with a can opener.

Powered now, we wound our way among floating bergs.
Father remarked that only a small part of a berg showed
above water. To be among these great masses of ice in a
boat which had an unreliable motor would ordinarily have
terrified me. But I knew Doc's boat was sacred. The most
restless of those bergs would behave in his presence.

As we were searching for the river channel, the cooling
system finally capitulated to the missing part. The muffler,
welded to a horizontal exhaust pipe, melted off and left a
gaping hole from which sparks flew out with each explosion. Someone murmured about the possibility of loose
gasoline in the cabin, but our discussion of the fire menace
was purely academic. No one could remember his physics
sufficiently to be sure of the combustible proportion of gas
and air. Doc didn't think there was much possibility of our
achieving an ignitable mixture. I was sure there wasn't. In

the *Simba* or the *Triton* we'd undoubtedly have been blown up. Doc gave heaven a chance.

We could not see the river channel in the opaque glacial water. On a flood tide, when the sea pushed inland, we could have navigated the shallows, but now the sea was leaving the river to its own resources, which were very meager. We made some progress against the current, although occasionally we dragged in soft mud. Heaven would undoubtedly have met our problem for us, but suddenly Doc became efficient and thought of the rock ballast.

We threw it over and, lightened, managed to make another few feet. There we stuck. Doc put on hip boots and splashed off to reconnoiter. He returned to report deeper water about fifty feet away, pointing it out while we lined up its position. We were very exact in getting these bearings, but no one seemed aware that a wide expanse of unnavigable shallows lay between us and water which would float us.

Since it was Doc's boat, I rather expected it to sprout wings and fly across the shallows. I'm not sure this miracle wouldn't have occurred if Doc hadn't lost his rating by that unfortunate efficiency in the matter of ballast. Our keel grated harshly. Everyone was mildly surprised, for Taku River was completely rockless, or at least it had been before we had brought up our own rocks to go aground on. Father, who went overside to investigate, reported that we were resting firmly on the stones we had carried from Juneau.

This unique bit of seamanship ended talk of reaching deeper water. I suggested that the weight of six people in a launch high and dry on jagged rocks was asking a good deal of heaven, but Doc didn't want the women to get wet and muddy. After all, he knew how far Providence could be pushed. We sat comfortably aboard.

"When the tide turns we'll have more water," Doc said.

That would be the flood tide on which we had expected to return home, but no one suggested that we abandon the project to visit the lodge. Mrs. Doc thought that Oscar, the caretaker, might come looking for us in the lodge's boat, the *Mud Hen*. I doubted this. Oscar must have developed a philosophical attitude during a year of caretakership. And his coming couldn't raise the level of the river.

During the wait we repaired the muffler. I had seen Vic mix an asbestos paste to bandage a hot pipe. The tool chest contained a package of asbestos fluff but not an inch of canvas. Dana, Bobs and I, in slacks, had no extra garments, but Mrs. Doc offered her slip. While we mixed asbestos and water, Doc made a professional job of the bandaging. On that he needed no help from heaven. When he had finished, the muffler was attached to the pipe in a workmanlike manner. Having a doctor aboard was very helpful.

While we sat marooned we watched for Oscar in the *Mud Hen*. Emotions regarding his arrival were a trifle mixed. Father, Bobs and I looked forward to his coming. Doc, Mrs. Doc and Dana rather dreaded being found aground on rocks which demanded explanation. When at last we saw him coming, Doc's family began to prepare a story accounting for our presence in the river on an ebb tide. Their fear of Oscar's disapproval led me to expect a ferocious individual.

We sat like chastened children as the *Mud Hen* bore down upon us. Quite suddenly it stopped. Doc and Mrs. Doc broke into gleeful shouts.

"Good!" they cried. "Now he's aground and can't say anything to us."

Oscar tried to pole off. His failure to get free made everyone laugh more heartily. He abandoned his boat and waded toward us. Doc assured him he could walk to us. But Oscar apparently had no heavenly underwriting for the next moment he stepped off into icy depths. His slicker ballooned above his head and as he went down he resembled an angry morning glory.

"Look!" Mrs. Doc cried. "Oscar's found the channel."

I was glad to know that Taku had a channel. Oscar proved this fact by swimming across it. After that feat no one tried to deceive him about the rocks. He didn't find the story as humorous as we did. When the tide finally floated us off our ballast, the men poled our gas boat to the channel, took the *Mud Hen* in tow and started up river. Oscar insisted on riding in his own boat. He need not have distrusted our craft for it gave an impressive demonstration of good seamanship a few moments later.

We were gathered at the stern telling Oscar about our adventures when he suddenly stopped listening. He was counting persons.

"Who's at the wheel?" he demanded.

No one was. But Doc's boats had had to learn to be self-reliant. The gas boat was following the twisting channel as well as with a wheelsman.

Then I knew that heaven was on our side and that Bobs and I would safely return to the *Triton*. I prepared to enjoy the events of the day.

Ten minutes later the bandaged exhaust pipe exploded in a snowstorm of asbestos fluff. A blizzard floated out toward Oscar astern. He didn't even ask what caused it. Apparently a year in Doc's employ had destroyed Oscar's capacity to be astonished. We brushed it off ourselves, but bits of fluff clung to hair, eyebrows and woolen clothing, giving us an odd newly hatched appearance.

We reached the lodge, a big log structure on the banks of the Taku. We ate a mid-afternoon lunch. We visited Oscar's trap line, also the Twin Glaciers. Oscar presented us with sourdough yeast twelve years old and apologized for its youth. He regretted that he had not borrowed some from a neighbor which was much better, being twenty years old. I was glad he hadn't, for I would have felt its charge to be as sacred as that of the virgin's lamp.

Oscar's yeast, white and sweet smelling, proved to me how deceived I'd been by the stuff Robert had introduced as sourdough years before in a north wood's cabin. I carried home a sample to confront him.

Toward evening when Oscar was in a panic lest we'd outstayed another tide, we departed. We had scarcely waved our good-bys to Oscar when the gas boat made a complete circle. Doc put the motor into neutral while we discussed this phenomenon and decided that it had something to do with the swift current. We tried again, and started off on another circle. This time we were near a bank, and when it was evident that we were about to strike shore, Father rushed to the bow to keep us off with a pick pole. He thrust the pole into the ground just as we struck and Father was catapulted in the most graceful pole vault I ever witnessed. It established some sort of distance record. We saw Father sailing through the air. Then he disappeared completely.

"Don't you think that was wonderful for a man of Father's age?" Mrs. Doc demanded.

I thought she meant the involuntary pole vault, but she was speaking of his quick dash forward.

Father's crashing return through the brush assured us

that he had not been killed. While we waited for him Doc deduced that something was wrong with the steering gear. He was proved right by Bobs and Dana, who reported that the disabled motor, which we were taking to town, was resting squarely on the steering quadrant. As Oscar had lifted the motor to the afterdeck, he appeared to have made an error. But Doc admitted that he had rearranged it for symmetry.

To go aground on the way downriver was only to be expected. Fortunately we had turned only one bend and could blow the whistle for Oscar, although Mrs. Doc said she would rather sit through another tide than hear what Oscar thought about our losing the channel. I preferred Oscar's comments to a night on the river.

We suffered neither. Perhaps Oscar spent the night on the river. We never knew. As he shoved the *Mud Hen* toward us through the shallows, he too went aground. He didn't seem happy about our laughter and he looked less happy when we managed to pole our boat into deeper water and went gaily down the channel, leaving our rescuer marooned. To leave the only other boat on the river high and dry on a sandbank seemed to prove that even the best of us make mistakes. Oscar's attitude toward river channels, sandbanks and tides was similar to Stewart's and Robert's. Heaven, apparently, leaves the efficient to manage for themselves.

At the lodge the men had propped the muffler with a piece of stove wood. The muffler did not entirely fill the hole in the exhaust pipe and a resultant shower of sparks seemed more ominous as it grew dark. I looked around the cabin for a fire extinguisher. A spot of clean paint behind a metal holder indicated an extinguisher had been recently removed. At the cost of being efficient, I whispered an inquiry about this to Doc.

"I hid it because I was afraid it might make you girls nervous," he said.

Doc was reasonable. He agreed that I might retrieve it from under gear in the forepeak and replace it in its holder if I didn't think it would be too terrifying an object.

Our next excitement was over Father. Someone noticed that he was missing and started a guarded inquiry.

"Where is Father?" was whispered up and down the rows of people sitting on both sides of the cabin. It was like a childhood game I'd played when each one whispered to his neighbor.

Now each looked around, studied the whole interior and gravely reported that he did not see Father, although a midget couldn't have concealed himself in that boat. Mrs. Doc lifted the stern curtains and said Father wasn't on the afterdeck. There was no panic and no dismay. We carried on an unhurried search while the boat continued downriver in the darkness. I was as sure as everyone else that Father had not fallen overside. That couldn't have happened on Doc's boat.

We looked under side benches. We moved loose objects. The tool chest was the only place we hadn't searched when Father materialized between the stern curtains and asked if he'd been called.

He'd been sleeping on the slat and canvas top and he returned to finish his nap, although Mrs. Doc reminded her husband that he had told Dana the fragile canopy would not bear her weight.

"Father's tired and needs a nap," Doc said comfortably.

A skipper who risked having upper works crash on him

for the comfort of guests was something new. I'd deduced that boats rated slightly above humans.

As we approached Taku Inlet, Doc tinkered with the searchlight. He remembered that it had not worked the last time he had run the berg-cluttered bay. When he succeeded in turning it on we decided that it had better be left burning. Bobs and Dana were sternly warned not to knock over the wood holding up the muffler or to go near the forepeak where the switch of the searchlight was precariously adjusted.

A moment later Mrs. Doc entered the bow window of the cabin and the light went out. Doc put the searchlight away philosophically.

"Too bad," he said. "Bergs look lovely with the searchlight on them."

My mind was on safety rather than scenic effects. Strain as I might, I never could quite get and hold a serene dependence on heavenly guidance. I worried lest my relapses into efficiency would cause our protecting spirit to desert the craft. We needed Providence as we wound in and out among the bergs. Mrs. Doc held a pocket flashlight. Doc took the wheel. We all shouted orders.

"Go ahead! Turn to starboard! No! No! Not that way! I mean to port! We missed that one all right. Here's another!"

Doc's equanimity was marvelous. While bergs passed like tall gray ghosts in the darkness, he listened not to one woman but to four who could never agree as to which two-story chunk of ice held the greatest menace. No one seemed to consider that we might be caught by two cruising bergs and become an eggshell between them. Collision hazard was enough to worry about, and through it all Doc dodged and weaved and maintained a cheerful calm. Stewart and Robert would have been not only jittery but sulphuric. Later they denied this accusation by assuring me that they wouldn't under any circumstances have been there to be sulphuric.

The icebergs past, we settled to a slow jog down the shore. The motor ran, stuttered, threatened to stop, but didn't. Doc diagnosed its trouble as "too much of something," or he added to be safe, "Maybe not enough." Bobs and Dana slept. So did Mrs. Doc. Father and I sat beside the pounding motor while he told me stories of his boyhood in the colorful Russian days of Sitka. Doc dozed off for forty winks while Father took the wheel. Those forty winks were our undoing. Doc wakened full of energy. He gave the motor the gun, whereupon it stopped, as if to say that since no one appreciated what it had been doing for hours it might as well quit.

Doc decided that we were out of gas and the gunning of the motor had exhausted the vacuum tank. This sounded reasonable. It was the only mischance left for us. Doc brought out the oars. At a mile an hour, it would take five hours to reach home, but we increased our route by hopefully chasing a bootlegging boat around a point. The bootlegger retreated into a deep bay to decide whether we were friend or foe. Doc was a friend and in need of help. We were far in the bay when Doc remembered that no one knew how to fill the vacuum tank anyway. So we continued on to Juneau.

It was four in the morning when Bobs and I crept into the *Triton's* deckhouse. Robert was in the galley making coffee before setting out to find us.

It was much too long a story to tell then. Had I been wise I wouldn't have admitted there was a story. He wakened me at nine to get details of the night, but as soon as I started he stopped me.

"Grab your coffee and come over to the *Simba*," he said. "Betty and Stewart can't miss this."

Any anxiety I may have had over their worry or the possibility of the *Simba* or the *Triton* faring forth on an unnecessary rescue was wiped out. I was back in the world of efficiency. The skippers denied they had even thought of rescue.

"What!" they cried. "There aren't enough women and children in the world to make us take our boats among those bergs in the dark!"

I was telling the last few details of the story when a mechanic came to fix Doc's boat. Stewart and Robert went along. They returned soon, doubled over with laughter.

"All the time Doc was rowing," they said, "he had five gallons of gas in his tank."

XXV

ALASKAN ADVENTURES

ALASKAN RIVERS COMPEL FOR-
giveness for the land's superabundant rainfall. Without its
excessive rain and snow, many lovely streams would not
find their way to the sea. From the first we were river ad-
dicts. As the seasons passed we came to have our favorites
and revisited them year after year. Even in our last summer we discovered new ones.

I became a connoisseur of rivers. The others jeered, con-
tending I cloaked an admission of indolence in an impressive title. I rarely traveled far and I almost never fished.
Rivers themselves were my hobby and I enjoyed a stream
as one does an etching through an intensive study of beauty
in small sections.

I spent hours beside crystal pools splotched with sunlight and adorned with mosses and huge ferns. I stopped
to watch play of sunlight and shadow on snowy mountainsides. Loitering, I would see a mink, his dark fur shining
in the sun as he carried on his day's tasks along the river.
Or a mother duck which had made a gallant effort to dis-
tract attention from her brood by a noisy pretense of
flight would return to collect her young and warn them
that there were people on the stream.

Alaskan rivers are different. They never have the parked
effect of New England streams flowing through rounded

woodland and between grassy banks. They are never smoothly strong, like rivers that pass between midwestern prairies. Like Alaska, they are steep and rough and violent. Their banks are mountainsides hidden by giant trees, narrow valleys dense with small growth, or broad flats of raw gravel. Always they carry scars of spring freshets, and always they are noisy and lusty and sparklingly new. If their passage is barred here, they go there. Always they go.

Variations in Alaskan rivers is a great part of their charm. Some run across shallow riffles, detour in sharp turns through huge gravel bars, deepen without warning to become sparkling sheets of snow water. Some are paralleled by bayous in which devil's club and huge-leaved skunk cabbage grow in rank abundance. Others twist between thick banks of elders. Many are barred by great trunks of spruce brought down by spring torrents and interlaced so thickly that one must crawl over, duck under or cross on them from bank to bank. Then river travel takes on some of the aspect of tight rope walking. Again rivers open to reveal vistas of valleys and distant peaks. Any river may leap off a cliff or fall through a rocky gorge and the traveler must leave the stream bed and climb steeply.

On such rivers I could, without twinges of that conscience which drove the others on, settle myself on a bank or on an islet. I could doze, lulled by the sound of falling water. I could read. I might see an eagle, an otter or a bear. But always I had a deep sense of peace.

Robert had to see what the river looked like a mile beyond, even though he knew it couldn't be any lovelier. Bobs and Lua straddled. If the going didn't look too tough, they followed Robert, but they were quite as apt to settle beside me and become connoisseurs.

Trout pools of Alaskan rivers are incredible. In some, trout lie thickly head to tail and side by side like columns of soldiers on parade. One afternoon when Stewart had caught all the trout we could eat, had caught many more and had returned them to the water, when he had brought in a trout on every cast and three when he used three hooks on a leader, he and Robert estimated the number of fish in the pool. The computation was two thousand trout, a figure so startling to them they cut it in half. Even then they never dared tell anyone. Later we found a pool with twice as many trout.

Alaskan rivers ended forever my faint interest in fly fishing. Trout in such numbers took all challenge from the sport. I never dared admit this publicly until the day I met an Alaskan who was planning a fly fishing vacation in the state of Washington. I looked surprised.

"I know all about our trout pools," he said. "I want to go where I earn a trout."

One member of our family devoted himself to fishing with an ardor which made up for our disinterest. Lua became a fishing fan. The sing of a reel was music to his ears and trembling with excitement he would sit beside a fisherman while a trout was played. He would look up coaxingly as if to say, "Let me have him now." And at the first nod of assent, Lua would dash into the icy water, dive, grasp the fish in his mouth and deposit it far up the bank. He didn't puncture the skin or displace a scale. The landing ended his interest in the fish and he would return to the bank to await the next strike.

Lua elected himself Stewart's canine landing net. He made this very plain one day when Charlie Drumm was experimenting with a rod. Lua heard the sing of a reel and rushed over to sit by Charlie. He was fond of Charlie and forgave him for losing the first trout. He even wagged an encouraging, "Don't mind, old chap. Accidents will happen." But after the second strike when a fine trout broke water and then the line went slack, Lua looked at Charlie reproachfully and departed for the next bar to sit beside Stewart.

Irish terriers are excellent hunting dogs, but after Lua's first fish, game had to wear scales and swim to attract his attention. He stared wonderingly at deer. He no longer dug for chipmunks or barked news of an animal ashore. A rat didn't stir any racial memories. He took no interest in a gun, but sight of a rod made him ecstatic. A fish on a line caused a trembling tension and if he saw a trout leap in a pool he would beg the nearest fisherman to make a cast.

But when salmon began to run up rivers to spawn and the water boiled and churned with hundreds of struggling fish, Lua was reduced to frenzy. He couldn't wait for a rod. He dashed in to do his own fishing. The fish came in droves and knocked him off his feet. He could handle a three-pound trout but a fifteen-pound salmon could flip him onto his back. But he never gave up trying.

He splashed and spattered through a mass of solid fish, looking more worn, baffled and crazy with excitement at each futile lunge. We rolled on the bank with laughter, but our laughter only added to his determination.

His last encounter with salmon went on for several hours and provided his most exciting day on any river. When we tried to call him out of the icy water he would look downstream, see another school coming, wag his tail and look at us beseechingly.

"Let me try just one more lot. There's a trick to this game, but I'll learn it."

After this apology for disobedience he would gallop down to meet them, and the oncoming fish would bowl him off his feet and roll him over while he lunged, snapped and shrieked with rage.

Bobs' sympathy was entirely with Lua. When he shivered all that evening from his long immersion in snow water, she covered him with blankets, tucked a hot water bottle beside him and held us responsible if he developed pneumonia or rheumatism.

She reminded us of a previous tragedy when her dog had died from food poisoning. The veterinary had blamed aging fish in a neighbor's garbage can.

"You know how dangerous fish poisoning is," she cried. "I've lost one dog. And I'm not going to lose Lua!"

That sobered us. The river banks were covered with dead and rotting fish. We decided Lua's battle with salmon was ended. Thereafter he was on a leash in salmon spawning season.

The skipper made partial atonement. When we saw a halibut schooner lifting gear we always stopped to buy a fresh fish, and one day Robert took Lua aboard. A line two miles long was being hauled in by a gurdy and on every few yards of it was a fish. Lua's excitable nature threatened to burst him asunder. Cod, gorgeous big red snappers and halibut up to sixty pounds came over the side in endless procession to flop on the deck. Lua talked about it for an hour after he got home. His sleep was twitchy all night.

Lua had another piscatorial outlet. Spring and fall each year he fished for salmon with me in the Yucluetaws and his tension and absorption were far in excess of mine. Because we feared he'd be caught on a hook, we trained him to keep away from a fish when landed in the boat, and being a gentleman he observed the rule.

But when Bobs landed her first salmon, a twenty-eight pounder, Lua decided his mistress was not going to see that fish flop out of the dinghy if he could do anything about it. He sprang upon it and line, heavy lead, dog and fish were in a snarl before the situation was straightened out. But Lua and Bobs were happy.

Lua spent his old age beside a garden pool in which a lone goldfish swam. He lay beside it for hours, staring at the yellow mite. But in the eyes of his memories I am sure it was a large, fierce salmon.

The salmon saga has been made poetic. But to me that devastating struggle to perpetuate a species is both brutal and repulsive. When the fish come in from the open ocean and are caught in traps and purse seines in sea water, they are active and beautiful. I've stood on a floating trap and looked into the heart and seen thousands of flashing uniform symmetrical bodies.

But when salmon leave the sea and ascend the rivers disintegration sets in. The head of one specie becomes horribly distorted. All are possessed by that remorseless urge for perpetuation which entails destruction. It is bad enough that salmon should have to fight their way up rivers, bruise themselves in shallows or in leaping up rocky falls, being attacked by bears and pecked at by gulls and eagles. But nature has saddled the distressed creatures with a revolting sadistic trait. In love-making the male strips the flesh from the tail of his mate. Then the potential mother struggles up stream with her caudal fin waving at the end of a skeleton.

The fight of the salmon to attain their goal only adds to the grimness. The whole surface of a river boils as myriads of fish swarm to destruction. They swim against swift currents, thrash through rapids and leap up falls.

Emaciated, misshapen, fins worn, tails shredded, the salmon reach the spawning pools at last. The weary mothers scrape out hollows, pushing down with lowered heads, whipping the water with their tails until the whole surface is splashed and broken.

And then they must die if their young are to live. A marine growth feeds on the decayed carcass of the parents and the next spring the new-born salmon become lusty on that growth.

Certainly nature has had her off moments.

Alaskan anchorages were adventures in beauty. In a sea country so vast and so intricately indented we could not know every bay and harbor. We had heard of the British Columbia inlets, Princess Louise, Knight and Gardner, and found them as magnificent as was claimed. But Alaskan cruising was exploration. We came upon breath-taking beauty without warning, and discovery added zest.

No one had told us of Red Bluff Bay, as magnificently sculptured as Princess Louise, and we found it on a gambling chance. We couldn't visit all the narrow sea slits in the magnificent coastal range of Baranof Island, so the skippers decided to stop in every third bay.

"We can't go wrong," Stewart added.

Red Bluff came up on the wheel of fortune, and the *Simba* and the *Triton* turned into the most beautiful harbor we had as yet encountered. The sheer walls were red. Eight waterfalls plunged from a high cliff. A cone-shaped mountain, set in the center of a broad valley, was adorned with the clear blue of a glacier.

It was a beautiful spot in which to catch up on odd jobs. There are always things to do about a boat, and we had added a home and a job of writing. At least once every summer the *Triton* had to be repainted; and every day meals had to be cooked, cabins cleaned, floors waxed, decks scrubbed, plumbing, water and electric systems kept going, three gasoline motors groomed. And fiction writing went on always.

In Red Bluff Bay by no prearrangement but some common impulse, the whole crowd was filled with sudden energy. Bobs took the vacuum cleaner and departed for her stateroom. Early in cruising we had found to our astonishment that there is dust aboard a boat, but Bobs and Lua added sand, dog hairs, bits of dog biscuit, odds and ends of seaweed, shells and marine vegetation to the usual fluff from blankets and woolen clothing. A cleaning day in the afterquarters was an occasion.

Betty and I re-stocked day store lockers and checked over main supplies. As the summer advanced we had to make sure a run on a favorite dish hadn't thrown the season's list out of balance. When we knew our long and short lines of groceries we met for barter. The *Triton* traded canned sweet potatoes for *Simba* pineapple and I rectified a spring plunge in lima beans with some choice hominy.

Stewart and Charlie scrubbed ship and even washed the hull. The *Simba* was so glistening I dashed back and put a coat of varnish on the foredeck bright work. Robert finished copying a story to mail at the next post office and invited the *Simba* for dinner. My remarks on ancient sourdough hardships had wounded his pride. He cheated a bit by asking me to make a clam soup, but his sourdough pancakes were as light and fine as he had claimed they would be.

Betty took a sample to the *Simba's* cook, who had regarded the antique yeast with suspicion. The cook retorted a few days later with some magnificent cinnamon rolls that put him one up on any sourdough expert. Sourdough may have been unknown in China, but he showed Alaska how.

XXVI

BROWNIES

OUR ALASKAN PLAYGROUND narrowed. We had favorite streams and harbors and chose the more spectacular waterways from a labyrinth of straits and arms, all of which are thrilling. The rugged ranges of Southeastern Alaska restrict the sea to thin ribbons winding beneath steep naked cliffs. Sometimes these ribbons meet in a superb concourse and then as far as the eye can see in very direction there is splendor.

In time we acquired preferences in lofty vistas, although I had never expected to become choosy about mountains. After days, weeks, months and seasons of sailing beneath majestic peaks, some became more impressive. This was especially true of the glittering ramparts on the east coast of Baranof Island. To me they excelled all others in bold grandeur.

The three great islands, Admiralty, Chichagof and Baranof, provided our main cruising region. We visited them when salmon surged upstream to spawn, for then the big brown bears, found in Southeastern Alaska only on these three islands, left their mountain homes and came down to the rivers to fish. Around any bend in almost any stream we were apt to come upon a great grizzly intent on catching his dinner.

In our early cruising days we were granted complete self-expression in any river. We traveled singly and in groups. Betty and I took naps in fine flat bear wallows. Lua and Bobs ranged through head-high grass. We were operating on the theory that the brown bear of Alaska, like other bears, would under all circumstances avoid an encounter with humans.

A man in the Forest Service convinced the skippers of their error. They returned from an afternoon's visit with the chap, bringing startling data on the brown bear of Alaska.

Most important was the theory of the twenty-fourth bear. Twenty-three bears will run, but the behavior of the twenty-fourth is unpredictable. He may have an uncertain temper. He may dislike man because of a previous encounter. He may be ill or nervous, may be unnecessarily apprehensive of danger. He may be the victim of some psychosis and not know why he dislikes humans. The reasons are unimportant compared to the fact that he feels truculent.

The bear situation would be immeasurably simplified if the twenty-fourth bear wore his number like a football player. But he doesn't. He announces himself by going into action. And not only is the brown bear of Alaska the largest carnivorous animal in the world, weighing up to 1600 pounds, but he can get into a charge instantly and come with astounding speed. In addition to weight and speed he is capable of intelligence. He carries out a maneuver known as "fish hooking," either circling for an attack from behind or waiting beside a trail ahead for his enemy.

And every brown bear in any river is a potential "twenty-fourther."

The skippers relayed this information and ended with stern new rules. Betty's and my predilection for walking bear-made trails and napping in bear wallows must end at once. Lua must be under surveillance lest he commit some overt act which would transform a peaceful brownie into a truculent twenty-fourther. No person should leave the group or get out of sight of the others for one moment. And a big game rifle must go up the river on every expedition.

That twenty-fourth bear worked havoc with personal independence.

After the rules were clearly understood by all, we went in for stalking brownies. The first bears we saw didn't see us. One was a scout who had evidently been sent down to see if the fishing season was on. He came off a mountain, crossed the wide flat to the river, looked at the water, turned and departed the way that he had come. His manner was one of business-like dispatch. He was on an errand and didn't know he had been observed.

Another bear was swimming in a deep pool in a river one warm day. He wasn't fishing. He was merely cooling off. Robert, who led our single file, motioned. Bobs, Betty and I crowded up to watch the bear lolling comfortably in the water. Stewart slipped around the bend and got a movie of him. That bear swam off upstream and never knew his picture had been taken.

Another day we were walking up a river which ran between high cliffs. Nearly thirty feet above the water a huge spruce tree lay across the canyon, both ends buried in the forest. It was a lovely thing to see even without action. But as we were admiring the effect, a yearling brownie stepped onto the stage. His coat glistened and he walked with a swagger across that natural bridge and disappeared in the greenery on the other side, completely unaware of his admiring audience.

Another brownie met us on a river flat as we were returning to the dinghies. The marsh grass was waist-high and he suddenly rose from it fifty feet ahead. We stood absolutely still. Reared on his hind legs, he stood ten feet tall. Most evidently he was an ordinary bear and merely curious. He looked us over and then turned and sauntered off to the forest. But the sight of those great forequarters and that huge head made me willing to subscribe to bear rules from then on.

Single file, as quietly as possible, Stewart with a camera, Robert with a rifle, Bobs, Betty and I herded in between the two men, we walked up many rivers. And we saw many bears. The excitement of turning a bend in the stream and coming suddenly upon a bear, or a whole family of bears fishing, never lessened.

Thick growth on river banks is cut by bear trails, for each bear or family maintains his personal road to the river. Some passages are straight and open and an approaching bear can be seen. These I stared down boldly. Other openings are low, roofed by greenery or hidden by a tree trunk, and the feeling that at any moment a bear might emerge into the shallow river made me cast apprehensive glances astern. After a few miles of these concealed bear doors, I always found myself staying in the middle of the stream.

A big brownie fishing often presents a comic picture. In his wild dashes at a salmon, his chagrin when he misses, his rueful expression as he watches a fish which has eluded him, he appears anything but a mighty hunter. I've seen a great bear who has made a half dozen attempts squat in shallow water with an "Oh, hell. What's the use?" air. Even when he finally lands a salmon and walks shoreward with the fish held by the middle and flapping in his face, he makes a very different impression than he probably believes.

When a brown bear attacks a man, he slaps him down and then bites him. He takes small nips until his quarry appears to be dead and then will leave him, returning to bite again if the man moves. This procedure is well known and men have saved their lives by lying absolutely still and pretending death. It is difficult, but it has been done. A prospector was chewed and lay for a day while the bear watched him. When the bear departed the man got off to town where his sixty wounds were treated. He lived.

Dr. De Vighne told us of treating a man who recovered from ninety-two punctures in his skin. A woman probably saved her life by promptly fainting when she wakened from a nap beside a river to see a brownie standing over her. Tracks confirmed her story that the bear was large. She spent two years in a sanitarium while her nervous system recovered.

Bobs listened to these stories and then prepared for a possible bear encounter by practicing immobility under torment. Being tickled was the worst experience she could imagine. We were all called upon to serve as ticklers. When she had worked up to such self-control that she didn't even twitch, she was sure she was ready for ordeal by bear.

Only once in our bear stalking were we in any danger, at least so far as we were aware. That bear was a twenty-three and a-halfer, hadn't quite decided to become a twenty-fourther. Betty, Bobs, Robert and I were on a river with a stream watcher, a guard placed to prevent illegal seining of salmon. He carried a 45-90 Winchester. We turned a bend and came suddenly upon a magnificent bear. We'd seen larger specimens, but none so gorgeously coated. He was unusually dark and every hair glistened in the sunlight. He had none of the clinging matted patches of winter coat which so often make the summer bear look rather moth-eaten.

That he resented the interruption to his fishing was very evident. He stood about forty feet away and looked us over. His retreat into his own private trail led us to believe that he had decided to forgive us. But he reconsidered, and a moment later he emerged. We stood absolutely still. So did he. But he could have crossed that forty feet of shallow water with two leaps.

When he pulled back his upper lip, showed his tusks and made the odd sound of truculence known as huffing, I heard the stream watcher cock his rifle.

"Don't shoot!" Robert whispered.

Frightened as I was, I was glad to hear those words. The bear was far too fine a specimen to die just because he had some odd complex about human beings.

Apparently the complex was no fixation. He backed into the underbrush, stood for a moment, came out again for another inspection. We hadn't moved. Moreover, we didn't intend to move until that bear had made up his uncertain mind. Neither had we spoken. This time the bear felt better about us. He didn't huff and he seemed to be giving the whole situation mature consideration.

We strove to show our amiable intentions, but trying to register friendliness toward a thousand pounds of truculent bear which could be in our midst with only a few seconds' warning is difficult. Any speech or movement might be misinterpreted.

I don't know about the others but my thoughts were a blank and wouldn't have influenced a mouse. I just stared at that bear, waiting to see if he tensed for a charge. He stared at us. And then like the gentleman he was, he swept his head downward almost in a bow. His gesture plainly said:

"The stream is yours."

His departure was unhurried but most evidently decisive. We didn't move for several minutes. Then the stream watcher let down the hammer of his rifle.

"The first move and I'd have shot," he said. "There'd have been no time for a second try."

XXVII

In Alaska we expected gales, fog and rain and were prepared for tough going, and we often got it. But we had days and days of smooth water and in some years much bright sunshine. All weather is unpredictable, but Alaskan weather is more so. We've known weeks of never-ceasing drizzle, and along the mainland we've known days of white peaks against cloudless skies.

Taking the long run to Southeastern Alaska is a gamble unless one can enjoy life even if he has to put on rubber boots when he arises in the morning and wear a slicker whenever he steps on deck. Our crowd could. Occasionally we might grumble about weeks of drizzle, but we didn't stop doing things. We cruised, explored rivers and carried on our ordinary life afloat.

The temperature is as variable. We spoke of cold and warm summers. There were days when we basked in sunshine, and there were days when the only reason we didn't wear another sweater was because we were wearing every outer garment we owned. Stewart was our champion sweater wearer. One evening when Betty and I were complaining he contended that we wouldn't be cold if we dressed warmly. We looked at him. He bulked so large we wondered how he got through a doorway. By actual count he was wearing six layers of coats, sweaters and leather jackets.

One dependable feature is the coldness of the water. Along the mainland, when there is an enormous drainage of melted snow, we have known it to be only 42 degrees, which is ten degrees above freezing. We took the temperature of the sea frequently, not because we were contemplating swimming but as support for our firm determination not to.

Bobs swam, even in rivers of snow water. Although assuring us these cold baths set her up, she began to look wan. Whereupon we became as firm with her as she with Lua. I suspected she was a bit relieved that parental authority saved her from the charge of being a sissy. I never believed she actually enjoyed those plunges.

Except for the four towns of Southeastern Alaska and the canneries, we cruised in a country practically unpeopled. Days and weeks passed when no boats anchored near us and we saw no dwelling houses ashore.

My chronic pioneering enthusiasm rose to fever pitch. I was tempted to start colonizing until the skipper reminded me that what I really lamented was lack of a prepioneering type that would be content with an existence reduced to the simplest formula. Few people nowadays are satisfied with only food and shelter.

"How are your potential settlers going to buy flour, sugar, tobacco and reading matter, not to mention an occasional drink and a boat and gasoline?" he asked.

He was right and I knew it. The men in coonskin caps and leather garments who moved westward, shooting their food as they traveled, are of a by-gone age. I, in a comfortable boat with electricity, modern plumbing, canned food from all over the world, sheets, soft beds and books,

was mourning the lack of people willing to exist on sea
food and game.

"But the right sort of family could build a life here,"
I always added.

"Sure," he agreed. "That kind could do anything it had
to do."

"If we're ever up against it, this is the country I'd
chose," I said. "We'd dig clams, catch crabs and trout,
shoot game and plant a garden."

"What would you do for money?" he asked.

I could only answer that there is always some way to
earn a little money. And then I'd cloud the issue with a
cheerful statement that anyhow it was a fine country to
know about.

It was a fine country, in wind, rain or sunshine. All three
couldn't come at the same time, but two could combine
most successfully. One combination was inevitable. When
a sou'easter roared, the heavens opened.

Once we spent six interminable days behind Mary Island
because of this last combination. Dixon Entrance was more
than smoking. We learned later that five floating traps
were not merely driven ashore. They were hurled into the
forest. We asked only five hours for the crossing of the
open water and were not given a minute. And throughout
those six days the rain fell. There were no drops, only
long pencils of water. The dinghies had to be emptied
twice a day. In the short row from one anchored boat to
the other we breathed rain.

We played dominoes, poker and pinochle. We read. We
entertained each other at dinner. Those who accepted
weather as it comes remained calm, and those of us who
didn't, and I was one, stared morosely at our gray world,

tapped barometers, listened to the hiss of rain and the howl of the wind, and grumbled.

When the gale was over and we made one of our finest crossings of Dixon Entrance, we forgot our indignation that we had been trapped. This is one of the eternal wonders of cruising. We forget so quickly the inexcusable behavior of the sea.

A second wonder is the capacity of the sea to spring surprises, to give smooth sailing in a crossing of ill repute and then heap on the grief when one least expects it. No wonder men have found old ocean a fascinating mistress, any day and any night unpredictable.

One late summer when the *Simba* and the *Triton* had left Alaskan waters with their constant threat of gales and fogs and were cruising blithely south through the Gulf of Georgia, we ran into our best anchor watch. It happened in the safety of a landlocked harbor, properly named Boot Cove. The narrow boot top entrance opened into a haven as protected as one could imagine.

We thought the cove a definite discovery, and the skippers wondered why they'd never anchored in it before. After we rowed home from the evening pinochle game aboard the *Simba* the last look around was a mere formality. We rode to a light anchor. The big hook and fathoms of heavy chain in that snug harbor would have been as senseless as mooring oneself in a bath tub.

At midnight I heard Robert leap from his berth.

"We're dragging!" he shouted as he dashed aft.

I grabbed my flannel trousers and ran to the wheelhouse. He counted on my being at the wheel when he started the motor and I knew he'd put it in go-ahead without a signal. When I reached the deck the *Triton* was more than dragging. In a sixty-mile gale she was speeding straight for the

Simba. Robert needed less than a minute to start the motor, but we were due for a collision in half a minute. I yelled to Charlie, who slept in the *Simba's* wheelhouse.

"Get over a mattress," I screamed. "We're coming!"

"Wait a second till I get my pants on," Charlie's sleepy voice responded.

Neither gale nor *Triton* could wait on formalities. We shaved the *Simba* by a hair'sbreadth. I couldn't have steered that close without crashing. I saw Charlie's astonished face in the wheelhouse as we passed. Then our motor started, and we went back against the wind without bothering to lift the anchor. When it had bitten again the skipper dropped our right bower, the heavy hook.

Not once in our years of cruising had those big flukes ever slipped and we went below feeling safe. But we didn't sleep. One doesn't with sixty-mile gusts careening the boat. The cove was a black hole under a mountain, the wind tore the tops off the waves and the bay was a shimmering sheet of phosphorescence.

We were still awake when the *Simba* dragged. Charlie had felt the hook let go, and he didn't bother with his pants.

"When I reached the afterdeck to call the old man," Charlie told us afterwards, "I could have stepped ashore."

He started the motor and jammed the clutch in without ascertaining if Stewart was at the wheel. If Stewart wasn't there they were due to pile up anyway. But Stewart was on duty and the *Simba* pulled away without striking.

When we looked out, Stewart was on deck, Betty was on deck, and also the cook. Every light in the boat was ablaze, decks, wheelhouse, cabins. The dignified *Simba* looked as bawdy as a river showboat while she ran in circles around us. The mystery of those circles took us to the deckhouse.

"For Pete's sake!" Robert muttered as the *Simba* made another dizzy circle.

In the meanwhile the gale was picking off loose objects from the deck. A pillow flew into the darkness. A bamboo table top waltzed neatly across the deck and disappeared over the rail. Betty and the cook were lashing deck chairs and retrieving odds and ends. Stewart was concentrating on circles.

And then we saw Charlie, in his pants at last, hanging over the bow with a boathook trying to dislodge what appeared to be a half ton of hay clinging to the anchor. Armsful of it whirled off in the wind.

"Eel grass!" Robert said.

The explanation didn't add to our peace of mind. We'd never tried our heavy hook in an eel grass meadow.

After cruising more than a thousand miles of tricky passages and lying safely in difficult anchorages, we had reached the peace of the banana belt—as we called the lower Gulf of Georgia—to stand our longest anchor watch. For hours every sudden movement of the *Triton* made us fear that our hook had become a hayrack and we were due to flee in the darkness.

These farther south adventures in smaller waterways are the more astounding because they are so unexpected. When we left Alaska in the fall without having had to fight a storm of gale proportions, I always drew a breath of relief. The North Pacific has a reputation to maintain. The wind blows hard and often. A "sixty-mile breeze," as the halibut fishermen call it, is not uncommon in summer. In the winter storms, which the fishermen do dignify by the word

gale, the wind blows harder and longer. Fishermen have
told us that they carry a thousand feet of heavy manila
and make fast to a big tree. Only thus can the crew sleep
in peace.

Yet the worst beating the *Triton* ever took was outside
Deception Pass in a late fall storm. Bobs' departure for
school made the boat seem lonely and the skipper and I
decided on a week at the Seattle Yacht Club while we had
a city bust. It was blowing hard against the tide in Juan
de Fuca Strait, but we thought we could get across. I
stowed the main cabin and galley for bad weather and took
all the usual precautions which usually brought us through
a storm without breakage.

But in that crossing, when tons of water crashed against
the *Triton*, things moved which had never moved before.
Books popped out from behind railings despite the towels
and napkins I'd stuffed around them. Cups vaulted off
hooks. Plates and bowls leaped out of cubbyholes like
jumping beans. When I heard my precious after-dinner
coffee cups go down I made a frantic dash toward the
companionway. At that moment they seemed more important than the ship.

"Don't go down there!" the skipper barked.

"But my dishes!"

"To hell with the dishes!"

The deckhouse was lying over so far that I could have
stood on the housing. As I scrambled up the inclined floor
to reach the seat behind him, I sorrowed for my cups, but I
was touched that he needed me in a crisis. The next moment the chart table disgorged fifty pounds of charts down
the companionway. They washed back and forth across
the cabin with books, pillows, a tray, a chair and a miscel-

laneous assortment which had poured out of a buffet. I made another move toward the cabin only to be yelled at.

When we were through the pass and in sheltered waters I asked coldly why the attack of skipperishness aboard the *Triton*.

Then I saw that his face was white.

"Just as that big one hit us, the steering gear jammed," he said. "I didn't want you below if we rolled over."

XXVIII

COASTWISE NEIGHBORING

SINCE THE SPRING WHEN WE rebuilt the *Triton*, our cruising season had gradually lengthened. April sailings had been put forward to March. November returns had stretched to December. Finally our nine months' home became a year round one. When we'd remained aboard through a winter I told Robert we'd become real stay-at-homers.

He was highly diverted by this label for a pair who spent their time moving from one harbor to another. But my point was sound. Instead of closing a summer home and traveling, we remained at our own fireside. That was what the *Triton* had become to me and I'd lost all feeling that we were wanderers.

Our fall, winter and spring life afloat was different from summer cruises to Alaska. When Betty and Stewart put up the *Simba* and departed for the south and Bobs went to school, we settled into a quiet home life.

We didn't cruise far or change anchorage often. A week, two weeks, sometimes longer, were spent in a harbor. We didn't go aground on our own tea leaves and beef bones, but sometimes I looked overside to see if I could catch the glint of our tin cans. We settled down to writing, long walks ashore and dinghy trips around the bay.

We carried on ambitious projects in overhaul. I made slip covers for the berths in the deckhouse and main cabins.

Yards and yards of heavy upholstery material filled the
cabin and the electric light plant ran overtime to supply
juice for the sewing machine. But it was a professional
job—glove fasteners, boxed edges, and, more important,
they fitted. Robert ceased to remind me of the famous
upholstery night session.

But the demise of that joke might have been due to a
new grievance. Refinishing mahogany trim in the main
cabin began very much like the upholstery. One evening I
regretted the varnished surface of our dark wood. It would
be much lovelier in a wax polish. Interested, Robert broke
out a can of varnish remover. I expected him to experi-
ment in an obscure corner but he applied the stuff to the
door of our most conspicuous buffet. When it bubbled up,
looking like some terrible skin ailment, I chuckled. Now
he had to go on.

"Damn you!" he said. "You're always steering me into
something. But look at the grain of that wood!"

He was off then, and spent the evening on the door. We
didn't know what we had started. Before we'd finished
doors, strips, buffets, dining table, trim and overhead car-
lines, we had hundreds of hours of homework to our
credit. And long before we were through, he was a more
passionate finisher of wood than I. The main cabin looked
magnificent and we'd discovered a new and fascinating
avocation.

Our life had been so thoroughly domestic I was astonished to discover Bobs considered it a hazardous existence.
She'd never spoken of her belief, but the summer she was
thirteen and the *Simba* and the *Triton* were cruising south,
she quite suddenly proposed an arrangement of auxiliary
parents.

The previous year a schoolmate whose parents were in the Orient had received notice of their deaths. The girl had been sent to English relatives whom she'd never seen. "Then I thought of you and Dad running around in fall storms and fog and of all the crazy things you do," Bobs said. "I'd like it understood at school that Betty and Stewart are my foster parents. Do you think they'd mind?"

I knew they would be pleased, but I didn't know how pleased they'd be until she asked them.

"One of the nicest things ever happened to us," Betty said. "Everyone should carry spare parents. And you don't have to kill your dad and mother off to make us that."

Stewart nodded and tried not to show how moved he was.

Robert and I talked it over and wondered if we had taken chances. Thereafter we made a tremendous effort to convince an adult-minded daughter that we were reliable and dependable. It seemed odd that the youngster over whom we had worried should begin to be concerned for us.

During years afloat we'd learned the distinctive charms of the different seasons.

Summer was the time for cruising, for sparkling water and long evenings on deck. Early fall was the time for walks ashore, hills of brilliant foliage, red sunsets and crisp nights. We always anchored in the Gulf Islands and occasionally Bobs and a school friend spent a week-end with us.

Later when the weather grew colder, frost formed on our decks in the morning and the air was sharp. We kept a fire day and night. We'd come in from an afternoon walk with our blood tingling. The sea was gray and very quiet between dark hills. And then we'd begin to plan that soon after the school Thanksgiving holiday we would cruise south to American waters.

In mid-winter months, when it rained, as it did very often, I loved the patter on the deck above us. It brought a feeling of snugness. In a house I'd always resented rain and felt imprisoned. But in the *Triton* I'd go up to the wheelhouse and look out at the gray curtain and hear the sharp hiss of raindrops on the sea and rejoice that we were a self-contained home and that I didn't have to venture out in it. Discomfort isn't entirely comparative. It's also a matter of viewpoint.

The skipper felt the way I did. He'd go up on deck for a last look around when we lay in a black pocket of a harbor, with the wind whipping the halyards against the mast, a sou'easter on outside, and the *Triton* riding safely to the big hook. When he came below and pulled the hatch closed, he'd remark comfortably that the sea was a safe place in a blow. Ashore power lines were falling, trees were crashing and lives were being endangered. Nothing could touch us here. That was also a matter of viewpoint. But it was the way we felt.

When winter was over and an early spring sun warmed the deck, we began the joyful task of preparation for the summer's cruise. That was a time of grooming and anticipation.

And at last, stowed and ready, the *Triton* turned her bow north. Food for the season was in the lockers. Fuel tanks were full. Cans of lubricating oil and kerosene for the cookstove jammed the lazarette. Three tons had been poured into the craft. We were chock-a-block. The skipper liked the solidity of the loaded ship. She had the feel of being able. And she was weighted with the needs of our living. We could sail away and laugh at stores and filling stations and purveyors of all the public utilities on which landsmen are dependent.

My greatest spring thrill came when I wakened in a sun-lit harbor and saw dancing flecks of refracted sunlight on the white deck above me. Then I knew that for months I would waken to that glad promise of a joyous day. One can see morning sunlight almost anywhere but only in a ship do jeweled wavelets signal a morning greeting through a porthole.

Bobs, we discovered, planned on the spring appearance of the *Triton* as much as we. The girls who were to be aboard for the Queen's Birthday week-end would have been invited months in advance. And all the stir and excitement of summer cruising would begin again.

Our instinctive adjustment to a non-stable world had come so gradually we were unaware of it. We discovered how firmly it was established when we were hauled out up the coast for an emergency bottom scraping. We lived aboard while on the ways and after a pre-dinner drink Robert went to attend to a task on the foredeck. He weaved around and came below definitely worried. I'd been staggering about in the galley, almost ready to take the temperance pledge.

"We're poisoned!" I cried, and I was so sure of it I made him get the bottle of Scotch and read the label.

One drink had never registered before. We worried over that mystery until after dinner. Food hadn't restored our balance. Then Robert burst out laughing.

"It's the *Triton*, not us," he said.

She was solid, fixed in one position, and we'd continued

to make involuntary compensations for a water-balanced craft. Solving the mystery didn't help, for our subconscious accommodation continued. Until the *Triton*, freshly copper-painted, slid down the ways and into the water, we dissolutely reeled about our home.

As the season passed and the *Triton* dropped its hook in small coves lying on either side of the international boundary, our ship began to engage in coastwise neighboring. We knew not one community, but many. Anchorages were homecomings, whether we rode at anchor with only waterfowl and the odd seal for neighbors, or blew the whistle at a house ashore or at a fishing craft whose owner popped up to wave us in.

At the time I knew only how the fellow in the boat felt. I liked to go ashore and see how the new fruit trees were bearing, admire the tennis court, hear who was high boat at Cape Flattery, or how well the children were doing in the new union high school. Since then, I too have lived on a harbor and I know how a boat at anchor furnishes the sea. A harbor without boats is not a harbor. I've had an oddly warm feeling toward boats I've never been aboard. I've watched a skipper drop the hook in the same spot he chose on a former visit, and have felt somehow that a friend had arrived.

I understand the old fellow who rowed out to us one day when we stopped in a strange harbor. He was beaming when he came alongside.

"I hoped you fellows would drop in some day," he said. "You're the writing boat, ain't you?"

That became our pet joke. A writing boat completed an assortment of vocations which had made it possible for sea lovers to go to sea.

A dentist had fitted up a small cruiser as an office and been so successful he complained dental work in every port put an end to his cruising. A photographer had better luck, for his clients didn't require such long appointments, but he'd had trouble with a limited supply of fresh water. A peddler's boat, with notions and dry goods, had worked the coast for years but regular customers had tied him to the same old courses. A junk boat, collecting bottles and old brass, accumulated a cargo too near Vancouver. A show boat reported a wonderful summer in the matter of a good time and hours of practice of dance routine on sand beaches, but settlements were so few and far apart the box office suffered.

"What's our professional grief?" I asked the skipper.

He grinned. "Boat work," he said. "We'd rather polish and paint and wax and doll up the *Triton* than pound the typewriters."

In December of our sixth year afloat we swallowed the anchor for three mid-winter months. Or perhaps we merely nibbled at it when we slept ashore after 522 consecutive nights aboard the *Triton*.

We rented a land home in the city of Victoria because Robert needed to be near a reference library and Bobs desired a Christmas vacation with her friends. Her letters were filled with reports of forthcoming holiday teas, luncheons and dancing parties, and heavily illustrated with sketches of the sort of frocks she thought she needed. A great deal of emphasis was placed on the absolute necessity of a sleek floor-length evening dress, completely backless and worked out preferably in black satin.

Robert looked at Bobs' sketch and laughed. "Tell her to be her age," he said.

From his male viewpoint it was all so simple. He even supported Bobs by admiring the sophisticated black satin frock we brought home from shopping. Bobs called it a compromise, but I knew better. It was my personal defeat. Robert said she looked lovely and I couldn't deny it, even while I knew she was dressed ridiculously in a gown ten years too old for her.

Adjustment to land life came slowly. For a week we walked about the apartment carefully pushing objects back from the edges of tables. I dismantled the china closet. All plates that stood on edge were laid safely on their backs before I realized the first arrangement hadn't been precarious. Only an earthquake could shake them down. Robert laughed about that, but I discovered two Chinese vases, pet possessions of the owner and which stood unlashed on the mantel, made him as uncomfortable as they did me.

In three months ashore we always missed the staccato double beat of our ship's clock bells. We were irritated by the pompous voice of a land clock on the mantel. The progression of ship's bells is so logical and convenient. Our Seth Thomas lived in the wheelhouse and we were able to tell the hour and half-hour anywhere within hearing distance. Land clocks stupidly repeat the single chime to mark each half-hour. Aboard the *Triton*, even in the middle of the night, there was never any question of half-past twelve, one or half-past one.

Ship's bells were evolved from the routine of four-hour watches and the scheme is sound. Anyone knows whether it is morning or afternoon, early evening or past midnight. But only a ship's clock raises its voice to inform how many of those eight half-hour periods have sped.

XXIX

OLD CHANNELS, AND NEW

In early June we made the run to Alaska without Bobs. She was detained by examinations. The school had frowned on our plea for an early departure and reminded us that in another year Bobs must go up for matriculation.

She came by steamship, joining us in Ketchikan. The young person whose bags the skipper carried from the wharf was not the youngster who seven years before had seen her first cruiser. The mop of blond hair, once brushed only under compulsion, was now trained in waves. Her head topped Betty's by three inches and was almost level with mine. She had made that transition from child to woman.

All recognized this except Lua, who still operated on the basis of complete equality. He considered that they shared ownership of the *Crab* and he sat in the stern like a dignified admiral. To him it was as in the old days when Bobs had been so concerned about his hours of exercise, but I detected an indulgent tone in her voice when she invited him for an airing.

Robert and I had seen the change coming. In early years Bobs and her boat guests had considered any harbor adequate for celebration of the Queen's Birthday, providing there was sufficient food to feed thrashers and an unlimited supply of fruit cake and ginger beer. But the previous May the girls had called the skipper's attention to a regatta and for the first time the *Triton* had ridden at anchor in a fleet of yachts. Dinghies had been tied to our railing, the afterdeck filled with young people and tall lads in white had taken the girls sailing. At the farewell party aboard a large yacht I'd noticed with amazement that Bobs was dancing with the same men who danced with me.

This young person wasn't going to care for an entire summer plodding up Alaskan rivers. She'd had years of brown bears, trout pools, mountains, glaciers and enchanting harbors. I broke this news to Robert.

"Bobs' school friends must think we're total losses," I said.

"All right," he said. "We'll go south early and be real yachtsmen."

There were other changes in our crowd. Betty and Stewart now had a new eighty-three foot craft, the *Kuru*. Charlie Drumm was its engineer and the galley was manned by Oscar, who had cooked in halibut schooners and also had master's papers. Robert and Oscar became pals and spent hours in the *Kuru's* galley drinking coffee while they pulled in skates of gear and sailed halibuters to the westward.

Robert and I had been murmuring about cruises we could make if we had a crew. But crew meant a larger boat. No one seems proof against that insidious idea, "a bigger boat." We took it up seriously one afternoon as we voyaged down a channel. We had thrashed out so many problems in the wheelhouse while we were under way.

"With a man aboard we could go out to the westward," Robert said.

That's what Alaskans called Southwestern Alaska, "out to the westward." Even the words were thrilling. They meant Kodiak Island, The Shumagins, Cook Inlet, the Aleutians and Dutch Harbor, higher mountains, larger glaciers and storms which even halibuters called gales. We got out the charts and noted the heights of the peaks and glaciers which threaded the coast like a string of pearls.

The six hundred miles of open crossing were not possible for a crew of one man and two women. Robert murmured about a halibut schooner, Diesel-powered and rebuilt for our needs. In another moment we were drawing sketches. "What a ship-home that would be," Robert said. "California for winter, summer out to the westward. With one good man, we could manage."

Emotionally we were ready for a larger cruising radius. Step by step, we had been pushing farther. First the *Yakima,* then the *Triton.* First a summer cruise, then a year-round home. First the inlets of British Columbia and then Southeastern Alaska. Now our imagination and our wishes had outdistanced both our bank account and our family orbit.

"You'd be no more willing than I to put two thousand miles of ocean between Bobs and us," I said. "After all, she's got to learn to be something more than an able-bodied seaman."

He smiled wistfully and admitted I might be right.

Doc's family in the *Chirikof* joined us in Sitka. It is the favorite harbor of all who have seen it. Ship captains claim it to be the most beautiful port in all the world. Studded with birthday cake islands, backed by the cone-shaped peak of Mount Edgecombe to the west and the majestic Baranof range to the east, it is a stunning haven that still shelters evidences of three regimes.

Doc, steeped in early Russian history and knowing every man, woman and yellow dog in the territory, interpreted its color. The first Russian colony in Sitka was exterminated by Indians in 1799. Five years later the Russians returned under Baranof, who made it the most important trading center north of Mexico. Ships from all the world anchored in its harbor. The mission bells of California were cast in a Sitka foundry and the Sitka church, a favorite of the Czars, was given priceless altar trappings, rich embroideries, carvings and rare paintings and gorgeous jeweled ikons. All these treasures were still stored in a small white frame church where Baranof had once worshiped.

Doc loved the place and its people, and the people loved him. As the party from the *Kuru* and the *Triton* walked up from the wharf, a townsman stopped to shake our hands. He wrung them gratefully.

"You're the folks who are taking care of Doc this summer," he said. "That's just fine!"

The village stirred in preparation. Barter was in the air. Indian women laid out wares along the wharf and the fronts of native cabins were strung with blankets, mocassins and miniature totem poles. The excitement was explained by a steamship whistle and as soon as the ship was against the wharf its passengers swarmed ashore for an intensive study of native life. A small Indian boy dashed down the road.

"Mama, mama!" he shouted. "The sights are coming."

I'd often wanted a name for tourists.

Fourth of July was properly celebrated by what was undoubtedly the only baseball game ever played on Admiralty Island. Our three boats had been joined by the

Katinka, owned and crewed by Mr. and Mrs. Hibbs. Our guests raised the number to thirteen and low tide gave us a field. Stewart captained the Bears and Robert the Seals. The game was close with both sides bringing in a flock of runs each inning. Competition was in errors rather than good fielding. The score was even, in the upper thirties, when the tide flooded the diamond.

Doc then built one of his so-called friendship fires, a conflagration of several cords of driftwood. Anything less would have been a feeble blaze to Doc.

We huddled at a distance and caught up on a year's news with the Hibbs. Robert and I had met them in Seattle when they had dropped down in the casual fashion of the Alaskan. Purchase of a pair of shoes, a longing for the theater, or no excuse at all, justifies the thousand-mile sea trip to the States.

The *Katinka* was now doing a super-patrol duty for a group of canneries, watching the watchers of the fish traps lest they sell out to fish pirates. The Hibbs lived aboard in Alaskan waters all year, and when I first heard of their encounters with winter gales, I stared in horror at Mrs. Hibbs. She wasn't a brawny person, not at all the bouncing outdoor type.

"Weren't you frightened?" I had asked.

"No," she said, "but I got so awfully black and blue."

Her answer proved to me that I would never be a real first mate.

When I learned we were going into Kootznahoo Inlet I hoped that Doc's heavenly underwriting was a blanket protection for all three boats. The Inlet was a broken system of narrow passages which penetrate to the center of Admiralty Island and Doc told us that twenty years earlier the Indians had not permitted white men to enter. Since the natives were of the tribe which had exterminated Russian Sitka, white men had not argued the matter. Nature had provided the Indians with a natural defense of their territory. Never have we seen a worse jumble of rocks and reefs and narrow twisting channels through which the tide rushed with great velocity. But once inside we were so well repaid we visited Kootznahoo a second time.

We had a feeling of isolation far back in the hundred-mile island. Streams were filled with trout and marshes with young wild geese. We discovered a bay filled with flounders. Deer were amazingly plentiful and so tame they would lie down and sleep while we passed with a noisy outboard motor. We followed a large river far into the island, and where the river entered the sea was a reversing rapids. On the ebb the river poured over a ledge, and on the flood the sea poured over in the opposite direction. In the churning mixture of fresh and salt water an unbelievable quantity of foam was piled up. The first time we saw it the white smother was two feet deep and had crowded onto the shore and buried the dinghies.

After three days' exploration of this remote paradise for wild creatures we decided to cruise to Rodman Bay to say good-by to Doc and the *Chirikof* with a crab picnic ashore. The harbor was over-populated with crabs—fighting crabs, too. Betty, Stewart and I encountered a colony of them when we had no dip net and made a sporting event of the occasion. I contributed two shoulder straps and Betty dug a nail out of the miscellaneous collection in her pockets. Stewart made a lasso and brought crabs over the gunwale while we cheered.

We now embroidered game harvesting with special features. Stewart struggled to keep his lure from attracting large trout that he might get a mess of smaller "eating fish." Then Robert decided to prove he could drive a thousand trout as he would cattle. Like Lua chasing salmon, he waded into the water and splashed and splattered, and looked about as frustrated. Every time he lost his herd he'd find the trout had merely circled around his feet and gone back into their original formation.

The *Chirikof* was to leave early in the morning. A sou'easter blew up soon after midnight and was howling at dawn. I murmured drowsily that it was a fine harbor in which to be wind bound and the skipper agreed that no boat would pull out that day. Betty and Stewart held much the same conversation.

We came on deck at the usual hour and stared in amazement at the place where the *Chirikof* had anchored. She was gone.

"For the love of Pete!" Stewart called. "Doc's gone!"

It was one of those incredible facts which must be put in words for belief and even then it didn't seem quite possible. Charlie reported he'd heard the motor start and Stewart asked why he hadn't stopped them.

"Why should I interfere?" Charlie asked. "Doc's got a better person than me taking care of him."

Muir Glacier was our farthest north. The land beside it is the newest on the continent. One feels the rawness of it even outside in Glacier Bay. We heard no birds and saw no animals. Stewart and Robert explored a river and reported they saw tracks only of a bear, and that he had been traveling fast to get out of that desolate country. On shore the only growth was prostrate willows, too young to stand erect, and, strangely enough, luscious wild strawberries.

One hundred and fifty years earlier Vancouver had reported the glacier at Icy Straits as a glistening rampart a mile high. Present day charts showed it as a great horseshoe lying in Muir Inlet forty miles back. We found it five miles behind the chart's location, and shrunken to one river of ice. Elsewhere were only great cliffs of mud and mountains of bare rock.

We gathered pieces of peat-like earth which had been buried and compressed through the ages under glacier ice, one to two miles deep. When we dropped the peat into a glass of water, it unfolded like Japanese water flowers and became stalks and leaves. It was a fascinating thought that we were seeing and touching plants of the pre-glacial era.

But the infant land, the rawness, the quiet, were as depressing to me as they had been to the bear. Like him, I wanted to leave.

In the evening at anchor in Berg Bay we concluded our hardest fought pinochle tournament. Rivalry had been intense ever since Betty had made an official pinochle flag, white with a red crab rampant. The winning boat flew the pennant from the masthead and we wanted it when we went south. There it set yachtsmen to hurried searching of code books to determine whether we were at home, or weren't, or at dinner, or taking a nap, or offering food and drink.

Our two-man team defeated the *Kuru* trio and we all went on deck to see Stewart pull down the pennant. There we discovered our most gorgeous display of northern lights. In the cold air we could almost hear them snap and crackle.

"They must have heard up at the North Pole that the

Triton finally won that flag off us," Charlie said as the skipper of the *Kuru* made a formal presentation to the skipper of the *Triton*. Sometimes our ship's manners were simply perfect.

In midsummer we left the *Kuru* and started south for our season of real yachting. Lua found himself again in familiar harbors. We didn't know how he catalogued scents' memories of more than two hundred bays in which the *Triton* had dropped anchor, but he knew them, and he distinctly remembered whether he had enjoyed them. When the motor slowed he would waken and rush to the foredeck. There he would sit with eyes closed and nose extended, reviewing the sort of time he'd had on a previous visit.

If the memory were pleasant and he had explored rivers and played on land, he would wait eagerly for a dinghy to go overside. He was under everyone's feet while he expressed approval of our choice. If he'd had a dull time, his ears and his tail would go to half mast and if the former visit had been marked by downright unpleasantness he would glance piteously at the skipper, then drop his head dejectedly and go below.

The latter part of that summer won Lua's complete approval. He loved people and had never known such sociability in the *Triton*. We anchored near yachts with dogs aboard. Girls were boat guests. Large teas were served on the foredeck where swimmers in wet bathing suits could lounge. Swimming parties became a daily affair, with the top of the deckhouse a diving platform. The diving covered the bright work and windows with salt spray, much to the skipper's horror. But Lua became so excited he often leaped from the top of the house.

Lua was shown off and much admired. We went ashore and met Bobs' school friends' families and also the school friends' dogs. Lua plunged into the gay whirl so fervently that we wondered if his social instincts had been frustrated.

Occasionally we anchored off a yacht club and the skipper wore white pants and a yachting cap. We attended club flannel dances. Bobs played tennis and went sailing. She and I went on day-long shopping expeditions to Victoria, where we selected school clothes and topped off at teas with other mothers and daughters who had spent similar days. When the excitement was over, Bobs went off to school, a dignified upper-sixth former.

We reserved an apartment for midwinter and departed for our fall cruise. September and October days were lovely, and so warm we were able to put a coat of varnish on all the bright work abovedecks. I painted the skipper's engine room and changed the color of the motor from gray to bright green.

"That's swell," he said. "We're going to put this ship up for winter in such fine shape we won't have much to do next spring."

XXX

SEVEN YEARS

As we had cruised south in late summer we'd left familiar harbors and old friends with the customary, "See you next spring." We didn't doubt but that we'd see them all again. Those harbors and those friends were woven into the pattern of our lives.

When Bobs came home for holidays in early November, the *Triton* was waiting for her as usual. We anchored near school friends and Bobs spent three days playing badminton. Guests came aboard in the evening or we visited ashore. The last morning of her holiday we ran to a small harbor on Vancouver Island where a taxi always met us to take Bobs back to school. The taxi blew its horn and we started shoreward in the dinghy. It was like so many departures—Bobs in her school uniform, and Robert, Lua and I to see her off.

Early in December, when snow was at sea level and the decks were iced, we ran to Seattle to put the *Triton* under cover during our short stay in Victoria. In the canal locks I held the bow line against the force of the water which boiled around us as the lock chamber was raised to lake level. On so many homeward voyages I'd stood on the foredeck of our ship and watched the inner lock gate swing open. I never doubted that I would do so on many more returns.

Even when we left the *Triton* in the shipyards in Lake

Washington, it was as one turns the key in the door of a home left for a short absence.

That is the way one should say farewell to a boat. We didn't know it then, but later we knew it was so.

When Christmas holidays were past we discussed our summer cruising. I said we couldn't voyage too far north because we must go to San Francisco in August. Bobs would matriculate in June and must make arrangements for her next school year.

"That means a short cruising season," Robert said.

We talked of where we might go, the Gulf islands, the inlets, possibly a quick run to Southeastern Alaska. And as always when cruising plans were being discussed, Robert brought out the chart. The history of the *Triton's* wanderings was recorded by a bold black line which traced inlets, encircled islands and criss-crossed larger channels.

But no line ran "out to the westward." Now we studied those distant waters, even though we knew we could not cruise them that season. Probably we never could. But eagerness to see them took all zest from planning a shorter cruise. Never before had Robert ended talk of our summer voyage by rolling up the charts without determining a course. The sketch of the converted halibut schooner had meant more than we had realized that afternoon when we had talked of a wider cruising radius.

I suggested that we were falling into the habit of repeating the same old courses year after year. Robert's energetic denial was an involuntary admission that he had the same misgiving. For a week we avoided the subject of our summer's cruise. Neither wished to admit what he was thinking.

A boat is different from a home ashore. A land home settles and grows mellow, blending more and more with its surroundings. But a boat lives only when she moves.

She stays young only when new waters lie across her bows. Like every other discovery which has radically influenced our lives, a realization of this truth came without warning. We make these discoveries only when we are emotionally ready for them. They stun us, even as we recognize their truth. Now we knew that a summer in which the *Triton* no longer found adventure might mar our memories of her.

So we admitted at last that our cruising days were over. Robert was completely adrift. "I can't imagine not being in the *Triton*," he said.

We had spent ourselves, our affections, our substance and our energies on her, but neither regretted the spending.

"And we'll never make a better investment!" Robert said.

He was right. We'd bought something with those years and with that devotion to a ship. And we'd had those years while we could enjoy them. Perhaps never again would we be free and young enough to wander in a sea country.

We didn't know how truly we had spoken when we discussed the wisdom of our investment. Overhaul, rebuilding, upkeep and cruising had held our attention and taken our earnings in the boom years. We understood that more stable people had grown wealthy, but that had not seemed so terribly important. Later we had heard reports of the depression and learned that some of that wealth had fled, but we didn't know the extent of the flight until we went to San Francisco and heard the investors' stories.

The stay-at-homers had lists, figures and old bank books, which now meant nothing. We had pages in a ship's log which meant very much. That seemed to indicate some sort of triumph of pure folly.

But we knew nothing of all this when we stood one

morning in early spring on the yacht club pier and watched a stranger put the wheel of the *Triton* hard over and turn the ship into the fairway for the beginning of a voyage to Alaska. I last saw the *Triton's* stern through a mist of tears. And as had her first owner, we turned quickly and walked away.

At the club house veranda we looked back to see an empty fairway. The *Triton* had vanished.

After a moment Robert spoke. "Anyway, he didn't buy those seven years."